Violence in the Name of God

Violence, Desire, and the Sacred

Series Editors
Scott Cowdell, Chris Fleming, and Joel Hodge

Volumes in the series:
Vol. 1. *Girard's Mimetic Theory Across the Disciplines*
edited by Scott Cowdell, Chris Fleming, and Joel Hodge
Vol. 2. *René Girard and Sacrifice in Life, Love, and Literature*
edited by Scott Cowdell, Chris Fleming, and Joel Hodge
Vol. 3. *Mimesis, Movies, and Media*
edited by Scott Cowdell, Chris Fleming, and Joel Hodge
Vol. 4. *René Girard and Raymund Schwager: Correspondence 1974–1991*
edited by Scott Cowdell, Chris Fleming, Joel Hodge, and Mathias Moosbrugger
Vol. 5. *Mimesis and Atonement: René Girard and the Doctrine of Salvation*
edited by Michael Kirwan and Sheelah Treflé Hidden
Vol. 6. *Möbian Nights: Literary Reading in a Time of Crisis*
by Sandor Goodhart
Vol 7. *Does Religion Cause Violence?: Multidisciplinary Perspectives on Violence and Religion in the Modern World*
edited by Scott Cowdell, Chris Fleming, Joel Hodge, and Carly Osborn
Vol 8. *Mimetic Theory and Film*
edited by Paolo Diego Bubbio and Chris Fleming
Vol. 9 *Mimesis and Sacrifice*
edited by Marcia Pally
Vol. 10 *Violence in the Name of God: The Militant Jihadist Response to Modernity*
by Joel Hodge

Violence in the Name of God

The Militant Jihadist Response to Modernity

Joel Hodge

BLOOMSBURY
NEW DELHI • LONDON • OXFORD • NEW YORK • SYDNEY

BLOOMSBURY INDIA
Bloomsbury Publishing India Pvt. Ltd
Second Floor, LSC Building No. 4, DDA Complex, Pocket C–6&7,
Vasant Kunj, New Delhi 110070

BLOOMSBURY, BLOOMSBURY ACADEMIC INDIA and the Diana logo are trademarks of Bloomsbury Publishing Plc

First published in India 2025
First published in Great Britain 2020
This paperback edition published in 2021

A catalogue record for this book is available from the British Library.
A catalog record for this book is available from the Library of Congress.

ISBN: 978-93-61310-01-0

Series: Violence, Desire, and the Sacred

Typeset by Newgen KnowledgeWorks Pvt. Ltd., Chennai, India

Printed in India by Manipal Technologies Limited, Manipal

Contents

Note on Permissions

Some material for this monograph has been used from the following publications, with permission. I wish to thank the publishers and editors for this permission, and for the reviewers of these essays for assisting me to improve them.

Hodge, Joel. "Terrorism's Answer to Modernity's Cultural Crisis: Re-sacralising Violence in the Name of Jihadist Totalitarianism." *Modern Theology* 32, no. 2 (April 2016): 231–58.

Hodge, Joel. "Why Is God Part of Human Violence? The Idolatrous Nature of Modern Religious Extremism." In *Does Religion Cause Violence? Multidisciplinary Perspectives on Violence and Religion in the Modern World.* Violence, Desire, and the Sacred 7, edited by Scott Cowdell, Chris Fleming, Joel Hodge, and Carly Osborn, 39–55. New York: Bloomsbury, 2018.

Acknowledgments

I wish to begin by expressing my gratitude to the Australian Catholic University (ACU), the Center of Theological Inquiry (CTI), Princeton, and the Center for World Catholicism & Intercultural Theology (CWCIT), DePaul University, for the support provided to me for this monograph to be undertaken and completed. I gratefully acknowledge the support of my home institution, ACU, and express my particular thanks to the Faculty of Theology and Philosophy, particularly Professor Dermot Nestor and Professor David Sim, for providing me with the time and resources to complete this project.

I am greatly appreciative of the supportive research environment provided to me by Dr. William Storrar and the trustees and staff at CTI, and Professor William Cavanaugh and the staff at CWCIT, especially Francis Salinel and Karen Kraft. In both places, I was able to engage with great scholars, gain valuable feedback, and enjoy new and old friendships. Thank you to Dr. Joshua Mauldin, who was responsible for the Research Workshop on Religion and Violence at CTI of which I was a member in 2019, and to my colleagues who participated in this workshop (or who were fellows at the time of the Workshop), Etin Anwar, Richard Davis, Willem Drees, Mark Eaton, Dirk Evers, Pauline Kollontai, Philip McDonagh, Paul Middleton, Peter Ochs, and Christine Schliesser. I'm grateful for their advice, feedback, and friendship. The workshop was a uniquely enriching experience.

My special thanks to the support of my family and friends during this project (and of me in general!). I am truly grateful to you all. My particular thanks to my parents, Vince and Susanne, who have provided unwavering support and love to me during this project and throughout my life. My thanks also to my siblings—James, Andrew, Samuel, and Mary—and their spouses and children—Jeab, James, and Jessica—for their support. Thank you also to Sr Eufemia Lacerda da Costa Fdcc and Fr Robin Koning SJ for your support and encouragement during this project.

I also thank my colleagues in the Faculty of Theology and Philosophy, ACU, with whom it is a pleasure to work and collaborate. I especially thank those who filled in for me in various roles while I was on research leave and with whom I've had helpful discussions, including Professor Ismail Albayrak. A particular thanks to Dr. Christiaan Jacobs-Vandegeer, Jennifer Jacobs-Vandegeer, and their family for their friendship and support.

I am also grateful to the members of the Australian Girard Seminar (AGS) and Colloquium on Violence and Religion (COV&R) for their friendship and assistance. I presented my work in progress for this monograph at COV&R conferences and gained valuable feedback. My work also greatly benefited from a COV&R/AGS conference on religious violence that I organized with my AGS colleagues, Professor Scott Cowdell, Dr. Chris Fleming, and Dr. Carly Osborn, which was a great success. This monograph builds on an edited volume which we produced following this conference, *Does Religion Cause Violence? Multidisciplinary Perspectives on Violence and Religion in the Modern World* (Bloomsbury, 2018). Some chapters from this volume were presented at a session at the American Academy of Religion, which I'm grateful to Associate Professor Grant Kaplan and Professor Martha Reineke for facilitating. I have also benefited from discussions with members of the Girard reading groups in Melbourne and Brisbane for which I'm grateful.

I am greatly appreciative to Rev. Professor Anthony Kelly CSsR, Professor Wolfgang Palaver, Dr. Drasko Dizdar, Professor Scott Cowdell, Professor Sandor Goodhart, Professor Ann Astell, Dr. Thomas Ryba, Professor Marcia Pally, Professors Joseph and Kelley Spoerl and Fatih Erol Tuncer, for their assistance or advice, including by reading or discussing different aspects of this monograph. Of course, any erroneous or problematic parts of this monograph only can be attributed to me.

Finally, my gratitude to Bloomsbury Academic, especially Colleen Coalter and Becky Holland as well as to Scott and Chris (my fellow series editors), for their assistance and support of this monograph. Thank you also to those who peer-reviewed or copy edited this monograph, and a special thank you to Chris Brennan for the index.

Introduction

Why Another Book on Jihadism?

Humanity is experiencing an age of escalating and absolutizing rivalry. This is the thesis of René Girard to explain the nature and trajectory of violence in modernity.[1] This thesis will be explored and analyzed in this study with reference to militant Islamism/jihadism and the state-based antecedents and responses to it. This study traces the trajectory of modern religious extremism in its most potent form—militant Islamism and jihadism—to show how violence is more intentionally embraced as the center of worship, order, and ideology.

The embrace of extreme and totalitarian forms of violence by jihadists is a response to modernity—though in two ways that have not been sufficiently explored or appreciated by the existing literature on religious extremism, jihadism, and terrorism. First, this violence is a manifestation of the unrestrained and escalating dynamics of desire and rivalry in modernity. Violent jihadists embrace these dynamics of escalating rivalry to fuel and justify their violence, and when they achieve victory, seek to unleash, control, and repress desire. Second, extreme violence is a response to the unveiling and discrediting of sacred violence. Violent jihadists seek to reverse this decline by more purposefully engaging in and valorizing sacred violence in the name of the one God. Violence becomes a form of worship for jihadists, even to the point that, for some, violence is worshipped in itself. Jihadists justify this sacred violence on behalf of the victims of a Westernized modernity. Both these aspects of modernity are examined in detail in this study to shed new light on the rise (and fall) of militant jihadism.

To contextualize jihadism, it is important to recognize the escalating and polarizing nature of rivalry as evident in modern politics and warfare. From the French Revolution through to the world wars, totalitarianisms, and terrorisms of the twentieth and twenty-first centuries, human violence has been escalating in rivalrous patterns. René Girard has provided important insight into why human violence is following this rivalrous pattern: it is moving according to the mimetic logic of human desire. As desire proliferates and fragments under the pressures of modernity, violence becomes more extreme and, in one sense, more unpredictable in its response to its rivals. In this violence, forms of identity, meaning, and solidarity are sought. In Islamist-jihadist violence, a manifestation of absolute rivalry and warfare can be identified in our own time. Its "all or nothing" attitude regards killing oneself and others as a sacred, absolute duty. In this, there is a return to what Girard calls the "violent sacred"—the cultural projection of sacred violence that channeled violence into controllable and awe-inspiring doses to provide social order and give stability to individual identity. The modern return of the violent sacred, however, moves beyond a search for order to a desire for absolute victory and totalitarian domination.

Nevertheless, the sacred projection no longer works as effectively as it once did, because the arbitrary violence and scapegoating that underlies it has been exposed. Thus, the "all against all," in Hobbes's terms, that turned into the "all against one" has returned to the "all against all." Except that this time, the rivalries that represent the human grasping for identity and being has escalated to new heights, to cover the globe. The global trajectory of violence—exemplified in violent jihadism—seeks a return to sacred violence, though in a more intentional form than in the past. Jihadism seeks to make sacralized and transcendent violence the center of culture again but in a much more radical way than in the traditional cultures: by claiming that the God of victims—the "Abrahamic" God—justifies such violence.

The appropriation of God by militant jihadists represents the revenge of violence in reasserting itself. Girard claims that the advent of extreme rivalry and the return of sacred violence have come about, ironically and inadvertently, because of that which reveals it: the revelation of the innocent victim of human violence, which emerged from the biblical traditions, or more broadly, the Abrahamic traditions.[2] The revelation of the innocent victim exposes sacred violence as scapegoating. Because such scapegoating has been revealed, it undermines new efforts to bring about unanimity through violence. When new victims are accused in modernity, there is a greater moral awareness of what is occurring than in the past. Thus, the desacralization of violence opens up the possibility for understanding and being free of violence. However, it also makes possible a more extreme and purposeful violence that seeks to recover its place at the heart of culture and religion.[3] Jihadism is a manifestation of this recovery effort.

In addition to challenging the modern consciousness of the victim, extreme violence represents a threat to the institution of the nation-state and the global order founded on it. The nation-state monopolizes violence in an intentional and controlled manner to maintain order (in some ways like the archaic or violent sacred). As an institution, it has been successful in providing a framework for order and prosperity, especially in the West. However, the legitimacy of this institution in many places is threatened by a postcolonial legacy, polarization, and terrorism. Its institutional reach remains uneven globally, particularly in sections of the Middle East, Africa, and Asia where the colonial and postcolonial experience has been fraught with difficulties and failures. In these places, the nation-state itself has been a vehicle for various dictatorships and forms of totalitarianism to repress and oppress populations. Building on discontent with modernity, violent jihadists reject nation-states (in the plural) and seek to build their own unitary state to cover the globe as an antidote to the problems and tensions of modernity. In this way, jihadism is an ugly mirror or double of the state that seeks to take the state's monopoly on violence to its absolute end. This possibility has been realized, at least for short periods, in places such as Syria, Iraq, and Nigeria. They have experienced the enforcement of a sacred totalitarian regime that is in absolute rivalry with all its "enemies" and uncompromising in its application of violence.

This study argues, then, that militant jihadism, as the most prominent protagonist of sacred violence done in the name of God, is a particular response to modernity that purposefully seeks to resuscitate the power of sacred violence to provide order and power. This violent revolutionary response to modernity directly contrasts with the unveiling of violence that occurs in the Abrahamic traditions. Each of the sacred scriptures of these traditions tells the stories of innocent victims, such as Joseph expelled by his brothers, and places God on the side of the victim. For example, the Hebrew Scriptures are centered on the liberation of the Israelites from slavery—from a permanent state of oppression and potential victimization—while Christianity focuses on Jesus unjustly killed at the Crucifixion (and his later rising). Islam focuses on the prophetic witness of Muhammad who is persecuted by his own people for his monotheistic witness (and later resists and converts his opponents). By contrast, Islamist militants seek to violently reclaim the victim from the nonviolent trajectory of the Abrahamic traditions. By claiming to be victims themselves of a Westernized modernity, these militants aim to relegitimize sacred violence. They do so on behalf of defending "legitimate" victims from modern oppression in the name of the wrathful and just order of their God.

Thus, there is an important struggle over the heart and soul of human culture and religion in modernity. It is the task of this study to shed some light on this struggle by analyzing the violent modern dynamics represented by militant jihadism and its struggles with the nation-state and other forces of modernity. Examining violent jihadism in this way involves understanding its history, key figures, and theology. Yet, more than this, it involves analyzing militant jihadism in a more fundamental way than conventional political, anthropological, and historical studies through a rigorous and comprehensive understanding of human desire, culture, and religion. In this way, new light is shed on the nature of militant jihadism, the threat it poses, and what it reveals about humanity at this stage of modernity. On this basis, it will be possible, then, to discuss an alternative to violent jihadism that provides political and social resistance to extremist violence.

The Inquiry

This study seeks to understand modern violence, particularly in its religious or sacred dimensions, in the form of militant jihadism, especially focusing on Sunni-Salafist groups. Jihadist violence is chosen as it is an extreme and potent form of violence in modernity (perhaps the most extreme). It represents one of the most pressing issues of our time and provides a case study of the violent dynamics of modernity. This study does not seek to attribute responsibility for violence to any particular tradition but rather to understand the nature of extreme violence, which in this case is perpetrated in the name of Islam.

Moreover, I do not wish to get into a fruitless debate about who is to blame for Islamist terrorism, such as "Islam" or "the West." Rather, I take an anthropological and theological approach to analyzing the features of Islamist violence. This approach provides a way of understanding the causes and dynamics of such violence. Through it, I identify how violence in modernity is increasingly sacred, totalitarian, and intentional. Militant Islamists and jihadists represent this trend in a particularly clear and virulent form. They do so in a certain way—through indiscriminate, apocalyptic violence that is explicitly sacralized in its dedication to God. There is one particular feature of Islamist violence that is distinctive and has not been much commented on: the subversion and reappropriation of the Abrahamic God to re-sacralize violence on behalf of the victimized. This particular feature is of the highest importance for understanding the danger and potency of Islamist violence.

The violence of the jihadist, or any terrorist or totalitarian actor, is deeply troubling. Yet, much literature around both violence and jihadism struggles to grapple with the origin and dynamics of violence and how violence is connected to human nature, historical contexts and developments, and religious doctrine and belief.[4] Connected to this problem, René Girard notes that the question of violence is actually a quite recent phenomenon:

> Violence is a new subject. In the past, people complained about insecurity, disorder, disorderly societies, and so forth, but there was no theme of violence as such. One can even ask the question whether ancient languages had a word that really means violence in our sense. To ask "why is there so much violence around us?" may feel like an eternal question, but in fact it is really a very modern one.[5]

To the challenge of understanding violence and its connection to militant jihadism, I draw on the thought of Girard,[6] one of the premier theorists of violence in the twentieth century. By utilizing Girard's thought in conjunction with the many studies of jihadism, I seek to trace and analyze its major characteristics, particularly in relation to violence. By drawing on anthropological and historical studies as well as the protagonists' own views and experiences, I contextualize Islamist violence within the political, economic, and social conditions of modernity, as well as the beliefs, ideas, and doctrines of the jihadists. Based on the outcome of this approach, I can undertake an anthropological and theological analysis of jihadism's connection to violence.

Aims

The study aims to analyze the motivations and dynamics of jihadist violence. The study primarily focuses on Sunni Islam in the form of Salafi-jihadism, while also analyzing Shia jihadism to note important consistencies and differences with regard to Sunni jihadism. Sunni jihadism has emerged as the most widespread militant form of Islamism. It is a global movement originating in Middle Eastern, north African, and Asian contexts, which has also gained Western followers, especially in migrant communities. It exports members, ideas, and violence to various locations, while also fostering violent actors (whether in the West or the Muslim-majority world) who cause violence in their own local sphere.[7]

This study utilizes Girard's mimetic theory to systematically analyze this contemporary form of religious violence in a way that has not previously been attempted. It does so with the aim to analyze the ideas and actions of jihadist militants, in order to understand how their violence is oriented to a particular type of re-sacralization. I argue that contemporary militant jihadism draws its identity and motivation from a form of idolatrous, re-sacralized violence that rivalrously mirrors major aspects of modernity in defense of select victims.

Terms

In this study, I refer to "extremists" in a broad way to refer to those in a social, religious, or ideological movement on its most extreme or radical fringe who seek revolutionary or radical change, often in a violent manner. When I refer to "Islamists," I am doing so in accordance with the common usage, that is, of a Muslim individual or group who applies Islam in a political fashion to bring about the presence of Islamic law, doctrine, or practice in political life. Islamism is a broad term that can be inexact or even pejorative. There are a range of Islamists, who deploy different types of tactics. According to Gilles Kepel, Islamisms generally emphasize moral order, obedience to God, and hostility to materialist, non-Islamic forces, such as communism, socialism, forms of nationalism, and foreign influences, especially "Western" forms.[8] Radical or militant Islamism is understood in this study as the politicization of Islam into an ideology and movement that regards Islam as a "total system." Those who use violent tactics in the name of Islam, then, are referred to as "violent/militant jihadists," "violent/militant Islamists," "Islamist/jihadist militants," or "Islamist/jihadist terrorists."[9]

Of course, not all those who believe in jihad are "violent jihadists." Jihad has a long, nonviolent tradition, which according to Asma Afsaruddin, is original to the term.[10] Afsaruddin argues it is problematic to use the term "jihad" to describe the violent activity of militant Islamists and terrorists because it obscures the more important nonviolent tradition.[11] Nevertheless, jihad has had a violent tradition (in association with the term for conflict or fighting, *qitāl*). Even if violence is a conditional feature of jihad (as Afsaruddin argues), it is at the center of the doctrinal justification and motivation of militant Islamists/jihadists.[12] Thus, I also use the term "jihadist" in line with other scholars to describe these militant Islamists, though I clarify this usage with the adjective "violent" or "militant."

For ease of reference, I refer to the different groups of militant Islamists or jihadists as a broad movement, with a particular focus on the Sunni-Salafi persuasion. While there are different groups and aims even within Sunni jihadism, they largely share many of the same ideas, doctrines, and histories, which are centered on violence (especially following the Afghan campaign of the 1980s). Though there are differences, many of the leading sociologists and theorists treat jihadi groups broadly as a movement. Even those who don't regard these groups as a movement still recognize their distinctive and unifying characteristic, which is of primary interest in this study: "that it's an individual's duty to engage in violence."[13] Regardless of whether militant jihadism is a movement, it is the connection between militant jihadist groups and violence that I particularly focus on in this study.

Why Militant Islamist and Jihadism?

Religious violence has been identified in various studies as coming in many forms in the past and present. Examples such as the Crusades, anti-Semitic violence, the Sikh Khalsa (military), Islamic expansionism, Israeli military and settler violence, Buddhist-majority persecution of minorities in countries like Myanmar, and Hindu fundamentalism in India are all presented as examples of religious violence. Religious groups are also claimed to be responsible for terrorist actions, such as the Jewish Defense League, the anti-abortion Army of God, and, of course, al-Qaeda and Islamic State (IS, ISIL, ISIS, or Dāʿish).[14] Each of these groups have committed violence for reasons connected to their religious beliefs and moral systems. These examples have led some to condemn religion as inherently violent.[15] This characterization, however, has been heavily critiqued, including in the landmark work by William Cavanaugh.[16] Cavanaugh argues that it is not possible to distinguish religion from political or social movements, such as nationalism or communism. Thus, he concludes that there is no unique category of religious violence. I return to this argument in more detail in Chapter 9.

Since 9/11, Islamist extremism and terrorism have gained the most widespread attention of any form of religious or cultural extremism and ignited a global debate about religious violence. Scott Atran argues that radical Sunni Arab extremism and revivalism is a "dynamic, countercultural movement of world-historic proportions" that has a fundamentally "revolutionary character" in that it seeks to re-make the world through violence.[17] Olivier Roy argues that Islamic extremism is a repository for nihilism in which death is embraced and violence "is an end in itself."[18] Yet, in many ways, militant Islamism parallels other extreme religious, nationalist, or ideological movements in their aims, demography, and actions. For example, Michael Cook claims that Islamic fundamentalism and extremism contains three important components, each of which have other religious parallels. The three components are: a widespread revival of Islamic piety and practice, the growth of Islamist politics (that champions Islamic identity, promotes Islamic values, and seeks to achieve the goal of creating an Islamic state/caliphate), and the rise of Islamic militancy (jihadism).[19] However, in contrast to other religious parallels, Cook argues Islamist extremism uniquely contains these three components at the same time fueling its potency.

Western foreign policy, moreover, has identified and prioritized the threat of Islamic extremist groups, especially Islamic State of Iraq and ash-Sham (ISIS) and al-Qaeda (AQ). Western and other intelligence and policing agencies regard militant jihadism as the most immediate terrorist threat to social order. Christopher Wray, the current director of the US Federal Bureau of Investigation (FBI), reported the following in testimony to the US Senate Homeland Security and Government Affairs Committee on September 27, 2017:

> Currently, the FBI has designated the Islamic State of Iraq and ash-Sham (ISIS) and homegrown violent extremists as the main terrorism threats to the Homeland. ISIS is relentless and ruthless in its campaign of violence and has aggressively promoted its hateful message, attracting like-minded extremists. The threats posed by foreign fighters, including those recruited from the United States, are extremely dynamic. These threats remain the highest priority and create the most serious challenges for the FBI, the U.S. Intelligence Community, and our foreign, state, and local partners.[20]

While the violent threat and potency of groups such as ISIS and al-Qaeda has been clearly demonstrated, there is also much fear and hyperbole regarding Islam and Islamic extremism. This has resulted in a counter-movement to prevent Islamophobia. This study is in sympathy with such responses, however these responses should not preclude full and robust academic study where appropriate, especially when such study can assist in understanding human violence and terrorism in greater depth. In particular, there are distinctive characteristics in militant jihadism—and in the state-based responses to it—that can bring to light important dynamics in modernity and the trajectory of human violence. Without wishing to exaggerate or demonize, this study seeks to understand these dynamics through the lens of militant jihadism as a revolutionary, violent force:

> This [Arab Sunni] revival is a dynamic, countercultural movement of world-historic proportions spearheaded by ISIS, (the Islamic State of Iraq and Syria, also known as ISIL, or the Islamic State of Iraq and the Levant). In less than two years, it has created a dominion over hundreds of thousands of square kilometres and millions of people. And it possesses the largest and most diverse volunteer fighting force since the Second World War.

What the United Nations community regards as senseless acts of horrific violence are to ISIS's acolytes part of an exalted campaign of purification through sacrificial killing and self-immolation: *Know that Paradise lies under the shade of swords*, says a *hadith*, or saying of the Prophet; this one comes from the *Sahih al-Bukhari*, a collection of the Prophet's sayings considered second only to the Quran in authenticity and is now a motto of ISIS fighters.[21]

Why Mimetic Theory and Militant Jihadism?

There have been numerous studies that have tried to come to terms with the jihadist "campaign of purification" in its political, social, and religious dimensions. In a chapter drawing on his academic study of Islam and background in intelligence work, Jonathan Cole claims that analysis of violent jihadism has been overly dominated by Western categories.[22] While Cole states that these categories provide avenues of understanding, "Western epistemological and ontological presuppositions" have led to inadequate forms of analysis that do not take account of "the *particular* worldview of jihadists."[23] Because of the difference from Western thought, Cole argues that Islamic-jihadist thought requires a sustained analysis as it provides the ideological and theological frameworks for violence. In this critique, Cole includes Girard's analysis of Islamic terrorism as he points out that it lacks an appropriate understanding of jihadist categories.[24] This critique poses an important question: what role does mimetic theory have in understanding religious violence and particular forms of violence?

Cole does not totally discount Girard's potential contribution to understanding violent jihadism, particularly in the ability of his theory to engage with empirical data and avoid "treating jihadist violence as utterly sui generis."[25] In this way, mimetic theory can assist in identifying the connections between different forms of religiously and culturally mediated violence. Nevertheless, Cole would like to see Girard's claims about violence tested in relation to jihadist thought. In *Battling to the End*, Girard makes similar claims that Islamic thought needs to be studied in relation to the terrorist violence committed. In particular, he speaks of the need "to try to understand the situation without any presuppositions and using all the resources available from the study of Islam."[26] Moreover, Girard is also critical of conventional Western rationalism as being inadequate to the task of understanding Islamist terrorism and its trajectory of violence:

> What we are witnessing with Islam is nonetheless much more than a return of the Conquest; it is *what has been rising since the revolution has been rising*,

> after the Communist period that acted as an intermediary. Indeed, Leninism had some of these features, but what it lacked was religion. The escalation to extremes is thus able to use all components: culture, fashion, political theory, theology, ideology and religion. What drives history is not what seems essential in the eyes of Western rationalists. In today's implausible amalgam, I think that mimesis is the true primary engine.[27]

While Girard's remarks about Islamist terrorism are suitably qualified regarding the Islamic nature of such violence, he also argues that important understandings of it can be gained through a historical analysis that is combined with a rigorous anthropological understanding of the human person. In *Battling to the End*, Girard suggests that Islamist terrorism is part of a historical spectrum of violence that can be understood in relation to other forms of violence, particularly from the French Revolution onwards. Girard identifies how mimesis is the key driver of this violence, and that mimetic causes for violence have compounded or accelerated in modernity (since the French Revolution). Thus, both a rigorous study of jihadism from within its Islamic categories as well as historical, anthropological, and sociological analysis can provide insight into this unique movement. This study seeks to bring together these two elements, as identified by Cole and Girard as important for understanding violent jihadism, to contribute to a new and deeper analysis.

One further issue that Cole identifies with Girard's claims about violence is that it requires assuming that jihadist conceptuality is delusional, "blinding jihadists to the operation of mimetic rivalry and scapegoating that is the real cause of their violence."[28] Girard argues that all forms of violence that humans enact involve a level of *méconnaissance* (misrecognition), resulting in the protagonists not properly recognizing the nature and dynamics of violent rivalry. For example, when one is on the inside of violence, one believes one is justified in pursuing the object of desire against "aggressive" rivals. One believes one's violence is not aggressive, but just. One will use various rationalizations to justify this violence, including using theological or religious categories. In contrast, when one is on the outside of violence, one can more easily recognize how each rival is delusional about their claims and is in thrall to the reciprocal dynamics of violence that escalate to extremes.

Cole is correct to point to the element of sincerity and truth in the jihadists' use of Islamic categories to justify violence. In fact, as I show, jihadists show a level of intentionality and conscious awareness that is unprecedented in violent actors. Thus, the lines of argumentation used by jihadists need to be analyzed (and, if possible, refuted). These categories are not insignificant for Girard; in fact, they are actually important for understanding how violence is rationalized and enabled. For Girard, nevertheless, it is important to recognize how mimetic violence is a fundamental driver in such rationalizations.

Girard's account of violence, further, requires on-going examination, testing, and substantiation in the gathering and analysis of data. Girard himself is strong on this point: his theory is based on scientific principles and must be tested in relation to the data.[29] This is why Girard states that his mimetic analysis of violence requires engagement with Islamic thought and practice: "We have to be able to think about both Islamism *and* the escalation to extremes at the same time; we need to understand the complex relations between these two realities."[30] While not claiming to be an exhaustive examination of Islamism, this study seeks to contribute to the task of bringing mimetic theory into dialogue with the concepts and activities of militant jihadism, particularly by drawing on the latest studies of jihadist actors, thought, and battlefield practice.

As a starting point, let me provide one example of how Girard's thought can be used to analyze jihadist discourse. The example is drawn from a communique from al-Qaeda to justify the 9/11 attacks on Washington and New York. It justifies the terrorist attacks as purely defensive against a greater enemy and shows no regard for the injustice perpetrated against civilians, including Muslims:

> Allah granted to a troop of youths of Islam by His favor and generosity—and the purity of His success and grace—to give back to the community some of its rightful due, and to cause the Crusader enemy to drink from the cup from which we have drunk for a long time. The heroes who put themselves forward in order to demolish the fortresses of the enemy did not put themselves forward because of an earthly reward that they would receive or an ephemeral position or a fleeting lust, but they put forth their spirits as a ransom for the religion of Allah, in order to protect the Muslims, who taught the American hands a lesson through them. …
>
> Our presentation of [the testaments of the 9/11 attackers] at this particular time is a confirmation to the community that is living in [a time of] troubles in every place that the only way to salvation from this humiliation is through the sword, as the enemy does not know any other language than it. …
>
> Through this document we are sending a message to America and to the entire world that we—despite what America is doing—are coming and that it will never be safe from the wrath of the Muslims, since [the United States] has started the war and will eventually lose it.[31]

The Communique focuses on the injustices caused by the "enemy" and the defensive and protective nature of the "operations" in New York and Washington. It is believed by al-Qaeda that it is reasonable and even altruistic for Muslims to strike back at the enemy, especially in a war that is supposedly not of their own making. In this way of justifying violence, al-Qaeda demonstrates aspects of Girard's analysis of violence. For example, Girard argues that violence is reciprocal and relational, and this is shown in the Communique when it states that the United States started the war and that Muslims are just responding. Further, Girard shows in *Battling to the End* that aggressive postures in modern conflicts are commonly justified as defensive.[32] Al-Qaeda claims its violence is defensive, in protection of the victimized Muslim masses who are troubled and humiliated. As Girard discusses, the discourse of victims is significant in modernity, and it derives from the revelation of human violence. Lastly, all violence is justified in the name of God, which points to the explicit manner by which jihadists seek to re-sacralize violence on behalf of the victimized. These are a few brief examples of how Girard's theory has some strong points of contact with jihadist thought, providing a basis for further analysis.

Nevertheless, there are also particular Islamic concepts and legal justifications given for violence in jihadist thought that one could argue move beyond Girard's analysis. For example, in the Communique as a whole, these features center around general theological justifications for violence and particular justifications of certain actions, such as the killing of Muslims as part of the 9/11 attacks. This specific Islamic theological discourse points to Cole's claim that Western thought alone is inadequate to understanding the nature of jihadist violence.[33] This study aims to address this gap, at least with regard to mimetic theory, through engaging with Islamist history and thought. In this engagement, I show that jihadist thought gravitates to positions motivated by violence, which Girard's analysis can help to contextualize and understand.

Furthermore, the work of Wolfgang Palaver, alongside other work in the area of mimetic theory and world religions,[34] helps to counter the claim that mimetic theory is a Western or Christocentric theory to the exclusion of other traditions. There is increasing engagement between mimetic theory and various religious traditions, such as Islam, Judaism, and Buddhism. As Michael Kirwan argues, the concepts in mimetic theory can provide fruitful points of dialogue and analysis if they are understood by analogy with similar concepts in different religious traditions, rather than with strict lexical equivalences (to the exact words, "mimetic desire" and "scapegoating"). In this way, then, "the truth of sacred violence and its overcoming is not the unique possession of any faith tradition, even if, at present, the language we have for talking about this happens to be Western in origin."[35] In this sense, a well-developed tradition in Islam around such areas as desire, violence, and victimization can be engaged with and analyzed. Moreover, such a dialogue requires an understanding that a tradition is lived contextually: "Nowhere does mimetic theory encounter world faiths in some purified, essential form, but always in the throes of powerful and unsettling processes of modernization, and under the shadow of apocalyptic threats and challenges."[36] This point is particularly relevant to this study in its engagement with militant jihadism, which is a particular and peculiar form of Islam formed within certain modern conditions.

This study, then, seeks to present the fruitful points of analysis that can be made as mimetic theory and studies of contemporary jihadist thought and action are brought into dialogue. As the author of the study, I do not claim to be expert in the field of Islamic thought but I have sought to engage extensively with contemporary studies of jihadist thought as well as military and anthropological studies of jihadist protagonists in the field. This engagement is aimed to provide the relevant data and analysis to enable a robust and rigorous understanding of contemporary jihadist violence, with mimetic theory as the key analytical framework.

Overview of the Study

This study will present two main arguments based on the following approaches:

1. The engagement of Girard's mimetic theory with accounts of modern jihadist violence and thought, including from actors in such violence, to show how jihadist violence is a reaction to and mirror of modernity within a "victim identity"; and,
2. The formulation of a theological and anthropological account of jihadism as an idolatry that distorts the Abrahamic traditions and intentionally re-sacralizes violence in a totalitarian effort justified in defense of select victims and in the name of a divinely sanctioned social order.

This latter point—the explicit re-sacralization of violence—is the distinctive characteristic of jihadism as the means to reinstitute violence at the center of social and transcendent order. Nevertheless, in explicitly re-sacralizing violence in the name of the victim, jihadism shares the same fundamental tenets as other modern forms of totalitarianism. It is an acceleration of modern totalitarianism that seeks to appropriate the nonviolent God of the Abrahamic traditions to reconstitute violence at the heart of human identity.

My approach is distinct within the context of recent studies of religious violence. For example, as discussed, many contemporary studies of Islamic religious violence focus on political and sociological factors. While these studies are helpful, they are limited in their analysis of the theological, religious, and anthropological factors.[37] On the other hand, the studies that seek to analyze the theological and religious categories used by actors in so-called religious violence, such as by the well-known sociologist Mark Juergensmeyer[38] (who draws on Girard's mimetic theory), suffer from problematic understandings of "religion." These understandings have been critiqued by scholars such as Jonathan Z. Smith and William Cavanaugh.[39] There are, nevertheless, numerous studies that have useful data and analyses of modern Islamist violence, which I draw on in my research. I have been able to use and build on this research to provide a systematic analysis of the anthropological and theological dimensions of jihadism.

The study begins in Part I with Chapters 1 and 2 providing an overview of key and relevant insights in Girard's mimetic theory for this study. In particular, an account of violent dynamics in modernity is given in Chapter 2 to contextualize the violence of the jihadist movement. Part II gives an extensive analysis of different features of the jihadist movement to understand its violence. It begins by examining the relationship between militant Islamism, violence, and modernity and shows how jihadism developed a mentality of righteous violence based on a victim identity (Chapter 3). It, then, moves to analyze how militant Islamism systematized its violent answer to modernity in the form of Islam as a "total system" (Chapter 4), with the emphasis on jihad as a necessary and violent action (Chapter 5). Chapter 6, then, analyzes in more detail the way violence is constitutive of the jihadist movement and becomes a form of worship, legitimized with reference to select victims and the divinity. An analysis of jihadist justifications for such violence in this chapter also shows how indiscriminate violence is driving jihadism. In Chapter 7, I examine why this violence is so virulent and strong within jihadism. I show how this violence seeks to provide an antidote to the crisis of personal and social identity that characterizes the jihadist movement. Jihadist violence seeks to construct defining differences to give weight to the jihadists' own identity and satisfy their underlying resentment. On this basis, I, then, show how jihadism becomes a totalitarian movement that re-sacralizes violence in the name of God, which is the subject of Chapter 8. In doing so, jihadism seeks to claim the God of the Abrahamic traditions for its extreme brand of violent transcendence.

Part III draws together the study's analysis of jihadism as a form of "religious violence" and discusses ways to counter it. Bringing together the conclusions of Part II, Chapter 9 addresses why God is referenced in extremist violence. Through theological and anthropological analysis, I identify jihadism as a form of idolatry that distorts the nonviolent trajectory of the Abrahamic traditions. Engaging various works from religious studies, theology, and the evolutionary and cognitive sciences of religion, the chapter discusses the nature of religion and transcendence. In this chapter, I identify an underlying desire for being and God that is distorted within jihadism and sacred violence more generally. Carrying on from the previous chapter, Chapter 10 discusses in more detail how the Abrahamic tradition is distorted by jihadism. It also identifies the specific areas in Islam that remain unresolved regarding violence, which jihadists exploit. This final chapter, then, discusses an alternative to extremist violence, namely, the nonviolent transcendence of "the holy" that cultivates peaceful and humble solidarity with the victimized.

Part I

The Context for Militant Jihadism

1

René Girard's Mimetic Theory

This chapter provides an overview of the main insights of René Girard's mimetic theory, as a foundation for the analysis of subsequent chapters. Girard's work traversed a number of academic disciplines, including history, anthropology, literary studies, philosophy, biblical studies, and theology. Particular attention is given to Girard's understanding of mimetic desire, mimetic rivalry (especially internal mediation), and the sacred, as these are key concepts deployed in this study. Girard's theory is conventionally divided into three major parts:

1. Human desire is mimetic or imitated, that is, it is stimulated by others.
2. Human cultures use scapegoats or victims to resolve mimetic rivalry and violence in order to create and maintain cultural unity.
3. Biblical revelation reveals the innocence of the victim and the nature of the scapegoat mechanism and charts a positive way for structuring human desire in divine self-sacrificial love.[1]

In the latter part of the chapter, I examine the implications of Girard's insights for understanding Islam and explicate a brief understanding of modernity based on mimetic theory.

Mimetic Desire: A New Basis for Understanding the Human Person

Girard's mimetic theory centers on one fundamental concept that has led to a reevaluation of human nature, violence, culture, and religion. This concept is "mimetic desire" (also called "triangular desire" or "imitative desire"), in which Girard identifies that humans desire according to the desire of another.[2] Girard argues that human desire emerges not *for* the other's desire (the Hegelian view) but *according* to the other's desire, that is, under the influence of mimesis.

According to Girard, the origins of human relationality and self-identity, as well as culture, violence, and religion, are to be found in the imitative or mimetic dynamics of human desire. Girard uses the term "mimesis" to denote the social, interpersonal dimension of human desire so to differentiate his understanding from a popular notion of "imitation" as a type of mechanical copying. Girard regards mimesis as the dynamic force within the inner life of the human that brings persons into closer relationship with each other through shared objects and purposes.

The capacity to identify and be stimulated by others' desires is so basic to human selfhood and sociality that humans generally do not even realize its true nature and influence.[3] Jean-Michel Oughourlian, a psychiatrist who collaborated with Girard, argued that the mimetic insight can help to answer the most basic question of psychology: "Why is there *movement* rather than nothing?"[4] Apart from physical appetites (required for survival), the subject is *moved* to desire by the identification of other people's desires in a sophisticated imitative process. Girard's notion of mimetic desire resonates with the Greek philosopher, Aristotle, who observed that humans are the "most imitative" of animals[5], as well as with more recent research that is demonstrating the importance of imitation to the lives and evolution of the human species.[6] Such research has shown, for example, that imitation is a sophisticated capacity in which humans spontaneously engage from the earliest stages of life.[7] Imitation enables humans to transcend their own limited consciousnesses and bodily needs, and it allows for an organic and efficient process of relating and learning. By imaginatively entering into the action and lifeworld of the other in a personal, but social, way, humans can share in common purposes or objects, providing a powerful basis for human bonding.[8]

A conscious self-identity emerges from the complex interplay of mimetic desire in relationship with others, which becomes capable of autonomous, self-determining action. However, imitation of the other's form or what the other has is not sufficient on its own to produce a sense of "self."[9] The complex interaction of these two types of imitation with the temporal dimension of mimesis (repetition) produces a third sort of imitation: "Wanting to *be* who the other is."[10] Thus, the mimetic draw of the model in mediated autonomy enables and structures the human's new-found "ontological need" *to be*: "A need which draws us to others and to imitate them in order to acquire a sense of being, something felt as a lack."[11] As mimesis stimulates patterns of desiring and bonding within groups, it provides the means toward identity within and between people that answers the fundamental yearning for being, which Girard calls "metaphysical desire."[12] Moreover, desire involves a certain fluidity and freedom that remains connected to but not determined by one's social context. In this way, desire has a "metaphysical" character, as it enables a capacity for self-determination whose end is not predetermined, and which must be sought through relationships.

Girard's view, furthermore, implies a reevaluation of the understanding of human consciousness, which is conceptualized in many fields (including in some evolutionary literature) in highly intellectual and individualistic terms. This also has important implications for how violence is understood. By understanding the precognitive nature of mimetic desire, consciousness can then be understood as the way we talk about "the relational (including, but not exhausted by, the linguistic) framework of human awareness and perception."[13] As one matures in the context of tightly bonded groups, human subjects are formed in their imaginative and interpretative skills in order to make decisions about what objects of desire to pursue and whether and how to pursue them, based on social interactions. The challenge for humans is how reliant they become on violent social structures and bonding to determine their mimetic identity and desires.

Mimetic Rivalry: The Key to Understanding Violence and Modernity

Girard's insights into mimetic desire provide a powerful analytical tool to identify and understand patterns of desiring and relating in and across groups and how these patterns motivate violence through mimetic rivalry. Girard's understanding of mimesis, then, helps to demonstrate how humans are formed relationally, but it also has the capacity to demonstrate why and how they engage in dangerous levels of violence.[14] Girard's understanding of the causes of human violence, however, contrasts with some conventional views about violence. He argues violence is customarily regarded as a result either of social or political factors (e.g., oppression) or of biological factors, as a spontaneous act of aggression from a subject to an object.[15] Girard rejects these views as superficial in their portrayal of a "violent person" as somehow different and deviant from an otherwise peaceful human norm. Girard claims that, in fact, violence comes from competition and rivalry over shared desires, which implicates all humans in violence, not just "deviants."[16]

Mimetic rivalry is a common occurrence across human groups and results from the distortion of mimetic desire through certain forms of acquisition and competition. Girard noticed that mimetic desire became pathogenic and distorted as objects of desire are fought over (rather than shared). A pathogenic denial of the other occurs when the model of desire becomes a rival to the subject who wishes to acquire what the model desires. The subject does this by grasping at the object of desire. In this circumstance, the subject asserts the ownership and priority of his/her desire over the other's desire. As part of this assertion, the subject comes to believe in the autonomy of his/her own desire. On this basis, a delusion develops in which one believes one's desire is spontaneously produced by the self rather than dependent on others. Girard calls this delusion a "romantic" sense of the self.[17]

Ultimately, the subject's attempt to grasp at the other's object of desire is an effort to gain the metaphysical or existential depth that the subject regards the model as having because he/she possesses a certain object of desire. The common result is that the model/rival feels his/her own desire heightened for the common object of desire because of the original subject's desire for it. Both, then, seek to secure possession of the object, to the point that relations can become physically violent.

According to Oughourlian, recognition of the dynamics of mimetic desire in rivalrous circumstances is a difficult process—one with which human beings in general have struggled.[18] The object of desire becomes so important to the two rivals that they cannot recognize how their mimetic desire is operating to cause and heighten their conflict. Interestingly, Girard observed that the focus of conflict shifts as mimetic rivalry escalates. Once the rivalry is established, as neither side backs off from their claims to the object, the rivals tend to become more focused on each other. They become mirrors or "doubles" of each other in their desires and actions (in what Girard calls "double mediation"), especially as they reciprocate and heighten the violent actions of the other.[19] At this point of the rivalry, relations are dominated by a "tit-for-tat" attitude in which the original object of desire recedes into the background and is even forgotten. The rival, then, becomes the focus of *scandal* in a competition over identity and being.[20] The rivals now want to win that "being" by defeating the other, so that one's very identity and social standing is at stake.[21] The rival seems to possess the absolute certainty of being that must be conquered in order for one to achieve it. Thus, mimetic rivalry moves to the level of the metaphysical.

On this basis, Girard argues that violence and rivalry are not, in the first instance, caused by differences between human beings, such as differences over culture or religion or between "good" and "bad" people.[22] On the contrary, humans come into conflict primarily over what they commonly desire but can't share. These conflicts can escalate to the point that they fundamentally concern one's identity. At this level, acquiring the object of desire by defeating the rival is about acquiring being *through* difference. By defeating the rival and acquiring the object, one shows oneself and others that "I" am better than the rival—that "I" possess "real" being and "deserve" the object of desire. Thus, a difference is constructed in the midst of sameness—the sameness that occurs through the mirroring of mimetic rivalry. Girard calls this a state of sameness "undifferentiation," when nothing separates the rivals as they become like each other in their desires and actions.

Underlying mimetic rivalry is a fear of undifferentiation: of desiring the same objects because one's rival does and so of being the same, or no better, than the rival. Thus, prior to acquisition, each human fundamentally fears that they have nothing of substance in oneself compared to the other—that one has no ontological or existential density, such that one's appearance of substantiality is only a disguise. This fear leads the subject to grasp for being through that which animates being: desire. It leads the subject to seek greater differentiation from the other, to whom one is integrally bound in "borrowed desire," that is, in rivalry.

In this way, human relations are conventionally structured by reciprocity, that is, by the imitation of desire which leads to actions that are received by the self and then given back to the other/model. For example, in violent rivalry, one responds to a violent gesture by the rival (that blocks one's achievement of a desire) with another violent gesture (that seeks to clear the block or obstacle, or block the other from obtaining the object). The response can be immediate, without deliberation. It leads toward escalation in which greater violence is used to overcome the rival-obstacle.[23] As the rivalry intensifies, reciprocity becomes increasingly metaphysical, that is, the focus of the rivals moves away from acquiring an object to achieving identity and being through victory at any cost:

> As rivalry becomes acute, the rivals are more apt to forget about whatever objects are, in principle, the cause of the rivalry and instead to become more fascinated with one another. In effect the rivalry is purified of any external stake and becomes a matter of pure rivalry and prestige. Each rival becomes for his counterpart the worshipped and despised model and obstacle, the one who must be at once beaten and assimilated.[24]

Girard calls this state of rivalry the *skandalon*, in which the rival becomes a block to the subject's desire so that the rival takes the subject's focus rather than the original object.[25]

In discussing mimetic relations and rivalries, Girard identifies two distinct modes: what he calls "external mediation" (when the model is external and distant to the subject) and "internal mediation" (when the model is close and radically internalized). In external mediation, the subject and model are socially and/or physically distant from each other, and so, rivalry is impractical or impossible. External mediation is usually characterized by a one-directional relationship where the subject is influenced wholly or primarily by a model, and the model is unaware of or uninfluenced by the desire of the subject. Thus, the relationship remains *external* as there is no actual or possible mimetic reciprocity between the subject and the model. Social barriers and hierarchies cultivate forms of external mediation (and so prevent mimetic rivalry), such as the social distinction between an aristocrat and a tenant farmer.

According to Girard, mimetic rivalry occurs when desire is in the state of internal mediation. In internal mediation, the social and/or physical distance between the subject and model is minimal (or nonexistent), so that each becomes the other's model and potential rival.[26] They enter intense forms of reciprocity such that they mirror and internalize each other.

In *Deceit, Desire, and the Novel*, after analyzing key modern novels, Girard poses the question: "Why are men [*sic*] not happy in the modern world?"[27] Girard argues that this is so because modernity is characterized by accelerating forms of *internal mediation*.[28] In modernity, social forms that encouraged external mediation have broken down in fundamental ways, especially since the French Revolution. Identity that rested on such structures is now fragmenting. Increasingly there are minimal barriers in a geographic or social sense to prevent competition and rivalry from escalating. There are no models that give some sense of long-lasting mimetic cohesion, direction, or satisfaction. The capitalist-democratic project stimulates and diffuses mimetic desire through multiple models, but none are ultimately satisfying.

While historically dominant, mimetic rivalry and crisis are not inevitable outcomes of the inner workings of mimesis itself but are a distorted possibility that results from the denial of the anteriority of the other's desire.[29] Mimetic rivalry results from a pathological self-deception based on a false view of the self and one's desire; a self that cannot pacifically come to terms with the other *and so must assert itself over against the other*. Violent rivalry is used to fill the hole created by the human inability to pacifically come to terms with the other, resulting in a violent mechanism that builds distorted identity. It is to this pathology that I will be returning when discussing jihadism.

The Scapegoat and the Sacred: The Heart of Human Culture

Girard further argues that the movement toward cultural crisis, as a result of accumulating mimetic rivalries, is a perennial problem for human societies. Girard demonstrates that this state of social crisis (which he calls a "sacrificial crisis") is actually a common theme across various mythological literature.[30] Even for societies with sophisticated forms of security, outbreaks of violence still occur, such as in urban rioting. A point of provocation or scandal in the midst of escalating or pent-up rivalries causes mimetic contagions and cycles of violence.

The problem of mimetic escalation and group breakdown is, according to Girard, the central hurdle that humanity confronted in the hominization process. Answering this problem enabled the formation of human culture. Through anthropological and literary analysis, Girard discovered that violence is commonly resolved across human cultures by the accumulation of rivalries ("all against all") being cast onto a victim ("all against one"). The accusatory gesture of each member against their rival is transformed into a common gesture against one victim or scapegoat, who is attributed with the blame for the mimetic crisis. Thus, the victim of violence becomes a scapegoat for the rest of the community to unanimously release and deposit its pent-up frustrations, tensions, and rivalries.[31] If and when this "scapegoat mechanism" works, Girard claims that it convenes and maintains human culture.[32]

The scapegoat mechanism, then, unifies disparate desires, as the social group is unanimously united against one other (or group) in "righteous violence." While it produces order and peace, this first social act, nevertheless, involves a repression of the real nature of the scapegoating violence. Girard calls this repression *méconnaissance* (misrecognition or misunderstanding), which results in a false consciousness. In mimetic rivalry, there is an opportunity for awareness of the constitutive nature of mimesis, as the rivals have the possibility to recognize their sameness with the other. However, this awareness is conventionally repressed in transcendent violence, which guarantees order.

This repression follows the shock of finding order in the midst of chaos. As discussed, social relations conventionally collapse into the free-for-all hostility of indistinguishable rivals. Following this, they can suddenly give way to a resolution through scapegoating. Peace, then, is "miraculously" given in the midst of an abyss of violence. This powerful experience of transcendence leads the group to believe (or project) that the victim was really responsible for the whole scenario of chaos in order to bring about peace and order. Peace now relies on the scapegoated victim, who, in the crowd's view, had generated both chaos and order in a manner that was awe-inducing and miraculous. The power of the scapegoating violence is, then, projected onto the victim through a process of divinization. The twin power of the group's violence—to cause and to resolve chaotic violence—results in a "double transference," where both order and disorder, good and evil, are ascribed to the victim through supernatural agency.[33] This transference onto the victim is the basis for the construction of what Girard calls "the (violent) sacred," a variation of which is found across archaic or traditional cultures.[34] It is, in fact, common for traditional cultures to worship gods that are both malevolent and benevolent, which is a sign of the power of "the sacred" to cause chaos and order.

The sacralization or divinization of the victim establishes an absolute difference between the crowd and victim, which is the foundation for cultural difference. It gives a sense of identity to a group and serves to obscure mimetic rivalry and violence. Based on the power of the "violent sacred," cultural groups then perpetuate themselves through the ritual repetition of the scapegoating act (most commonly in sacrifice). This ritual is justified through myths that tell the mob's story of the miraculous experience of the divinized victim. Human cultures also establish taboos or prohibitions, based on their experiences of conflict, to prevent mimetic rivalry from occurring or escalating again. These "pillars of culture," as Girard calls them, lead to the construction of social structures or institutions that are regulated by rituals, taboos, and codes. "Foundation [of institutions] is never a solitary action; it is always done *with others*. This is the rule of unanimity, and *this unanimity is violent*. An institution's role is to make us forget this."[35]

Girard has provided extensive examples of scapegoating, and its central importance, in ancient, medieval, and modern periods. Girard has identified features of scapegoating in the stories that humans tell of their scapegoating acts. He identifies particular features in ancient mythology, such as in the Oedipus myth, and of medieval accounts, such as of the persecution of Jewish people in Europe. Girard found these features to recur commonly across cultures and presented the recurrence of violence and scapegoating as follows:

1. A crisis within the community that results in a generalized loss of distinctions or differentiation between the members of that community (e.g., in Oedipus' case, this was the plague).
2. The identifying and accusing of a victim (e.g., Oedipus as the cause of the plague because of patricide and incest).

3. The presence of certain characteristic traits in the accused, such as being from a minority, high/low position, or having some illness, deformity, or other unusual mark (e.g., Oedipus had a disability and was a foreigner and of high status).
4. The climax with collective violence/persecution occurring against the victim to restore order (usually veiled or symbolic) after which peace is restored and order is regenerated (e.g., Oedipus is expelled from Thebes and the plague is eliminated).[36]

As part of the fourth feature of collective violence, a crucial transformation of the scapegoated victim occurs. Because the scapegoat is at the center of a process that dramatically transforms chaotic violence into order, the power of unanimous violence is transferred or projected onto the victim by the mob, which thus experiences the victim as godlike. In the rise of human societies, Girard argues that the double transference onto the victim has acted as the means to stabilize human groups through an indivisible nexus of religion, language, and culture. In Girard's view, "religion" and "culture" are fundamentally inseparable as "religious" rituals, myths, and laws develop from the "violent sacred" to become the foundation for all cultural order. Nevertheless, despite their violent foundation, Girard regards religion and culture as inherently orientated toward peace. This is shown in the way human societies fear disorder, constantly guard against it, and use limited amounts of violence to maintain order. As part of this, though, the responsibility for violence is repressed and projected onto the sacred. The group externalizes the power of its own violence, so to allow it to continue to have an effect in repressing mimetic violence (and avoid any sense of guilt).

Thus, the externalization of violence—in the form of the sacred (the divinized victim)—is key to group survival because it enables the effect of the violently ordered peace to continue. The group lives under the protection of its projected violence in fear of the wrath of the sacred, which the group seeks to avoid provoking (through taboos and prohibitions). If, however, the sacred is provoked (by some crime against divine law), the group believes that its sacrificial rituals and sacred knowledge (myths) will restore relations. In other words, humans continue to participate in rivalry and distorted desire, which leads back to social disorder and requires regular recourse to unanimous, sacrificial violence to reestablish order.[37] In this sense, religion and culture address the "excess of desire" that humans experience in their mimetic relations. They provide a form of vertical transcendence that attempts to regulate disordered horizontal relations. However, Girard calls this violent transcendence deviated and false because it is "a caricature of vertical transcendency" that sacralizes forms of horizontal relations.[38] It is this "caricature" that violent jihadists (and other totalitarian movements) seek to resuscitate in modernity through their forms of scapegoating violence.

Revealing the Innocent Victim of Human Violence: The Biblical and Abrahamic Traditions

In comparing different cultural myths and anthropological studies, Girard discovered that the Judeo-Christian tradition uniquely undermined scapegoating myths and rituals by proclaiming the innocence of the victim. This biblical proclamation, culminating in the life, death, and resurrection of Jesus, exposed sacrificial violence as wrong and sought the transformation of distorted desire and mob violence through loving forgiveness. While deeply influenced by and emerging from a world dominated by sacred violence, Girard shows that the Bible continually takes a stance that identifies God with the innocent victim (rather than the mob). Girard demonstrates this with reference to biblical texts about victims such as Abel, Joseph, Job, the Suffering Servant in Isaiah, the Psalmist, John the Baptist, Jesus, and Stephen. Moreover, the Israelites' founding experience, the Exodus, is about God saving an enslaved people from large-scale persecution and victimization.[39]

The distorted condition of human relationships and cultures is exemplified, according to Girard, when Cain kills Abel or when Joseph is expelled by his brothers in the book of Genesis.[40] The Cain and Abel story seems to be connected to the other myths that relate how a rivalry, usually between brothers, founded a city, such as between Romulus and Remus that led to the founding of Rome.[41] Girard argues that Genesis relates the story of rival brothers but, in contrast to the myths, the victor and founder of the city is not venerated but is condemned as a murderer.[42] Genesis pointedly shows how Cain kills his brother Abel and identifies the cause of this violence in Cain's envy of Abel.[43] Following this, Cain is said to establish a city, which shows the culturally foundational character of Cain's murder.[44]

The condemnation of Cain made by God in Genesis occurs, according to Girard, because the victim is regarded as *innocent*.[45] Girard states that "Abel is only the first in a long line of victims whom the Bible exhumes and exonerates."[46] For example, in the story of Abraham, God prohibits those in covenantal relationship with him to violently sacrifice humans, particularly their children.

In the book of Exodus, God liberates an enslaved and victimized people from the violent wrath of an oppressive power. In the Psalms and "the Songs of the Suffering Servant" in Isaiah, the cries and sufferings of the victim are explicitly recounted.[47] Furthermore, Girard particularly highlights the story of Joseph, which shows the collective character of mob violence when envious brothers expel Joseph.[48] The biblical text shows the innocence of Joseph, who remains loyal to God and is reconciled to his brothers through forgiveness.

Furthermore, Girard argues that the passion, death, and resurrection of Jesus particularly reveal the innocence of the victim and God's solidarity with the victim, which transforms sacred violence through divine forgiveness.[49] The Gospels clearly proclaim Jesus' innocence as a victim of mob violence and even admit the guilt of Jesus' followers who initially acquiesce to such violence by abandoning Jesus. These followers realize Jesus' true innocence and their own guilt after experiencing God's gratuitous forgiveness and self-giving love in Jesus' resurrection. They are, then, able to resist the mob's condemnation of victims, which is demonstrated in the way the New Testament tells the story of Jesus and the early church: "The God of the Bible is at first the God of the sacred, and then more and more the God of the holy, foreign to all violence, the God of the Gospels."[50] In particular, the Bible presents that death does not have the ultimate say over the victim, nor is violence the ultimate arbiter of human life:

> The essential factor … is that the persecutors' perception of their persecution is finally defeated. In order to achieve the greatest effect that defeat must take place under the most difficult circumstances, in a situation that is the least conducive to truth and the most likely to produce mythology. This is why the Gospel text constantly insists on the irrationality ("without a cause") of the sentence passed against the just and at the same time on the absolute unity of the persecutors, of all those who believe or appear to believe in the existence and validity of the cause, the *ad causam*, the accusation, and who try to impose that belief on everyone.[51]

In addition to the revelation of the innocent victim, Girard came to affirm the loving and self-giving dimension of sacrifice. Initially resistant to the terminology, Girard recognized that this loving form of sacrifice—in which one nonviolently offers oneself for the good of the other—provides an alternative to violent sacrifice as a foundation for human relationality and identity.[52] He saw this form of sacrifice in the example of Jesus and in Solomon's famous judgment whereby, in a dispute between two women over a child, the true mother is willing to give up her claims to her child to save the child's life.[53]

Furthermore, according to Girard, the Christian tradition's insistence on the importance and divinity of the human victim, Jesus, is not the result of the mob violence that killed him. Rather, it is his loving self-giving and forgiveness that expresses the true nature of humanity and divinity, which Jesus demonstrates on the Cross: "Father, forgive them for they know not what they do" (Lk. 23:34; King James Version).[54] As Girard insists, "Love is the only true revelatory power because it escapes from, and strictly limits, the spirit of revenge and recrimination that still characterizes the revelation in our world, a world in which we can turn that spirit into a weapon against our own doubles, as Nietzsche also showed."[55]

However, in contrast to his study of Judaism and Christianity, Girard does not devote much attention to Islam. In his final work, *Battling to the End*, Girard makes some preliminary remarks about Islam, though he begins with a qualification that he has not done extensive study of Islam and that such study is required to properly evaluate Islam and the nature of terrorist groups.[56] Nevertheless, he puts forward a tentative hypothesis that Islam seems to rebuild archaic religion in a more powerful way than previously, supported by aspects of the Bible.[57] In his reading of the Qur'an, Girard sees a recognition of how violent sacrifice prevents vengeance.[58] This awareness implies some understanding of the dynamics of violence, though it can be used in the service of the violent jihad.[59] He also believes that the escalation of violence in modernity has taken advantage of Islam (as it has of other ideologies and nationalisms). Further, he also states that terrorism is a new phenomenon that is not related to classical Islamic thought and requires radical new ways of understanding.[60]

Wolfgang Palaver argues that Girard's remarks about Islam must be qualified by Girard's own admission of a lack of expertise and analysis regarding Islam, and Girard's own cognizance of not making Islam and Muslims into rivals and scapegoats.[61] Palaver argues Islam actually belongs to the Abrahamic tradition or "revolution" in the way that Girard understands Judaism and Christianity breaking from archaic religion by revealing the innocence of the victim.[62] Palaver demonstrates the consistency between Islam, Judaism, and Christianity by showing how stories in the Bible and the Qur'an are treated in similar ways. For example, in both the Bible and the Qur'an, the story of Abraham and Isaac prohibits human sacrifice, which is an important development in the history of violence. Moreover, both sacred books see the pivotal figure of Joseph as an innocent victim who reconciles with his fraternal persecutors.[63] On this basis, Palaver attempts to show that Islam has a consciousness of the victim in the

Qur'an and also an awareness of the dangers of human desire and violence. Moreover, Islam allows for expression of desire in a way that is driven by individual conscience before God and guided by certain laws/rules.

If Islam belongs to the same trajectory as Judaism and Christianity with regard to how human violence is understood and treated, it does not mean that these three traditions have an easy relationship with violence. On the contrary, it makes them prone to outbursts of violence within the societies in which they operate because violence is no longer constrained in the traditional fashion of scapegoating. In the Christian context, Girard refers to "historical Christianity" as the site of innumerable manifestations of sacred violence that have used the sensibilities of the Christianity tradition to create new victims, such as different Jewish populations in Europe.[64] Invariably, violence is justified in defense of victims against perceived persecutors. In this way, the dynamics of sacred violence take advantage of the concern for the victim by persecuting new victims who are claimed to have been persecutors themselves.[65]

Nevertheless, in Girard's view, this historical distortion does not discredit the essential insight into and solidarity with the innocent victim that is present within the Abrahamic traditions. In fact, it shows that violence has been unleashed from its previous constraints and that members of these traditions are still coming to terms with how to live without sacrificial violence. The fact that there is a contestation within these traditions between sacred violence and nonviolent solidarity with the victim actually presents the slow breakdown of the violent sacred and its attendant social structures, and the slow outworking of the implications of this breakdown for humanity's attachment to sacred violence. Thus, while violence discredits the witness of the Abrahamic traditions, it does not negate their essential trajectory—namely, to reveal violence and grow in solidarity with the innocent victim.

Modernity and the Concern for Victims

As a sign of the effect of the Abrahamic traditions in history, Girard argues that the concern for the victim is the distinctive driver and characteristic of modernity. While modernity is marked by a negative trend toward violence (e.g., world wars and terrorism), it is also marked by a positive trend in which victimization is recognized as morally wrong and nonviolent forms of solidarity are being developed. Girard states,

> The theme of human rights has become a major sign of our uniqueness as far as the protection of victims is concerned. Nobody before us had ever asserted that a victim, even someone who was unanimously condemned by his or her community, by institutions with legitimate jurisdiction over him or her, could be right in the face of the unanimous verdict. This extraordinary attitude can only come from the Passion as interpreted from the vantage point of the Gospels.[66]

Yet, Girard also argues that, despite the concern for victims, modernity is capable of the most destructive violence because violence has been unleashed from its sacrificial restraints: "The [Christian] Revelation *deprives* people of [archaic] religion, and it is this deprivation that can increasingly be seen around us, in the naïve illusion that we are finished with it. ... It is the loss of sacrifice, the only system able to contain violence, which brings violence back among us."[67] Thus, there are parallel and opposing trends in modernity caused by the revelation of the victim: "Our world is both the worst it has ever been, and the best. It is said that more victims are killed, but we also have to admit that more are saved than ever before. Everything is increasing. Revelation has freed possibilities, some of which are marvelous and others dreadful."[68]

In the first place, then, modernity is characterized by the positive concern for victims that has generally sought to resist and expose forms of violence. Growing out of this, modernity has been the site of efforts to protect victims (e.g., human rights, the responsibility to protect doctrine) and promote peace and reconciliation, based on nonviolent forms. In an unparalleled way, it has sought to promote respect for the dignity of the human person and social justice initiatives that seek to eliminate sacrificial violence among members of a community or state.[69] Second, and contrarily, there are escalating mimetic rivalries and forms of violence in modernity, such as terrorism, world wars, the Cold War, and the development of atomic weapons that are not kept in check by scapegoating and sacred violence. These two trends in modernity dangerously coalesce in totalitarian forms such as Nazism, communism, and jihadism, in which destructive and escalating forms of violence are justified against perceived persecutors in defense of the so-called victims of modernity. For example, in the name of the victimized Aryan people, Nazism undertook genocidal violence in the Holocaust, which, Girard argues, "was an attempt to divorce the West from its dedication to saving victims."[70] Thus, totalitarianism seeks to destroy victims in the name of victims. In a similar way (as I will show), militant jihadism twists the Abrahamic insight into the victim to resuscitate sacred violence.

Furthermore, while the injustice of scapegoating the innocent has become evident to modern people (especially in the West), this moral advance comes at the expense of weakened cultural protections. It leads to the possibility of unrestrained, "apocalyptic" violence, according to Girard.[71] Notable examples of this trend are world wars, indiscriminate "extremist violence," and terrorism, with violence escalating to unforeseen extremes.

Conclusion

According to Girard, the breakdown in the effectiveness of cultural institutions to restrain violence can be broadly attributed to one major cause: to the biblical/Abrahamic traditions. In the Abrahamic traditions, human violence is definitively exposed and the possibilities for a cultural shift away from violence occur. Thus, the cultural crisis that seems to afflict the modern world is really the emergence of a definitive choice for humanity: for or against violence. In the next chapter, I analyze the trajectory of modern violence in the context of this modern crisis, particularly in the unleashing of violence from the restraints of cultural institutionalization. The next chapter, then, examines the historical and cultural factors that contribute to the conditions for extremist violence.

2

Violence in Modernity

To understand contemporary terrorism and militant jihadism, situating them in the modern context is key. This context is sharply brought into focus by Girard's analysis of the dynamics of violence in modernity. According to Girard, Western-led modernity is characterized by a breakdown in the religious and cultural structures that have conventionally restrained violence, most particularly the institution of warfare.[1] This breakdown has been accompanied by the unleashing of mimetic desire (in the form of internal mediation), resulting in the escalation of rivalries and violence. In this chapter, I examine this breakdown with reference to trends in modern violence and how the identification of such trends contributes to understanding the context for violent jihadism and terrorism. These trends have resulted in the escalation of violence, in forms such as terrorism. They have also given rise to institutional responses to address such violence.

Forms of Violence in Modernity

There are some broad trends in violent activity in the modern period, particularly since the eighteenth century, that are important to consider in order to analyze contemporary extremist violence and terrorism. These trends have many of their origins in the West but have been internationalized through colonization and globalization. The most prominent trends in violence that are relevant to this study include:

1. The rise of revolutionary and totalitarian regimes.
2. The outbreak of world wars and the atomic bomb.
3. The Cold War and Mutually-Assured Destruction (MAD).
4. Genocide and genocidal civil wars.
5. Terrorism.

These five trends represent distinctive developments and extreme manifestations of violence in modernity. I provide a brief rationale of their importance:

1. The rise of revolutionary and totalitarian regimes enabled states to mobilize whole societies for "total warfare" and form standing armies, often justified in a moral or ideological cause (e.g., to liberate victims of inequality and oppression).[2]
2. The outbreak of world wars represented the closest realization of "total warfare" in human history, with most of the world engulfed in absolute warfare (in what Clausewitz might identify as the concept of war meeting its reality).[3] The atomic bomb was, of course, used at the culmination of the Second World War—a sign of the developing capacity of humanity for total, mass destruction following the deadliest and most widespread war.
3. The Cold War and MAD represent a phase of modern politics and warfare in which a global rivalry of nuclear-armed "superpowers" predominated. It revolved around the capacity for mass destruction, with the ability to target and destroy much or all of the enemy's (and world's) military and population with nuclear strikes.
4. Genocide and genocidal civil wars are another feature of modern warfare in which an armed group or state has sought to completely destroy whole identifiable populations. Infamously, Nazi Germany and the Second World War are known for genocidal aims, especially against the Jewish people. Internal discord in a state is sought to be resolved by the genocidal targeting and destruction of an identified group. According to the attacking group (or state), total destruction of the enemy group is the only satisfactory solution for whatever problem they identify, usually concerning the group or nation's woes. The Rwandan genocide in 1994 stands out as the most prominent and brutal example of contemporary genocide based around postcolonial ethnic divisions and national discord.
5. Terrorism parallels nuclear warfare and genocide in that it is the asymmetrical effort to destroy the enemy, even to the point of sacrificing of one's own life to kill others. As I will show in the following section, jihadist violence has developed to the point that terrorism is not just a tactic but an expression of an underlying theology: namely, that the enemy should be totally destroyed or, alternatively, should be converted and submitted to a totalitarian Islamist rule.

These five trends demonstrate the distinct and extreme trajectory of violence in modernity. They revolve around certain forms of rivalry, which, when such forms escalate to their absolute state, present the end or logic of mimetic rivalry: total destruction or total domination. For example, Girard argues that the European rivalries of the nineteenth century, especially between France and Germany, are crucial for understanding modernity and its violence, especially in the way that they led to the global wars of the twentieth century. These rivalries escalated to destructive proportions in the search for territory and identity, especially by newly developing states and empires. As the European experience shows, if mimetic rivalry escalates according to its own logic then the state of absolute competition and fixation with the rival can grip whole populations. The mobilization of populations and the destruction of the world wars show how modern states, especially Germany and Japan, entered into a state of total warfare, with destructive invasions and bombing campaigns.[4] Militant jihadism is the most recent and virulent manifestation of escalating mimetic rivalry in the contemporary world.

Warfare and Desire in Modernity

The destructive forms and patterns of violence in modernity is, according to Girard, connected to the breakdown of sacred systems (desacralization) that previously provided order. In particular, extreme forms of violence are attributable to the breakdown of the institution of warfare and the parallel rise of the "secular" state in conducting total warfare. Girard argues that the institution of warfare was historically an important sacrificial institution to restrain and channel violence. It was deployed in the manner of scapegoating, by directing a group or tribe against an enemy in a regulated way. The regulation of warfare continued into the medieval period and was reconstructed in a particular way to control outbursts of violence and warfare in Europe. Warfare was institutionalized through aristocratic codes and rules, like that of duels and tournaments, and allowed for relatively controlled expressions of violence. These codes and rules sought to restrain warfare and channel intergroup violence in meaningful structures (bestowing honor and status, for example), which established stability in medieval Europe and "new equilibria over an ever growing geographical area."[5] However, with the onset of revolution and total war in modernity, warfare was released from its regulatory restraints, under the pressure of mass mimetic dynamics.[6]

The origins of absolute rivalry in modernity are to be specifically found, according to Girard, in the outbreak of total warfare following the French Revolution and under the direction of Napoleon.[7] In the Napoleonic Wars, warfare lost its particular institutional character and was no longer the preserve of the aristocracy and its codes and strategies. As these codes were overcome, war became "total," unrestrained by the rules and conventions that had structured it as a sacrificial activity, that is, as an activity that cathartically released mimetic tensions in a controlled and regulated fashion.[8] In total warfare, the conventions and structures of war are purposefully disregarded so that a whole populace is mobilized for violence against a nation's rival(s).

Total warfare represents a crucial development in the trajectory of violence in modern history. Girard argues that warfare is unleashed to act according to its nature, which he shows to be fundamentally modelled on the dynamics of the duel (which escalate to death). In other words, modern warfare is a manifestation of the logic of mimetic rivalry that escalates to victory or death. In modern Europe, then, warfare became a vehicle for the release of violence in an absolute and destructive fashion as whole societies, often only newly formed (e.g., post-Revolution France and Germany), were mobilized for warfare. This trajectory of total warfare culminated in the world wars of the twentieth century and the race toward nuclear weaponry, with its potential for absolute destruction.

Warfare in the modern period (after the French Revolution) expanded so that it included the whole of society—in the provision of soldiers and weapons—and produced a military–industrial complex. Standing armies were the result of this process—showing that warfare was shedding its previous temporary character and taking on a more permanent, total character. In fact, Girard argues that standing armies and conscription united individual Western nation-states in an unprecedented way by centralizing the monopoly over violence and homogenizing civilian allegiance to the state.[9] Thus, the state became subject to, and could even direct, the mass feeling or hatred of the people in a unilateral way like "the crowd converging on a third party" in the manner of a scapegoat.[10] In this way, warfare moved from a codified game or art to a "religion," undergirded by sacred acts of violence.[11] The most comprehensive and violent forms of this secular "religion" appear in totalitarian regimes, and in a parallel way, in militant jihadist groups.

Girard argues that the breakdown of regulated warfare in modern Europe was due to increasing polarization and competition in modernity among nation-states. He argues that escalating nation-state rivalry, especially the French–German competition for identity and supremacy in Europe, contributed to total mobilization.[12] Within early modern European nations, the previous cultural system based around firm hierarchies (with the monarchy and aristocracy at the apex) was superseded by the nation-state where the old hierarchies were swept aside by a more egalitarian mobilization of the whole populace.[13] This change was driven by the outbreak of what Girard calls "internal mediation," that is, the intense form of desire in which there is less distance between subjects and models/rivals and so a greater chance for flatter social relations and more rivalries and competition. According to Girard, the democratic revolutions unleashed desire from preexisting social hierarchies, through the explosive power of internal mediation. Thus, the new democratic situation did not just mean universal suffrage in shared power and values, but on its darker side, it meant anyone could be in competition with anyone else:

> Who is there left to imitate after the "tyrant"? Henceforth men shall copy each other; idolatry of one person is replaced by hatred of a hundred thousand rivals. In Balzac's opinion, too, there is no other god but envy for the modern crowd whose greed is no longer stemmed and held within acceptable limits by the monarch. *Men will become gods for each other.*[14]

Modernity is characterized, then, by widespread competition in a manner previously unknown, spurred on by forms of internal mediation. Girard argues that the political and cultural drive for equality in Europe (which is laudable in principle) became dominated by forms of rivalry and violence, such as when the lofty principles of the French Revolution descended into class warfare and executions. This descent into class warfare and violence occurred because of the destruction of previous social hierarchies and norms. The revolutions of early modern Europe destroyed the prerevolutionary class system by removing its central pillar: the divine right of absolute monarchs.[15] For most of their history, traditional or premodern societies were built on the acceptance of social hierarchies that provided order, mediated desire, and structured relationships, within a defined social and existential framework. In medieval and early modern Europe, the rise of absolute monarchs invested with the divine right of kings effected a definitive social distance from (and victory over) the aristocracy, building on the distance between the aristocrat and the serf/peasant. It meant that the monarch was at the pinnacle of the social hierarchy, always to be imitated and never to be rivalled. The divine right acted as a taboo to prevent violence and social breakdown. By making the monarch's position subject to a supernatural taboo and licence, the monarch was largely removed from being a participant in the rivalries of the aristocracy. These rivalries could have resulted in the monarch's removal, scapegoating, or assassination. This structure gave social power and protection to the absolute monarch, especially to eliminate private feudal wars and centralize state power.

The democratic revolutions destroyed this system by taking the last step to expose the arbitrary nature of the class system—the divine right of kings—which was also culture's ultimate protection. The old hierarchies were no longer sacred. The monarch could be challenged by anyone, and so by implication, anyone could be in competition with anyone else. Even worse, anyone could be killed by anyone else, especially if one had a plausible justification to suit the guillotiners.[16] Girard states that, following the French Revolution, no one in France could "be privileged without knowing it."[17] The bourgeoisie and the "common people" could desire and take what the king had, namely wealth, power, and status. The masses were "entitled," which, as Girard states, only exacerbates the desire for more and greater, in "ontological sickness."[18]

Thus, the killing of the king unleashed internal mediation in a vicious fashion in France and across Europe, under the ideological cover of "equality."[19] Power and sovereignty became internally contestable and accessible, ostensibly driven by an ideology of equality, but in its violent manifestations, motivated by internal mediation. For this reason, the violence during and after the French Revolution was not directly caused by strong and oppressive class barriers. Rather, such violence had its roots in the growth in mimetic competition made possible by increasingly ineffective class barriers (made redundant by the killing of the monarch), in which the distance between subject and model was collapsing. A truly effective social hierarchy could have repressed the violence of the democratic revolutions, but instead, the social hierarchies were destroyed by these revolutions:

> The increasing equality—the approach of the mediator in our terms—does not give rise to harmony but to an even keener rivalry. Although this rivalry is the source of considerable material benefits, it also leads to even more considerable spiritual sufferings, for nothing material can appease it. Equality which alleviates poverty is in itself good but it cannot satisfy even those who are keenest in demanding it; it only exasperates their desire. When he emphasises the vicious circle in which the passion for equality is trapped, Tocqueville reveals an essential aspect of triangular desire. The ontological sickness, we know, always leads its victims toward the "solutions" that are most likely to aggravate it. The passion for equality is a madness unequalled except by the contrary and symmetrical passion for inequality, which is even more abstract and contributes even more directly to the unhappiness caused by freedom in those who are

> incapable of accepting it in a manly fashion. Rival ideologies merely reflect both the unhappiness and incapability; thus they result from internal mediation—rival ideologies owe their power of persuasion only to the secret support the opposing factions lend each other. Fruits of the ontological scission, their duality reflects its unhuman geometry and in return they provide food for the devouring rivalry.[20]

Alongside the fragmenting of traditional cultural hierarchies in internal mediation, human identity also becomes unstable and atomized. Mimetic models and patterns multiply, but none are definitive. None have authority and sacredness, or compel a decisive choice: "It is in internal mediation that the profoundest meaning of the *modern* is found."[21] The acceleration of mimetic desire has led to a distinctive crisis—the crisis of the "underground man" whose mimetic desire is uncontrollable and whose metaphysical identity is totally insubstantial.[22] In this context, it is possible to understand the underlying dynamics to which the violent totalitarian or extremist is responding. They seek to reassert control both culturally and personally through ever-escalating forms of violence.

The outbreak of internal mediation and the drive for equality also help one to understand the causes of warfare in modernity. Equality was, for example, the justification that was used to mobilize the French people in the Revolutionary and Napoleonic Wars. The French people were supposedly tasked with the liberation of the European continent from its dictators. With this justification, the chaos of internal mediation was focused on defeating internal and external enemies. Thus, while old social hierarchies were destroyed, the Revolutionary and Napoleonic Wars provided a new form of sacred structure, in which violence was done for a sacred moral purpose: to free the oppressed from the inequalities and injustices of the absolutist-monarchical state. The masses were, of course, entitled to better conditions and rights, however the mimetic dynamics of the conflict exaggerated legitimate demands as rivalry escalated desire. As desire was heightened, the moral purpose of the Revolution was exploited to justify the violent conduct of the Revolutionary politicians and the imperialist conquests of Napoleon and his followers. It was this moral purpose that provided a cover for mimetic desire to be unleashed across the continent, providing the sacred justification for total warfare. This total mobilization provided structure and meaning again to French public life.

In modernity, then, violence and warfare have entered a new, unpredictable phase: the moralization or "theologization" of warfare, as Schmitt identified.[23] Modern wars are marked by their extreme violence and motivated by the desire for total victory against the morally monstrous enemy.[24] Modern moralism provides a new incitement and justification for violence as it allows for the scapegoating of people by labelling them as "evil" and "oppressive." For example, according to the revolutionaries, the absolute monarchs of Europe had failed in their moral duty to their citizens and were inherently oppressive and so were deserving of death. This "moral" violence was prone to extremes. According to Clausewitz, "moral wars" removed the motivation and strategizing of warfare from the political arena, which generally sought limited objects through rational negotiation, to the ideological and moral sphere.[25] These moral wars allowed violence to be cathartically expelled to extremities, though often in extreme ways, even becoming genocidal in some cases. Thus, this type of warfare becomes, according to Girard, "absolutely unpredictable, truly undifferentiated violence."[26]

Furthermore, moral wars turn the biblical insight into the innocent victim on its head through a renewed form of sacred violence. Moral wars are "*total wars*," according to Dumouchel, in that they are undertaken to persecute and destroy the enemy in the name of protecting or liberating the victimized.[27] The victim becomes the new sacred category that affords protection to those who can claim it effectively and licenses violence against those labelled as persecutors. Thus, the moral crusade in revolutionary times to liberate the oppressed and victimized from the "tyrant" led to an outbreak of unfathomable violence in France and across Europe. Similarly, movements to liberate the oppressed peoples of Germany under Nazism or the working classes under Communism resulted in unprecedented levels of violence.

Girard warns that defending victims by persecuting the so-called persecutors is the most efficacious grounds for a new form of "sacred" religion ("paganism"). It alone provokes the most scandal to mobilize a population in (near) unanimity to scapegoat new and "deserving" victims.[28] It is a "secularized" or disenchanted form of sacred violence, not motivated by supernatural license but by moral and political absolutes. Palaver argues it relies on combining mimetic violence with the victim consciousness and suppresses a nonviolent mimetic ethos or practice.[29] It focuses on violent retribution and punishment for accused oppressors or victimizers.

Thus, the defense of the oppressed and victimized constitutes the major moral justification and incitement for mimetic rivalry and violence in modernity. Yet, as discussed in Chapter 1, it also constitutes a motivation for positive political and social changes. However, when the concern for victims cannot be combined with a nonviolent ethos, then violent revolution and warfare becomes possible.

In modernity, it is this justification that retains the greatest force to unify people, most often in violent moral campaigns. It twists the awareness of the innocent victim as a tool for righteous violence. This characteristic is even present in the jihadist movement. For example, violent jihadists claim to undertake righteous violence for similar moral reasons as the revolutionaries: "You think we are the aggressors. That is the number one misunderstanding. We are not: we are the victims."[30]

As I show in more detail in the next section, jihadist violence has the same structure as modern secular violence—it is justified in the name of the victimized, in a perverse distortion of the consciousness of the innocent victim. Jihadism is different, however, in that it claims an explicit supernatural justification for its violence and totalitarianism. This supernatural or transcendent justification parallels the emphasis on race or ideology in Nazism and Communism, though jihadism more directly seeks to appropriate God and the Abrahamic tradition to renew sacred violence and suppress nonviolent alternatives.

Terrorism, Jihadism, and Absolute Rivalry

The outbreak of total warfare and the disintegration of the rituals and institutions of warfare in the modern period are crucial for understanding the trajectory of violence represented by terrorism. Girard (drawing on Clausewitz) states that "the escalation to extremes"[31]—the polarizing and escalating nature of violence and rivalry—now occurs "on a planetary scale."[32] This is demonstrated by how the United States and its allies have been drawn into an intense conflict with militant Islamist extremists in places across the globe, despite the USA's geographical distance and military superiority. The globalization of modernity means that distance and strength do not imaginatively or mimetically deter weak and small parties from engaging in violent rivalries, as it would have in the past. Instead, escalating mimetic rivalry opens up the possibility for violence anywhere. Asymmetrical warfare—enabled by an intense form of rivalrous feeling and armed with new technology—makes it possible to inflict unlikely violence on a much stronger enemy.

Girard further argues that the escalation to extremes is identifiable with what Christianity describes as the "apocalypse."[33] For Girard, the violence of the apocalypse is not driven by divine intervention or punishment but rather can be identified with the outworkings of unrestrained human violence through escalating rivalry: "*When sacrifice disappears, all that remains is mimetic rivalry, and it escalates to extremes*."[34] The advent of total warfare and terrorism is, for Girard, a premonition of the apocalypse, that is, of the possibility of absolute destruction through human violence.

In Girard's view, then, violence is becoming more unpredictable and absolute in its pretensions as humans embark on pure rivalry and destruction, exemplified by forms of terrorism.[35] Yet, while Girard regards terrorism as part of a trajectory of escalating violence in modernity, he also sees something new in terrorism that takes advantage of Islam (and other political ideologies and nationalisms).[36] Terrorism regards itself as "a superior form of violence" that seeks an absolute victory at all costs, particularly in the effort to counter Western technology.[37]

Louise Richardson argues that terrorism expanded in the latter half of the twentieth century as a tactic to combat large, sophisticated military forces (some with nuclear weapons).[38] Terrorism became the tactic of choice by smaller groups bound together in powerful ways by shared bonds, goals, and beliefs.[39] Though it breaks the distinction between combatant and civilian, Richardson argues terrorism is consistent with the behavior of soldiers in seeking to kill an enemy and protect one's group by offering one's own life.[40] While it is true that terrorists act with a similar aim to modern military forces, their logic departs from the proportionality of modern warfare and presents the potentiality of total warfare. This departure is exemplified in one key area (which it shares with other forms of totalitarian violence): the indiscriminate nature of terrorist violence. As I show in the next section, indiscriminate violence has been increasingly deployed by violent jihadists as an explicit religious and moral duty, not just as an unintended consequence or unfortunate aspect of defensive measures. In this form, jihadist violence moves beyond proportionate military actions, doing so in a way that twists or disregards laws and prohibitions in the execution of total warfare. Such violence gives these groups their identity and unity, much like totalitarian states mobilized by total war. Furthermore, these extremist groups do not try to hide the victims of their indiscriminate and brutal violence, as some previous totalitarian regimes have attempted to do. Rather, they celebrate their violence in an explicit fashion and trumpet their targeting of combatants and civilians.[41]

The lack of distinction between civilians and combatants manifests a characteristic of modernity present in militant jihadism, though in an extreme way. Based on Schmitt's genealogy of terrorism, Girard argues that at the same time as Napoleon unleashed total warfare, irregular warfare (and the roots of terrorism) developed, as "partisans" sought to combat invading armies.[42] In irregular warfare, the distinction between soldier and civilian is purposefully confused (often for defensive purposes). Moreover, Girard notes that as "regular" armies developed in early modern Europe (able to mobilize all able-bodied persons in a standing army), irregular warfare developed as an equivalent.[43] In the confrontation between standing armies and local guerrilla forces, the respect for civilian status was eroded.

Nevertheless, guerrilla warriors and partisans generally target soldiers. By contrast, terrorists are purposefully indiscriminate in their targets. The terrorist takes the collapsing of the traditional distinction of civilian and combatant to an extreme. The terrorist is both a member of a civilian population and a covert combatant, targeting both combatants and civilians as enemies. According to Girard, this attitude "ensures the passage from war to terrorism" in which total war has escalated to the point where there are no longer legitimate armies but only fighters "ready to do anything."[44] Thus, the terrorist is intentionally orientated toward total destruction, as a vital means toward victory. Terrorist groups can be strategic in their choice of civilian or combatant targets, but such calculation is meant to inflict the most damage in an indiscriminate way to weaken and destroy the enemy. Thus, the order of the militant jihadist is not the sacred order of archaic societies that carefully engaged with violence ritualistically, or even medieval ones that codified violence, but rather, it is a radically modern one that has moralized and totalized violence. As I will show in the next section, the jihadist "all or nothing" mentality involves the complete destruction of one's enemies and is externalized and justified in a new form of sacred violence.[45]

While terrorism is a premonition of total destruction, it also represents a failure: the failure to mount an effective symmetrical campaign against an enemy. Gilles Kepel argues that, despite the revival of Islam as a political force across the Muslim-majority world in the twentieth century, militant Islamism has largely been a failure. It has failed to mobilize Arab and other Muslim populations against local "apostate" regimes and to defeat those regimes and their Western allies by force (despite some successes such as in Iran).[46] Because of this failure, militant jihadism becomes more extreme in seeking a violent, apocalyptic solution. The jihadist-terrorist solution is to engage in the most extreme and devastating asymmetrical warfare in order to catalyze a global war, in which it is thought that true Muslims will be moved to support the jihadist movement.

In order to apply this solution, militant jihadism has globalized, especially following the Afghan campaign in 1980s. It has expanded its ability to mount campaigns and attack targets across Western and Muslim-majority countries and has even been able to take territory in the Middle East (though that has been lost). Furthermore, it disregards national boundaries, rules of warfare, and the international system of nation-states. This transgressive quality of violent jihadism results in the legitimation of such acts as killing civilians, not only as a means to an end but as a good and praiseworthy act in itself.

In this way, the trajectory of the jihadist movement represents the escalation to extremes—intentionally embraced, ritualistically enacted, and doctrinally justified. Even or especially in defeat, jihadists more purposefully engage in violence. Connected to this, then, jihadism is not only a military threat but an existential one: it is willing and ready to use indiscriminate violence, such as chemical weapons and Weapons of Mass Destruction (WMDs), to achieve its stated aims of total victory. For example, ISIS undertook research into chemical weapons after it gained territory in 2014 and is reported to have deployed such weapons multiple times in battle: "The world's ultimate terrorist organization remains very interested in the ultimate terrorist weapon."[47] The escalation of jihadist violence has already manifested itself in unexpected ways. They have catalyzed an unexpected number of people to rally to the jihadist cause in the Middle East, across Asia and the West, and beyond. In Iraq and Syria, violent jihadist groups were able to take large amounts of territory.

Despite failures, militant jihadist groups have developed, particularly over the course of the twentieth century, to strategically inflict major damage on nations with significant Muslim populations and Western nations. According to Kepel, militant jihadism has moved through three phases from initial mobilization against apostate Muslim regimes, to defensive jihad against the West and its Muslim allies (exemplified by al-Qaeda), to offensive jihad with dispersed cells and fronts (exemplified by ISIS).[48] Violent jihadists have been able to transform a terrorist movement into a guerrilla army and even into a full-blown military in some places, consistently retaining indiscriminate tactics and a violent apocalyptic worldview.

As Girard discusses, rivalries and conflicts can take time to build up and develop, as has occurred with the development of militant jihadism in twentieth century.[49] Rivalries are typically subject to strategic concerns in which resentments are left to fester and ferment until one can achieve the means for victory. In some ways, jihadist groups have been strategic in their planning and operations, increasing their adherents, supporters and capacities, and exploiting divisive social contexts or conflict situations. At the same time, however, they have allowed their militant zeal to drive their actions. For example, they have deployed forms of indiscriminate violence against much stronger enemies, while misjudging the public mood regarding support for such actions, leading to failure and repression.

Nevertheless, despite their failures, jihadist groups are becoming increasingly adept, though often still frenetic, in their use of violence. For example, while jihadist groups have scandalized many nations and peoples around the world by their extreme use of violence in terrorist attacks, they are also willing to fight conventional wars when they are able, such as in Iraq, Syria, and Nigeria. These wars are fought in order to bring about a new theo-political system. Almost any kind of extreme and brutal violence can be used to bring about this aim, though some groups (like al-Qaeda) are more strategic in their use of violence than others (like Islamic State or IS/ISIS). Moreover, Islamic laws and doctrines can be twisted for jihadists in service of their violent agenda against the enemy/infidel. In this way, they exemplify a key facet of the crisis in modernity: rather than rules and prohibitions to restrict and channel violence (like in institutionalized warfare), such rules are instead distorted by and facilitate the most extreme and destructive forms of violence. These jihadist groups seem to take modern violence and war to their extreme: anything is justifiable, meaning in effect that there are no rules except victory.

Yet, on the other hand, jihadist violence and victories seek to institute systems and rules purportedly handed down by God in order to bring salvation and order. In this way, they seem to parallel the archaic sacred: they destroy in order to create anew. Moreover, the leaders of radical jihadist groups such as al-Qaeda and ISIS have made great efforts to justify their violent acts with reference to Islamic doctrine, particularly to respond to criticism from within and beyond the Islamic world.[50] These justifications seek to bring the radical jihad of modern Islamists into line with traditional legal norms so to be "noble, righteous, and innocent."[51] Although the justifications for violence from the jihadists are at times painstaking, the result is that even the worst kinds of violence and abuse against civilians, including "infidel" women and children, are justified in jihadists' understanding of *shar'ia* (law).[52] In undertaking such violence, jihadism has revealed deep fault lines in modernity, in both the Islamic world and the West, and provoked institutional responses to repress jihadist violence.

Institutional Responses to Jihadist Violence

With the rise of extreme violence and terrorism in modernity, there have been corresponding institutional responses to address and repress them. As discussed in Chapter 1, an international system based around a human rights ethos and deeper diplomatic relations has developed since the Second World War. As part of this, there has been a heightened effort to prevent and prosecute war crimes and crimes against humanity, which has helped to re-instil a respect for the distinction between combatants and civilians. Nevertheless, parallel trends toward escalating violence—evident in terrorism and genocidal wars—have been present in the latter half of the twentieth century and the beginning of the twenty-first century. These trends follow the trajectory that collapses the distinction between combatants and civilians.

In order to address the escalation of violence, Girard identifies the rise of "security" apparatuses and discourses (rather than ones based around warfare) as representing the new institutional (or sacrificial) paradigm for addressing terrorism and containing violence.[53] Through the use of advanced intelligence networks and technologies as well as coercion and force, "security" has become the overriding concern and motivator for institutional violence: "We have gone from an era of codified war to an era of security, where we think we can 'resolve' conflicts just as we cure sickness, with increasingly sophisticated tools."[54] On this point, the US use of drones and "black sites" are an exemplar of sophisticated tools used to "cure" extremist violence (with ambiguous consequences).

There are a few important rationales given for the operations of these national and international "security" apparatuses. The containment of terrorism and the use of WMD have become primary motivators for the construction and deployment of large state-based and private security apparatuses. Such security apparatuses and their "strategic interventions" are justified under the rationale that they "protect innocent people" and civilian populations (rather than just advance the self-interest of particular nations). Though a security paradigm has arisen to combat contemporary violence, Girard argues that political rationality has failed to comprehend the full nature of violence in its reciprocal, unpredictable, and escalating character.[55] In this, Girard is questioning whether sacrificial violence can really repress chaotic and indiscriminate violence any longer.

Nevertheless, the United States and its allies have undertaken some successful efforts in countering jihadist violence. Yet, in doing so, domestic and international laws of warfare and imprisonment have sometimes been qualified or disregarded in the "War on Terror." There is a danger that the United States may become like the enemy they are trying to resist. Yet, there is an internal capacity for critique in Western nations such as the United States, and in the international community more generally, that has led to contestation over the means and use of violence in the War on Terror, especially following abuses such as in the Abu Ghraib prison in Iraq in 2003. This internal democratic debate, which contains sympathy for victims of violence, is key to maintaining some balance in the use of violence, though the use of drones and "enhanced interrogation techniques" retain ambiguity.

Conclusion

A global cultural crisis in modernity around the deinstitutionalization of violence and outbreak of total warfare has opened up a major cleavage, of which militant jihadists are both a symptom and a most potent exploiter. This chapter has argued that modern violence, including militant jihadism, is being motivated by this cultural crisis. The identification of this crisis clarifies the underlying conditions for modern violence, especially in the form of totalitarian and extremist groups. These conditions have given rise to an escalation of violence according to the logic of mimetic rivalry. Jihadism, like other totalitarianisms, constitutes the most extreme manifestation of this rivalrous logic. In this way, it represents the most extreme response to the crisis of desacralized violence. In the next section, I systematically analyze militant jihadism's relationship with violence to show how it intentionally engages in indiscriminate violence as the sacred means to a divinely ordained order that provides a solution to modernity.

Part II

The Sacred Violence of Militant Jihadism

3

The Islamic Modernity

In this section, I show how violent jihadism is a theological–ideological movement that intentionally engages in extreme and indiscriminate violence to construct a sacred totalitarian order. To begin, this chapter traces the emergence of violent jihadism in the Islamist movement of the twentieth century. This movement largely grew as a response to a perceived crisis in Muslim-majority countries during the colonial and postcolonial periods. Islamists proposed Islam as a "total system" to solve the problems of modernity experienced in the Muslim-majority world. For some in the Islamist movement, violent jihad was argued to be integral to arrest the malaise of the Muslim world and achieve the aims of an "Islamic modernity." This chapter identifies the main figures, groups, themes, and developments in the Islamist-jihadist movement in the twentieth and twenty-first centuries. It does so with reference to how these jihadist figures and groups construct a resistance-terrorist movement based in a vision of an Islamized modernity and state.

In particular, the chapter shows how militant jihadism developed as a theological and ideological response to modernity among radical Islamists. It contextualizes this development within the political, social, and economic conditions of the Muslim-majority world and the Islamic ideas and doctrines used by radical Islamists. Despite its marginalization in many places, Islam retained popular appeal across the Muslim-majority world and provided social and ideological resources for a response. The reinterpretation of Islam provided the basis for Islamists to provide an alternative to a "Westernized modernity" and even form a violent response. The chapter, like this section, primarily focuses on Sunni jihadism, which contains different national strands that come to particularly gravitate around Egyptian groups and figures such as Sayyid Qutb and coalesce in the latter part of the twentieth century in the Afghan campaign.

The Crisis of Modernity

The rise of militant jihadism in the twentieth century has its roots in Muslim-majority nations, such as Egypt and Saudi Arabia, in which circumstances of alienation combined with a revolutionary Islamist ideology/theology to produce a global violent movement. The violent efforts of Islamist-jihadists represent an attempt to cope with and re-form modernity, dominated by Western forms such as the nation-state, capitalism, and new technologies. A crisis has been especially felt in the Muslim-majority countries because of political and economic failures during colonization and decolonization, and particular cultural and religious attitudes in the Islamic world that have felt disappointed in or subjugated to a "Westernized modernity."

The crisis was initially a slow-burning one that began in many ways with the fall of the Ottoman Caliphate in 1924 and the creation of independent nation-states in the Islamic-majority world. Initially many of these states, especially in the Arab world, relied on nationalist and socialist sentiments to provide legitimacy. However, the rise of authoritarian states, which often harshly repressed Islamist movements, and the failure to gain any regional or global supremacy, especially with regard to Israel and the West, undermined the popular legitimacy of these states and led to questions about their Islamic credentials. In Iran, this situation infamously led to the Islamic Revolution. In the Sunni world, various countries were affected by the crisis of the postcolonial consensus, most especially Egypt, Syria, and Jordan after their defeat in the 1967 Arab–Israel War.

Furthermore, modernity in the Middle East and other Muslim-majority states was characterized by a mass movement of people to cities, especially following the oil boom, seeking the "fruits of modernity and prosperity."[1] However, nationalist and socialist regimes in Muslim-majority countries failed to cope with the major demographic changes and economic challenges that occurred in 1950s to 1980s. Some Muslim majority countries experienced a doubling of their populations, leading to major urban pressures as large numbers of young people sought education and work in the cities.[2] Economic prosperity also floundered in a number of Muslim-majority countries, especially with the inflationary pressures and oil price fluctuations in 1970s.

The imposition of secular and authoritarian forms of nationalism, which in some places was combined with forms of socialism and pan-Arabism, alienated many people following the independence of a number of Muslim-majority nations. Moreover, the loss of honor and theological legitimacy after the collapse of the Ottoman Caliphate in 1924 and the pivotal defeat in the 1967 Arab–Israeli War, eventually brought the crisis to a head. Islamists grew as a response to this crisis to put forward their own solutions to the perceived malaise of the Muslim-majority world, particularly in the Middle East. Cesari argues that political Islam is a response of the Islamic tradition to the "dual processes of nationalization and reformation/westernization."[3] Drawing on the work of Bobby Shayyid and Nathan Brown, Jocelyne Cesari argues that changes in Islamic thought have responded to modern political conditions, including the rise of the postcolonial nation-state.[4] In a similar vein, Charles Tripp argues that Islamism is shaped by modern politics, especially burgeoning nationalisms.[5] Further, Farhad Khosrokhavar argues that the Muslim-majority countries have been the subject of distorted forms of modernization, such as colonialism, repressive and ineffective postcolonial regimes, economic stagnation, and exclusive, semi-secular forms of nationalism and socialism.[6]

Fouad Ajami describes the tension of a Westernized modernity in the Egyptian context, where the militant Islamist movement has its roots and out of which Mohamed Atta (one of the leaders of the 9/11 attacks) arose:

> There had come to Egypt great ruptures in the years when the younger Atta came into his own. A drab, austere society had suddenly been plunged into a more competitive, glamorized world in the 1970's and 1980's. The old pieties of Egypt were at war with new temptations. There must have been great yearning and repression in Mohamed Atta's life; it is the torment of Atta's generation. They were placed perilously close to modernity, but they could not partake of it.[7]

Islamism grew in parallel to the inability of Muslim-majority nations and populations to cope with modernity, especially because of the unpreparedness of these societies to deal with modernization and secularization. There was a lack of cultural and political resources and strategies, such as an effective nation-state supported by civil society, to enable these societies to adapt to modernity, without resorting to repressive state violence as a means of forming unity. In response to this struggle with a postcolonial modernity, Islamists claimed the lack of true Muslim faith and the often oppressive attitude displayed by authoritarian regimes had led to the failures and malaise of the Muslim world, especially after the 1967 war.[8] A reinterpretation and representation of Islamic history—as a successful tradition which had been unjustly oppressed by authoritarian rules and the Western colonists—as well as the "revival" of Islam as a cultural and/or political force—drawing on particular Islamic concepts and moral codes—was able to gain wider support to address the crisis that Islamists were professing to address. This movement came to regard Islam as the site to reconstruct and integrate culture, politics, society, and religion as a "complete and total system," which responds to and refashions modernity on Islam's terms.[9]

The Islamic Revival and the Rise of Islamism

The Islamic revival and the rise of Islamism as a political solution to modernity showed how in the middle and latter part of twentieth century Muslim-majority countries were experiencing a deepening crisis of political and cultural legitimacy within the existing global order. Regional and global identities grew around Islam to confront the failures of modernity, often with the ideological and financial support of Saudi Arabia and Iran. In the Islamic revival, a number of groups developed to provide clear and strict ways for Muslims to live Islam faithfully and authentically. This came at a time when intermingling with non-Muslims and/or secular state authorities had increased, forms of modernization were encroaching on Muslim lives, and regimes in the Muslim-majority world were foundering. Some of these Islamic movements and groups sought to reclaim Islamic belief, practice, and politics as a "total system" that would help the Muslim to live faithfully in the modern world, especially when local authorities were not supportive of Islam.[10]

Islamist groups grew out of a larger Islamic revival in twentieth century, driven by civil society rather than the government. According to Kepel, this growth in Islam was particularly evident in the more devout rural populace, urban poor, and petit-bourgeoisie (small businesspeople or bazaar traders). Many people in these groups found the appeals of the Islamist clerics or intellectuals compelling, especially regarding their own sociopolitical and economic situation.[11] With their support, Islamists ignored unsupportive state authorities and selectively used religious judgments (fatwas) and aid from local or foreign governments to support their political and cultural cause.[12]

According to Kepel, the strength of the Sunni-Islamist movement has been its focus on "re-Islamization from below" that engaged civil society in order to confront the forces of modernity and resist "apostate" or "infidel" state regimes. This movement dated from at least 1920s but particularly gained momentum in 1970s. While Islamic adherence and associations experienced difficult times after the independence of the Muslim-majority states, Islamic groups were able to endure and grow their support, especially politically oriented Islamist groups. In this time, Islamic movements assisted Muslims to live their faith more authentically (and often more strictly) in a way that addressed the modern context, especially in countries where Islam was not dominant or was in a minority position.[13] Muslim groups, mosques, and welfare organizations, especially with Islamist leanings, spread throughout civil society and various institutions such as the universities in Muslim-majority countries and in Western countries with Muslim populations:

> By its influence over the groups of "true believers" who were breaking with the "godless" societies they lived in, it [the Islamic revival] offered a refuge to individuals who felt wholly at sea in an atmosphere of rapid modernization, flight from the countryside and the breakdown of the old, close-knit rural society. Re-Islamization "from below" is first and foremost a way of rebuilding an identity in a world that has lost its meaning and become amorphous and alienating.[14]

While states and traditional structures struggled to cope with the pressures of economic and demographic changes, Islamic welfare organizations and other Islamist groups provided various forms of support and social networking and offered frameworks for personal and collective meaning. For example, Islamist groups were able to fill a gap for young people struggling in the education and economic systems of Muslim-majority states. In the latter part of the twentieth century, education and literacy became more widespread. Universities were opened by Arab states to advance the economy and cater for the growing number of young people moving to the cities. The goal of access and equality (similar to the post-revolutionary regime in France), however, led to a dysfunctional and corrupt system which alienated the poorer young people who could not afford to pay to get ahead. Kepel charts how Islamist movements organized to assist these students in places like Egypt.[15] They combined material support with social, religious, and moral structure. This included instituting rules and mores around various areas of life, such as personal conduct and gender, within the promotion of an Islamic worldview and practice. For example, these groups helped protect women from unwanted contact from men. In this way, they connected "charity and social concern with political and religious aims," instilling "an attitude of 'Islamic break' with the surrounding world."[16] Moreover, from the point of view of Arab and Western governments, supporting these Islamic groups was initially preferable to leftist revolutionary groups.[17]

Furthermore, Islamist groups helped Muslims to cope with the "secularization process" in the Muslim-majority world, especially in the Middle East, Asia, and North Africa. This process, to a large degree, grew out of the postcolonial independence movements. Secularization was often imposed by authoritarian states with nationalist, socialist, or pan-Arabic orientations. This process largely came to be regarded in a dubious light by many Muslims, especially because of the forceful way it was imposed. It generally involved de-emphasizing or delegitimizing traditional Islamic structures, practices, beliefs, and ideas. Nevertheless, Islamic ideas and structures were not completely eliminated from the public sphere. They even found new energy as nationalist or socialist states in the Muslim world failed to cater for all sections of the population during times of major economic and demographic changes. Islamist groups provided aid, support, institutions, rules, and structures to help people cope in difficult social, economic, and political conditions, especially those people on the fringes of urban centers. As the Islamic revival gained momentum in Muslim-majority countries, state authorities increasingly had to make appeals to Islam to legitimize themselves and gain popular approval, particularly from 1970s onward.[18]

In particular, the rise of an educated Muslim middle class and large numbers of urban youth in Muslim-majority nations posed particular challenges for political authorities as well as existing mainstream Islamic scholarship. These educated Muslims, who were generally not trained in Islamic schools of higher education, reinterpreted the Qur'an and Islamic history and concepts to put forth a robust and radical version of Islam as an answer to modernity and the particular crises they experienced. They also drew on the more conservative or radical elements of Islamic scholarship, bolstered by the ready supply of Salafi texts from Saudi Arabia.[19]

Moreover, because the ulemas (experts in Islamic law) were weakened by authoritarian regimes (particularly in 1950s to 1970s) and lost their independence to the state in most Muslim-majority countries, Kepel argues a vacuum was created by tight state control.[20] The irony was that in creating a religious and theological vacuum, the state potentially delegitimized their best defense against Islamism, namely, the ulemas who were generally conservative and regarded themselves as "voices of conscience," not revolutionaries.[21] When the state's version of Islam did not appeal as authentic among those disenchanted by nationalism and modernity (especially the rural poor and the large generation of young people who came of age in 1970s), then this opened the door to alternative versions. These alternatives were often provided by Islamist intellectuals and movements, drawn from the middle class and urban poor, who were not aligned with the state.[22]

An Islamic Modernity

The Islamic revival presented a political, religious, and sociological alternative in many Muslim-majority states to the nationalist and socialist projects of these states. Moreover, because Islamic countries have not undergone the same processes of secularization as in the Christianized West, Khosrokhavar argues that Islam remained a viable vehicle for social frustrations and aspirations to be channeled within a wider political vision or project.[23] One of the earliest and most influential Islamist movements to have emerged with a vision for an Islamic modernity was the Muslim Brotherhood in Egypt. Founded by Hasan al-Banna, the Muslim Brotherhood spread throughout the region as a leading organization for Islamists, providing the impetus for more radical stances. One of the most popular chants of the Muslim Brotherhood exemplifies al-Banna's position and the tone of an Islamist modernity: "God is our goal. The Prophet is our leader. The Qu-'ran is our constitution. Struggle [jihad] is our way. Death in the service of God is our loftiest wish. God is great, God is great."[24]

Drawing on the thought of the radical reform movement of the nineteenth and early twentieth centuries (particularly Al-Afghani's pan-Islamic and pan-Arabic vision), al-Banna argued for Islam as a "total system," exemplified in the Muslim Brotherhood's unofficial motto, "Islam as the Solution":[25]

> Banna and his disciples managed to politicize this religious zeal [of the Islamic revival] by shifting its focus away from the traditional realms of piety and religious ceremony and onto urban colonial society. The Islam of the Brothers raised the standard of "Islamic modernity" as an alternative to the modernity of Europe. The exact meaning of Islamic modernity has never really been settled, and this ambiguity has allowed a wide variety of social groups to assemble under its umbrella. If we describe European modernity as the dividing of society, politics, religion and culture into separate fields or discourses, then the Brothers were opposed to it during the 1930s, just as their heirs are today. Their Islamic version of modernity entailed a "complete and total" blend of society, state, culture, and religion, a blend with which everything began and ended. The social order they envisioned contained no internal contradictions. Political parties were scorned because their quarrels disturbed the unity of the Community of the Faithful [the *umma*], thus weakening it in its struggle with the enemies of Islam. Espousing this philosophy, the Brothers could thrive among the politically marginalized and discontented among the lower middle classes in cities. … In each case, the Brothers preached the unity of the faithful, placing special emphasis on personal morality.[26]

This vision of an Islamic modernity that could provide a modern interpretation and adaptation of Islam was regarded as urgent by many Muslims especially amidst the repressive attitude of the state and the major changes and intrusions of modernity. Many states in the Muslim world were able either to marginalize the clerical class and then put forward their own statist version of Islam, or co-opt clerics to provide Islamic justifications for their semi-secular, pan-Arabist/nationalistic ideologies. These justifications (mostly up until 1970s) even included arguing that forms of socialism and nationalism were consistent with Islam.[27]

According to Kepel, certain social groups were crucial for the growth of Islamist movements, from which were drawn jihadist activists and revolutionaries seeking to transform the secular and nationalist state. One was the growing numbers of young people from lower socioeconomic groups. The other was the devout merchant class or small business owners, who did not have political or economic power due to monarchical or military regimes. According to Kepel, these groups were committed to *sharia* law and an Islamic state but had different visions of the state. These differences were mediated by an Islamist intelligentsia, often made up of technically educated, though nonspecialists in Islamic law or theology, who focused on the moral and cultural dimensions of Islam so to unite both groups in the pursuit of political power.[28] Kepel argues that this model was successful because it was vague in its social agenda but strong on reform, charitable activity, personal morality, social ties, and religious practice.[29] It often included the targeting of religious enemies, such as the Shia, Copts, or other minorities regarded as impious and evil.[30] In some cases, Islamist groups were even able to establish themselves as mediators of social order in situations where they had won over population areas (through force and ideology) and state authority was weak. In these places, they resolved disputes and vendettas and exacted protection payments from businesses and individuals.[31]

As disappointment with the ineffectiveness of nationalist and socialist states grew, radical Islamist ideas and groups particularly appealed to those dislocated or disenfranchised by modernity. For example, the urban youth in Muslim countries were usually at the forefront of Islamist growth and action. As a group, they underwent large amounts of growth in the second half of the twentieth century. They were the beneficiaries of a modern education, however they also experienced dislocation from their traditional homes. They also had limited opportunities to gain a meaningful life and employment in the modern political economy of many Muslim-majority states, especially in the 1950s to 1980s.[32] Conservative and revolutionary Islamist groups appealed to those undergoing modernization and experiencing various forms of spiritual, social, political, and economic alienation. Islamist groups provided an alternative way of engaging in modernity, particularly in those places where political or economic failures or social or religious tensions arose:

> Neo-fundamentalism is particularly appealing to alienated youth because it turns their cultural alienation into a justification for forging a universal Islam stripped of customs and traditions and thus acceptable to all societies. It appeals to the well-educated, and the disenchanted, offering a system for regulating behavior in any situation, from Afghan deserts to American College campuses.[33]

There were particular conditions and motivations, then, that aligned to provide such potency for Islamist radicalism. Identity issues and alienation led the disenchanted, as Roy indicates, to be attracted to ideological and religious systems that offer a total solution. For this solution to become violent and for terrorism to grow, Louise Richardson argues that there must be disaffected individuals, a supporting community/organization (with effective leadership), and a legitimating ideology (religious or secular).[34] These three conditions were met in an overwhelming way in many Muslim-majority countries, particularly from the 1950s. Dislocated populations were cut off from traditional structures and became particularly receptive to Islamist solutions, especially where the state was not perceived to be representing the interests of the people or Islam, such as in Afghanistan, Pakistan, Egypt, Algeria, Sudan, Nigeria, and across the Middle East.[35]

In response to this postcolonial situation, radical Sunni-Islamist intellectuals such as Sayyid Qutb proposed comprehensive, provocative, and politically risky solutions. Qutb argued for a vanguard to imitate the Prophet Muhammad and the early generation of Muslims to renew Islamic society. This renewal had to be modelled on the Prophet and his early followers because they embodied true Muslim virtues and a true Muslim society under God's sovereignty (not the sovereignty of the "apostate" ruler or "infidel" state).[36] This meant following the Prophet Muhammad's example personally and politically in what was regarded as a literal way. This imitation included withdrawing from the corrupt world and returning to bring about an Islamic society/state under God's sovereignty and law (which coincide with interpretations of the Prophet's Medinan and Meccan periods).[37]

Another influential Islamic philosopher and leader, Abul A'la Maududi (or Mawdudi), who lived in India and Pakistan around the same time as Qutb in the middle of the twentieth century, also advocated for an Islamic vanguard (modelled on Leninism). This vanguard would live an Islamic way of life as a total political and social system and would challenge impious colonization and nationalism with a sharia-based Islamic state. He established a system for Muslims to live by with rules and habits that took a literalist approach to imitating the Prophet. This approach was meant to ensure separation from modern and un-Islamic ways of living, though, of course, it was very modern in its literalism.

While Maududi has been influential in radical Islamist circles, his own approach was to advocate from within the political system in Pakistan and create an Islamic state (through his organization, Jamaat-e-Islami). This approach contrasted to those promoted by intellectuals such Qutb, who wanted a more radical (and violent) overhaul of the state. Nevertheless, like Qutb, Maududi wanted a renewal of Islam among the Muslim population and to ensure its political dominance. He advocated for "Islamization from above" and resistance to Western imperialism, secularization, and nationalism.[38] Along with Qutb and others, Maududi's thought and rules have been adapted by radical groups in their violent pursuit of an Islamic state.

While Islamism was a reaction to authoritarian regimes, Western supremacy, and rapid demographic and economics shifts in 1960s and 1970s, most Islamist groups were content to engage with the benefits of modernity, particularly in the form of science and technology. Thus, the call from Islamist intellectuals like Qutb for a withdrawal or resistance to the modern world (in combating Qutb's sense of *jahiliyya*) did not mean an Amish-type reversion to a premodern age of simple living. Rather, Islamist groups were more concerned with asserting their rights to the benefits of modernity, which many of their members were promised but were lacking. They particularly wished to reassert the rules and status of Islam in the face of political, military, and economic failures. For Islamists, the Prophet Muhammad and their early generations of Muslims were essential guides to how to cope with modernity and undertake appropriate forms of withdrawal and resistance. Islamist groups generally wished to re-create the "righteous" world of the early Muslims by interpreting and applying Muslim precepts as a way to Islamize modernity (often in what they regarded as a literal sense), while rejecting foreign ideologies, failed authoritarianism, and perceived Western imperialism.

Both Qutb and Maududi were leaders in the radical Muslim intelligentsia who exemplified—along with the movements they emerged from or formed—the way in which Muslims were grappling with how to live and interpret Islam in modernity. The issues they grappled with were acute given the context of fragile, newly independent nation-states in the Muslim world, experiencing major changes under the influence of a Westernized modernity. Though the early generations were an essential guide, radical and militant Muslims (especially in the Sunni tradition) were divided on what kind of withdrawal from the modern world was required in order to bring about an Islamic renewal. Qutb did not provide exact guidance in this area except to condemn complete physical withdrawal and exhort violent resistance to the state, as he was executed before further developing his thought.[39] This situation resulted in different opinions and experiments, which had to adapt to local political conditions. Interestingly, though, by focusing on the nature of withdrawal or break from the modern world (especially because of the repression of authoritarian regimes), Sunni radicals became more theologically narrow and initially less able to use Islamic ideas to appeal to general and diverse audiences with social grievances (as Khomeini was able to do in Iran).[40] Thus, some radical Sunni movements have been more theologically rigid and less politically effective than some Shia groups.

The Militant Radicalization of Islam

Within the re-Islamization movement, the concepts of *jihad* (struggle), *takfir* (a type of excommunication), and *jahiliyya* (a pre-Islamic state of ignorance) became increasingly important, especially among radical Sunni groups. For example, al-Banna argued that jihad was a Muslim duty, involving (strategic) fighting (*qital*) that was necessary to achieve an Islamic modernity.[41] In the postcolonial era, the writings of Qutb, a prominent member of the Muslim Brotherhood, were particularly influential in the radical use of such concepts as *jihad* and *takfir*. These concepts were deployed in a violent and exclusionary way, contrary to much prevailing scholarly opinion. This narrowing of terms enabled jihadists to strictly divide the world into believers and nonbelievers and to justify violent action.[42]

Jihad, for example, had a long theological pedigree, with different meanings and uses within the Islamic tradition, such as spiritual struggle, defensive armed action, and offensive war.[43] Within radical Islamist thought, jihad took on a decidedly violent, offensive tone. Gerges argues that "Qutb was the first contemporary radical thinker who revolutionarized the concept of jihad and invested it with new meaning—waging an 'eternal' armed struggle 'against every obstacle that comes into the way of worshipping God and the implementation of the divine authority on earth, hakimiya, and returning this authority to God and taking it away from the rebellious usurpers [rules].'"[44]

The use of such terms as jihad revolved around Qutb's identification of the obstacles that were in the way of true Islamic worship and living. These obstacles were identified as part of the condition of *jahiliyya*, which denoted a pre-Islamic state of ignorance. For Qutb, since Islam had been abandoned by rulers and the elite in the Muslim-majority world, and was only present in the hearts of believers, a pre-Islamic state of ignorance (*jahiliyya*) was dominant in modernity.[45] Qutb's popularization of this term became an influential foundation for radical Islamist/jihadist thought. Violent resistance and struggle (jihad) became the primary or exclusive means to destroy the obstacles that prevented *jahiliyya* from being overcome in order to bring about a true Muslim society.

In order to specifically address the problem of *jahiliyya*, Qutb argued there needed to be some kind of break with and withdrawal from the surrounding "infidel" state and society. Shukri Mustafa argued that the Muslim vanguard was to withdraw physically, while the more dominant view among Islamists focused on moral, intellectual, and spiritual withdrawal so as to confront the obstacles that prevented *jahiliyya* from being overcome.[46] Reference to strict interpretations of *sharia* (law) and jihad were important in this regard. While the boundaries of *jahiliyya* were strictly applied, they could be difficult to define, with groups and movements developing detailed rules and manuals.[47] These strict boundaries were used to clearly define Muslim identity.

These boundaries, however, did not necessarily translate into violent radicalization. Some Islamist groups regarded *jahiliyya* primarily as the obstacles faced by individual Muslims in the conduct of their private life (especially in modern societies) rather than the obstacles produced by the state. By contrast, for Qutb and later radical Islamists such as Muhammad 'Abd al-Salam Faraj, the major obstacle was the infidel-authoritarian state, especially the Arab socialist/nationalist regimes, which they argued had to be confronted with violent jihad.[48] While Western powers were also regarded as a threat, it was subsequent jihadist thought (particularly from bin Laden and Zawahiri) that focused on the West as the primary target.

While Qutb argued that jihad was not about coercion, it was required to remove "systems or circumstances" (as part of *jahiliyya*) that impede "the freedom to choose" Islam.[49] He regarded jihad as more than spiritual purification and defensive war, but as requiring offensive approaches to remove the obstacles that stood in the way of Islam being preached and implemented.[50] These approaches involved both preaching/discourse (with those of the Book) and a (violent) "movement" to remove the obstacles that prevent "pagans" from engaging with and converting to Islam.[51] In particular, to overcome *jahiliyya*, the local despot needed to be overthrown by jihad in order to bring about an Islamic state governed by sharia.[52] Connected to the despots was the corrupting influence of the West, which was ignorant, barbaric, and Islam's historic enemy, according to Qutb and other leading Islamists such as Maududi and al-Banna.[53] Nevertheless, Qutb regarded the local "infidel" state as requiring the most immediate attention. His thought was formed particularly as a response to the repressive violence of the authoritarian state which he experienced in Egypt. While highly contested, Qutb's thought has been widely drawn upon by Muslim radicals and has been used to justify subsequent applications of jihad as primarily about violent fighting and warfare.

Despite the repression of Islamic groups in some countries, some radical groups actually came to benefit from local or foreign state assistance that helped them to develop and promote their radical understanding and practice of Islam. This support came from regimes in the Muslim-majority sphere seeking to increase their Islamic credentials or through foreign oil money. In the latter case, Saudi Arabia gave large amounts to Islamic causes across the Muslim-majority world (and beyond) as a way to promote its version of Wahhabi Salafism and undermine Arab nationalisms and Western influences. This support came at a time when, as mentioned, many citizens in Muslim-majority states, in nations as diverse as Egypt, Pakistan, and Algeria, became disillusioned with local nationalisms and modernity more broadly. This disillusionment came to a breaking point when the nationalist rhetoric of key states, especially in the Arab world, was undermined by their own failures with regard to their foreign enemies. The most spectacular failure occurred when Egypt, Jordan, and Syria were defeated by Israel in the Arab–Israeli War of 1967 ("Six Day War"). This surprising failure allowed Islamic groups to become more publicly prominent and influential in the Arab world, as the socialist, pan-Arabic, and nationalist ideologies of the middle of the twentieth century lost their legitimacy. From this point, regimes in the Middle East engaged more positively with Islamist groups to bolster their own popularity and provide assistance to the charitable and social works of these groups.

This support enabled radical Islamist groups to more easily appeal to urban and poor youth who, for political, economic, and demographic reasons, were left disenfranchised in the second half of the twentieth century. As part of their Islamization, young people in places such as Egypt, Pakistan, Palestine, and Algeria were particularly influenced by religious and moral values and rules (such as dress standards), which were used as identity markers.[54] The more radical Islamist groups were able to draw on the ranks of these young people to promote their own violent brand of Islam. For example, in Palestine, Hamas (an off-shoot of the Muslim Brotherhood) was successful at channeling the "random fury and resentment" of the young and disaffected into "pious zeal" and violent forms of jihad.[55] This included using moral and religious values and practices as identity markers and boundaries. These boundaries galvanized the young and poor over against secular classes and groups, who were said to be supported by "corrupt" foreign values, such as from Israel or the Western colonizers/imperialists. On the basis of this rivalry, Hamas was able to put forward violent jihad as the way to solve the Palestinian situation rather than negotiations or compromises. This served to differentiate Hamas from its competitors, such as the Palestinian Liberation Organization (PLO). Hamas became increasingly important during the First Intifada because it was able to draw on the large numbers of disaffected young people, who had recently come of age, to undertake violent jihad.[56]

Radical Islamist groups were also able to draw on foreign support because of great power rivalries, which contributed to the solidification and internationalization of their version of Islam. Most importantly, the United States and Saudi Arabia supported the *mujahideen* (holy warriors engaged in jihad) in Afghanistan against the Soviet Union (USSR) in the 1980s.[57] For the United States, the Afghan campaign was a convenient tool to channel jihadist violence against a common enemy. It also gave prestige to Saudi Arabia and other Islamic nations who supported it, while allowing such countries to "enrol potential troublemakers, divert them from the struggle against the powers that be in the Muslim world and their American allies, and above all keep them away from the subversive influence of Iran."[58]

Yet, in as much as they were used, jihadist groups were able to turn such support to their long-term advantage. The Afghan campaign allowed jihadi fighters to build international networks, undertake common training and experiences, and gain vital battle experience. It resulted in the extreme radicalization of numerous fighters, such as the Saudi, Osama bin Laden, who became fixated on a worldwide jihadist campaign.[59] Further, while militant Islamist groups have at times relied on support from nation-states, they have increasingly developed independent networks, funding sources, and radical ideologies to drive their international campaign, following the Afghan experience.

As the militant Islamist movement globalized, the antipathies to the "near enemy" (local apostate or infidel governments) and "far enemy" (primarily Israel, Russia, and the West) gradually coalesced around a desire for a universal caliphate (Islamic rule under a caliph or righteous Islamic ruler).[60] This desire for a caliphate represented for many Islamists and ordinary Muslims an overthrow of authoritarian-apostate regimes and the hegemony of the West in favor of an Islamic modernity that would bring justice and prosperity. In effect, the caliphate stood as a proxy for the desire of Islamists to achieve the goods of modernity on their own Islamist terms, over against repressive nation-states and Western dominance.[61] The era of modernity, which came to be regarded as the vehicle of Western nations and local elites, stood as the model-rival that had to be overcome in order to achieve the object of desire: prosperity and supremacy.

Among radical Islamists, the desire for an Islamic modernity is supported by a construction of Islamic history built on lost supremacy, modern failures, and a sense of grievance. It relies on a theology that sees God's providence as bestowed on the righteous and successful. For the more radical Islamist, true righteousness leads to the duty of jihad to fully restore Islamic practice and rule. For jihadists, taking and grasping what is desired and "deserved" from the enemy is the only way to achieving it. Jihadist groups absolutely insist on this duty of jihad, as the means to violently radicalizing the more general support for an Islamic modernity.

Thus, Scott Atran claims that for jihadist groups, such as Islamic State (ISIS), the caliphate does not represent a return to the past. Rather, it is the realization of the desire for an Islamic modernity that radicalizes legitimate desires and grievances through violent assertion:

> [T]here is a subliminal joy felt across the region [of Muslim majority nations] for those who reject the Islamic State's murderous violence yet yearn for the revival of a Muslim Caliphate and the end to a nation-state order that the Great Powers invented and imposed. It is an order that has failed, and that the US, Russia and their respective allies are trying willy-nilly to resurrect, and it is an order that many in the region believe to be the root of their misery. What the ISIS revolution is *not,* is a simple desire to return to the ancient past. … "We are not sending people back to the time of the carrier pigeon," Abu Mousa, ISIS's press officer in Raqqa, has said. "On the contrary, we will benefit from development. But in a way that doesn't contradict the religion."
>
> The Caliphate seeks a new order based on a culture of today.[62]

The aspiration for a caliphate, then, expresses a desire for an Islamic modernity that would address the failures of nation-states in the Muslim-majority world and the cultural tensions produced by modernization. The two most destructive and well-known international jihadist groups, al-Qaeda and ISIS, both have the caliphate as their aim and use similar legal reasoning to justify their violence, though with different approaches and tactics. According to Kilcullen, al-Qaeda regards the caliphate as a vague aim to be achieved by attacking the United States ("the far enemy") and ending its support of regimes in Muslim-majority countries. These attacks are undertaken to build a popular front guided by a well-trained vanguard which could lead the people to violently overthrow the apostate regimes in the Islamic world.[63] By contrast, Islamic State (ISIS) and its precursor, al-Qaeda in Iraq (AQI), have made the caliphate their immediate aim (true to their name), with sectarian provocation and intimidation tactics.[64] They have attacked states in the Middle East, appealed to and terrorized local Sunni populations into supporting them, and provoked Shia nations and groups into conflict.[65] While ISIS has provoked attacks in the West, its priority is the caliphate in the Middle East and the expansion of this caliphate by violence. Regardless of their differences, both jihadist groups have violence at their core and the general aim of an Islamic system that is in total dominance.[66]

Conclusion

Radical Islam in its different forms—whether as a social movement or a militant one—grew in reaction to the tensions of modernity particularly experienced in the colonial and postcolonial periods. In particular, the failure of nation-states in the Muslim-majority world to effectively cater for major groups within their territory, especially as various political, economic, and social changes occurred, exacerbated tensions and alienated many Muslims, especially Islamists. Amidst these failures and tensions, radical Islamist and jihadist groups have sought to accentuate the crisis of the Muslim-majority world and put forward radical answers in response. This response centers on a vision for a new and pure "Islamic modernity" over against local elites and the West. Militant jihadist groups particularly emphasize the one Islamic state and caliphate as their ultimate goal in reasserting supremacy. This goal is to be achieved by violence.

Particular circumstances of alienation in modernity have combined, then, with a revolutionary Islamist ideology/theology to produce a global violent movement. In the next chapter, I trace the foundational elements and vision of the militant jihadist response to modernity that lead it to commit extreme violence. This violence is deployed in the pursuit of establishing Islam as a "total system" that replaces the Westernized form of modernity. I argue that this effort hinges on the reactionary "victim identity" of jihadism, as part of which violence became essential to the construction and expression of the "Islamic modernity."

4

The Militant Jihadist Response to Modernity

In this chapter, I analyze the fundamental experiences and theological attitudes of jihadists that justifies their violent revolutionary pursuit of an Islamic modernity. I demonstrate how the jihadist movement is characterized by a radical attitude of "righteous violence," undergirded by a "victim identity." The experience of or identification with victimhood is key to understanding the mentality and motivation of the jihadist movement. As victims or in defense of the victimized, jihadists use ever more extreme violence to destroy their enemies and create a new social system founded on their interpretation of Islam. This chapter begins by examining how this "victim identity" developed and how it led to the collective attitude of "righteous violence" that drives militant jihadism.

Before undertaking such an analysis, it is important to note that identifying oneself as a victim does not automatically result in violence. Wolfgang Palaver argues that the consciousness of the victim can either combine with a nonviolent mimetic spirit of forgiveness or a violent mimesis of acquisition and rivalry.[1] This violent mimesis manifests itself in different forms, in violence against oneself or others. To trace the roots of the victim identity in militant jihadism, it is necessary to identity key concepts, experiences, and events that shaped the movement, especially in its use of and connection with violence. This is the task of this chapter, which will be further developed in Chapters 5 and 6.

The Experience of Repression and the Victim Identity

In fighting in defense of those Muslims aggrieved by modernity, the jihadist movement has increasingly identified itself with and as the victimized. This stance has justified ever more extreme violence. Khosrokhavar argues that the sense of "absolute victimization" is intrinsic to the jihadist reaction to modernity. This sense is directed against alienating political systems in the Muslim-majority world or by the feeling of "despondency and deep injustice within the Muslim diaspora."[2] The most infamous jihadist act, the 9/11 attacks, was justified by Osama bin Laden as defensive measures against on-going victimization. Al-Qaeda was justified, according to bin Laden, in violently responding to the attacks, policies, thieving, occupation, and destruction (including of religious sites) undertaken by the United States and its "client" governments in the Muslim-majority world.[3]

At the center of the militant jihadist's hermeneutic, particularly in justification of violent jihad, is the identity and attitude of being victimized. In jihadist discourse, "true Muslims" are victims of the West and their "apostate" allies. Maher comments: "The underlying ingredients [for radicalization] are always the same: righteous indignation, defiance, a sense of persecution and a refusal to conform."[4] Radicalization and the call to jihad are undergirded by "a sense of persecution" which has contributed to a "victim identity" among jihadists. This identity of persecution results in violence being justified in the name of the victims of modernity and its nation-states.

The experiences of violent repression in the twentieth century, primarily perpetrated by nation-states in the Muslim-majority world with Western support, form the basis for the jihadist victim mentality. Some Islamist groups experienced such repression at the hands of authoritarian socialist or nationalist governments in the second half of twentieth century, such as in Egypt, Iran, Iraq, and Algeria. The state justified such action because it perceived a threat from radical Islamist groups, whether real or exaggerated. For example, Kepel argues that the Muslim Brotherhood became the "scapegoats" for the Nasser regime to bring unity in Egypt, following the social and cultural upheaval of the end of the monarchy.[5] This is not to deny that there were radical elements in the Muslim Brotherhood threatening or perpetrating violence, but rather, that the identification of those elements became a justification to brutally repress the whole movement and reinforce state power and legitimacy.

Kepel states that in the 1950s the Muslim Brotherhood was the strongest intermediate institution standing between the state and civil society. This status gave it protection at the beginning of the regime but made it a target once the state had the requisite pretext and strength for destroying it.[6] In some ways, it is possible to equate the Egyptian situation with the French Revolution, when the violent end of monarchy led to the collapse of an existing social hierarchy and order. In the monarchy's place came authoritarian regimes looking for enemies to destroy and scapegoats to blame. In the Egyptian case, Kepel describes how different groups within the state structure were actually competing with each other to find plots against the president and state in order to institute a new round of purges, gain favor with the president, and defeat their internal rivals.[7] The Egyptian state's violent tactics against its enemies were often harsh, with destruction of villages, arbitrary imprisonment, torture, rape, and executions.[8]

Egypt was representative of the experience of a number of Muslim-majority nations, such as Algeria, Syria, and Iraq. In these countries, the state took a repressive approach to those who were part of Islamist movements, particularly in their early development. While the threat was real in some places, it was often exaggerated and used as a means to establish "secular" state power, such as during successive regimes in Egypt and following Islamist electoral victories in Algeria in the early 1990s.[9] Radical Islamist groups or parties were construed as a major threat to the state or the populace, as well as to the interests and ethos of the political and military elites. The state's reaction usually led to persecution of these Islamists. Murawiec documents this brutality across a number of regimes, quoting the following from Makiya that exemplifies the sacrificial violence which sought to unite the populace against radical Islamists in Iraq: "Hangings, involving only a few victims but permitting mass identification with the ritual, were crucial to the legitimation of Baathism in Iraq."[10]

Furthermore, in the latter part of the twentieth century various regimes in the Islamic world sought to accommodate the Islamic revival in states such as Egypt, Iraq, Pakistan, and Malaysia. The embrace of Islam and Islamists acted as a way to bolster these existing regimes, which were searching for social and political legitimacy. These moves eventually resulted in the marginalization of various Islamist groups, including the more radical ones, in a number of Muslim-majority countries. Radical groups in particular were repressed by the various regimes, which, after building up their Islamic credentials, claimed to be the main bastions of Islamic orthodoxy.[11]

These repressive actions contributed to radical Islamists developing and intensifying their victim identity and transforming it into a violent attitude. The violence by the state in Muslim-majority countries did not bring about unanimity in support of its cause but rather a sense of resentment, resistance, and retaliation among an alienated segment of the populace. Such experiences of victimhood led greater radicalization, such as when the Muslim Brotherhood's repression by the Nassar-led state in Egypt from 1950s contributed to Qutb and his followers' militant stances.[12] These experiences have been interpreted by militant Islamists in a rivalistic way, providing the motivation for a violent ideology and theology.

In the West, a similar phenomenon of identification as "victims" among some Muslim citizens developed in the second half of the twentieth century.

A significant number of first-, second-, and third-generation Muslims grew to feel alienated or rejected by their country of residence (often combined with dissatisfaction or alienation from their ancestral home). This alienation resulted in a sense of lack or loss of identity which they identified with being "victims" of Western culture and elites.[13] Khosrokhavar states that these conditions were easily exploited by militant jihadists: "Ignorance of Islam in the Muslim diasporas where people bear a grudge against society makes identification with Jihadism easier."[14]

The Victim Identity and Violence

This victim identity became characterized by rivalry with the state and a yearning for a true Islamic regime and age. For the militant groups in Egypt who could not or would not come to terms with the state, new radical forms of thought that were centered on a victim identity were developed. For example, as discussed in Chapter 3, the Egyptian state's repression of the Muslim Brotherhood led to new theological tools being developed to ideologically equip Muslim groups in their fight against the apostate state. In addition to the use of *jahiliyya* and jihad, a view developed that the accusation of *takfir* (a type of excommunication that labels a Muslim as a nonbeliever) could be more widely applied in a legitimate manner. In other words, the break between believers and nonbelievers became more strict, which became a basis upon which violent actions could be justified.[15]

In this context, individual and permanent jihad, interpreted violently, became essential to the fight against apostasy and idolatry, which expressed itself in the repression of Islam within its own lands. According to radical Islamist thinkers, violent jihad was necessary to defend Islamic lands and pivotal in provoking an offensive to ensure the true faith's worldwide dominance against apostasy and imperialism.[16] Drawing on the thought of al-Banna and Maududi, Sayyid Qutb was crucial to making jihad more central to Muslim identity: "Jihad is necessary for *da'wa* (preaching, calling others to join Allah's religion). … Although Islam aims at peace, it does not seek it at a cheap price. … Islam wants a peace in which religion is totally Allah's, the worship of the people is entirely directed towards Allah, and people do not take each other for god."[17]

Muhammad abd-al-Salam Faraj, Abdallah Azzam, and other radical thinkers built on Qutb's thought to emphasize jihad as an individual Muslim duty that was absolutely necessary and foundational for the practice of Islam itself. Muslims had to engage in or support violent jihad to be known as such and to be truly worthy of their religion. While jihad is conventionally divided between lesser jihad (physical struggle) and greater jihad (spiritual struggle) in Islamic thought, the former is absolutely privileged while the latter is de-emphasized or rejected by these jihadist thinkers. Moreover, to protect and promote Islam to its proper place, the duty of jihad was argued to not just be a collective responsibility of Muslim civilization but an individual duty incumbent on all Muslims to perform or support.[18]

In particular, Qutb's life and thought took on a foundational status in radical Islamist circles, especially in militant jihadist networks. A member of the Muslim Brotherhood, Qutb was influenced by the reformist–revivalist thought of its founder Hasan al-Banna. As discussed in the previous chapter, al-Banna's conception of Islam as a "total system" formed the basic vision of the Muslim Brotherhood and, for some in the movement, its increasingly militant stance against the Egyptian regime.[19] Nevertheless, Maher argues that the origins of the Muslim Brotherhood were not confrontational with the state, with the Brotherhood seeking to support Egyptian culture, especially where the state was unable to provide important services.[20] The Brotherhood sought to address a colonial/postcolonial context in which Egyptian and Muslim cultures were perceived as under threat and requiring protection.

However, as the postcolonial state sought to consolidate itself, the relationship between President Nasser and the Muslim Brotherhood deteriorated. The Brotherhood came to be perceived as a threat, particularly for its more radical and militant stances. During Nasser's repression of the Brotherhood, elements of the movement became more radicalized under the influence of Qutb who was imprisoned, tortured, and executed in this period.[21] Qutb drew on al-Banna's line of thought of the "total system" and of jihad, and developed both as a way to address modernity and an increasingly repressive context. Though he was not a trained Islamic scholar, Qutb's intellectual and literary skills gave him the ability to develop novel theological concepts and Qur'anic interpretations. His work appealed to and assisted disaffected Muslim radicals who lacked such concepts. It helped them make sense of their unexpected context—repression by a regime ostensibly governed by a Muslim leader with Muslim collaborators—and discern how they should react.[22] However, Qutb's novel approach was controversial in mainstream Sunni-Islamic circles, even within the Muslim Brotherhood.[23] Qutb helped to turn a nonconfrontational Islamic revivalist movement in the Muslim Brotherhood into the beginnings of a more radical and violent political movement.[24]

Qutb and other radical Islamists exemplify the manner in which authoritative interpretation of the Qur'an, Islamic law, history, and the Islamic tradition in general, was shifting in a typically modern or "postmodern" way. Qutb's unconventional scholarly background and approach exemplifies that of many Islamic militants and intellectuals. The authoritative clerics were no longer the gatekeepers of the tradition, but rather, authority was shifting and becoming more disperse. This occurred particularly in response to increased education levels and technological access among Muslim populations as well as the sense of urgency among citizens in Muslim-majority countries of the need to respond to modernity. Sunni extremists were often at odds with Sunni scholars and ulemas whose independence and credibility had been weakened by association with various postindependence Arab or Muslim-majority governments and their oppressive measures.[25]

While often providing alternative interpretations to the established clerics and scholars, militant jihadist leaders and intellectuals such as Qutb also used mainstream scholarship and legal statements to support their positions. As Maher discusses, militant scholars and leaders engage the Islamic tradition in a clear and often convincing fashion. They draw on traditional interpretations of the Qur'an, the early history of Islam, medieval scholarship (such as by Ibn Taymiyya), and modern Salafi scholarship in order to support their more violent positions.[26] Militant arguments use mainstream or historical positions and extend or distort such positions to justify their own stances in such areas as the necessity for and conduct of violent jihad, terrorist attacks, or martyrdom operations especially against Israel or Western targets.[27] Moreover, the violence of militant jihadist groups has usually been justified in defensive terms against the repressive state regime or the West. David Cook notes that jihadist thought is actually consistent with significant historical legal justifications in Sunni Islam for aggressive jihadist violence except regarding the need for a properly established authority to commission such jihad.[28]

While traditional scholarship is used, jihadist thought often uses idiosyncratic Qur'anic exegesis and applications of medieval or contemporary sources to justify new and more violent positions. For example, jihadists have appropriated and extended mainstream Salafi-jihadi concepts and opinions on various matters, such as jihad, *takfir* and *al-wala' wa-l-bara'* "to licence its war against the West as a legitimate and necessary defensive measure."[29] Moreover, jihadist interpretations of the Qur'an and Hadiths have been channeled through particular theological lenses and methods that have favored a selective interpretative approach, such as through the use of abrogation, in order to raise the authority of particular interpretations and verses such as of the notorious "sword verse."[30] As Khosrokhavar states, "In the Koran, Jihadists usually choose those verses that denote antagonism, war, and damnation toward the impious, the miscreant, the Hypocrite (inauthentic Muslims who spread dissent within the Muslim community), and disbeliever. These are mostly verses belonging to the Medina period, when the Muslim community was exiled from Mecca and felt under siege by its opponents."[31] Some of the aggressive jihadist actions, such as toward Christians and Jews, rely on certain suras, which involve enforcing submission through taxation or conversion. Afsaruddin argues that this selectiveness on the part of jihadists means that they overlook the nonviolent strands of jihad.[32]

The experience of repression, and the development of a violent victim identity, is reflected in the experiences of leading figures in the radical Islamist movement. Their subsequent reactions to repression were important for the development of militant jihadism. For example, key Islamist leaders, activists, and theorists, such as al-Banna and Qutb, were subject to torture, imprisonment, and/or assassination/execution by the state. Qutb particularly identified with and drew on the story of Joseph to come to terms with his imprisonment and torture, especially his witnessing of the brutality of the Muslim prison guards, in order to construct an approach to state repression.[33] Based on Joseph's words in prison about revering God alone (who wields real power), Qutb argued that the guards and torturers had forgotten God and were instead worshipping Nasser and the state. They were ignorant of Islamic principles of justice. In effect, "they were pagans. Only the imprisoned Brethren were still true Muslims."[34] However, rather than imitating Joseph's forgiveness and reconciliation as a victim of imprisonment and scapegoating, Qutb drew on the tradition of violent jihad and absolutized it in service of his rivalry with and resentment of the state. He rejected the Egyptian state and those like it as infidel regimes that needed to be violently resisted and overthrown. He regarded the state as lacking any Islamic legitimacy as it did not follow Islamic principles of justice.[35] Instead of the state, for Qutb, the suffering of the "martyrs" stood as the true sign of Islam. This suffering was motivation for violent resistance rather than reconciliation (or nonviolent resistance). Violent jihad, then, was the appropriate response to oppression in order to bring about a true Muslim society.

As discussed in Chapter 3, in order to justify his position, Qutb applied the concept of *jahiliyya*, which denoted a pre-Islamic state of ignorance and godlessness, to the contemporary situation, particularly with regard to the Egyptian state. Appropriating this term from Maududi via Abul Hasan Ali Hasani Nadwi, Qutb argued that there was no longer any Islamic society in the contemporary world as it had been cast out.[36] This was a significant move for Islamist-jihadist thought because it departed from traditional Islamic theology that regarded the Muslim nations as part of *dar al-Islam* (the domain or lands of Islam) and professed Muslims to be worthy of certain protections and rights, including rulers. Even unjust rulers were generally meant to be brought into line with Islamic law peacefully by the ulemas (clerics/scholars), though violent jihad was a possibility. Qutb rejected this consensus, effectively declaring the Egyptian state un-Islamic or pre-Islamic and so providing the intellectual foundations for a violent campaign of resistance and conquest to establish a true Islamic state.

Qutb's discussion of *jahiliyya* and its antidote were greatly influential on radical Islamist thinkers, activists and groups, including Abu Muhammad Maqdisi, Shukri Mustafa, and others.[37] *Jahiliyya* spread as a concept among jihadists and was expanded by them to apply not only to unjust rulers but to whole sets of people (including those who self-identify as Muslims), whole political systems, and even to the international order led by the West.[38] This wider application occurred as the postcolonial disillusionment with authoritarian regimes increased and Western foreign policies, culture, and education increasingly affected everyday life in Muslim-majority nations. Radical Islamists sought to provoke "true" Muslims into a choice to stand against the apostate and infidel regimes.[39] In particular, Qutb particularly exhorted his followers to destroy the obstacles that stood in the way of truly Islamic worship and living.

In this way, Qutb and his Islamist followers gradually turned their experience of victimization into a rivalry with the state and any other people, ideas, or practices that stood in the way of their stated goal—true Islamic living and dominance. For example, in his justification of the 9/11 attacks, Osama bin Laden mentions the obstacles that apostate governments and the West had put in the way of "establishing the Islamic Sharia."[40] For Girard, obstacles commonly recur as part of rivalries because the rival becomes the obstacle to the achievement of desire (such as to achieve power or dominance). The identification of these obstacles by Qutb and later Islamist thought—which are really rivals to Islam's liberation and proper place in modernity, and in later thought, its worldwide dominance—presents the increasingly mimetic and rivalrous state of thought that came to dominate the radical Islamist movement.

In particular, the realization and identification of the Islamic illegitimacy of states in the Muslim-majority world, especially following the experience of repression, effected a major shift in Islamist thought. In many ways, this shift was traumatic as it identified an alienation with rulers and political arrangements in the Muslim world, which shocked and disappointed Islamists. This shift parallels the state of affairs in Europe when the divine right of kings was eliminated: anyone could be in rivalry with anyone, even with the local despot. The local state and ruler did not have protection of religious or divine sanction. This opened up the possibility for violent rivalry. For Qutb and his successors such as Faraj, jihad against the ruler who does not implement the precepts of Islam was necessary, even if the ruler professed to be Muslim. The ruler had to be destroyed as an obstacle to a truly Islamic society and state. This attitude resulted in Faraj and other members of the radical group, "Jihad," assassinating the Egyptian president, Anwar Sadat, in 1981.[41] Thus, it was in opposition to both the local nation-state and the West that militant Islamist thought was developed. It was a reactionary response to the postcolonial, Westernized modernity from which it felt excluded and inferior.

The Revenge of the Victim

Thus, the victim experience and identity were and remain key for the global Islamist-jihadist movement. As the militant Islamist movement developed, adherents found solidarity in a shared sense of victimhood. On this shared victimhood, they developed an outlet for meaningful activity and camaraderie through righteous violence. According to Murawiec, the jihadist struggle "is always the deadly, bloody struggle of the victim against a world wholly dedicated to persecuting the victim, who 'must' in turn strike 'back.' "[42] It is this "striking back" which has come to increasingly characterize the tenor of the militant jihadist elements of the Islamist movement. This violent reciprocity and retribution are characteristic of jihadist discourse, exemplified in Osama bin Laden's own public statements (such as to justify the 9/11 attacks). The justifications given by jihadists seek to mask the real violence against rivals and victims with a cloak of righteousness in what Jonathan Sacks calls "altruistic evil."[43] What may present itself as just, and even believe itself to be altruistic, is really a brutal mimetic impulse to reassert domination over the rival.

Furthermore, the "intense community" experience that comes with "defending the victimized" is an antidote to the desacralizing effects of modernity and the Abrahamic traditions, which undermine "intense" forms of negative social bonding over against others.[44] Jihadists seek to reconstitute "the tribe" in an absolute way through defending the justice and honor of its "sacred" cult of victims. Moreover, in the age of mass media and the internet, it is easy to encourage a distorted and violent form of solidarity with the victim. It also easy to spread poisonous messages, and as Sacks argues, "demonise whole populations," especially as the internet is increasingly driven by anonymous forms of mimetic rivalry: "Jihadist and suicide-bombers are recruited by nonstop streams of images of the humiliation of Muslims at the hands of others who then become the Greater or Lesser Satan and can be murdered without qualms since you see them as persecutors of your people."[45]

In fighting for select victims against their perceived persecutors, jihadists are driven by a form of scapegoating violence that Girard identified as specifically modern, which is now facilitated and accelerated by media technologies.[46] This cult of the victim is a distinctly modern conception that jihadists have appropriated in an extremely violent manner. Chris Fleming sums up the new era, "Here we witness an intensification of 'victimhood' as a frame in which culture and history are viewed, but one in which a mixture of a concern for victims and the competitive striving for claiming victim *status* often becomes difficult to tease apart."[47] According to Eric Gans, "victimary thinking" has particularly emerged after the Holocaust as the foundation for what could be called postmodernity.[48]

The victimary claim of jihadists exemplifies both the characteristics identified by Fleming. Jihadists inadvertently display the Abrahamic concern for the victim by claiming to be *the* victims of modernity. In seeking to universalize and absolutize their claim, they put themselves in competition with others claiming victim status. They effectively reduce their absolutist vision by becoming one of the petty competitors for violent supremacy over modernity. Their claim to victim status, furthermore, is connected to their particular interpretation of Islamic views about the status of apostates, hypocrites, polytheists, Jews, and Christians. These views represent an extreme exclusionary position in their condemnation of anyone not on the jihadists' side.

Thus, it is the modern worldview that justifies violence with primary or exclusive reference to the category of victimhood. It does so by twisting the consciousness of the innocence of the victim and the injustice of persecutory violence to victimize those accused of being persecutors. The knowledge of the scapegoat mechanism has deprived violence of its absolute, sacred, and moral self-transcendence. In order to counter this desacralization, new attempts are made to claim moral and supernatural justification for violence by appropriating the category of the victim. This occurs by claiming victim status in which the so-called victim is given moral priority and agency over against the unjust mob and persecutor.

For example, the "suicide-martyr," rather than a passive victim of mob violence, is celebrated by jihadists as a glorious combatant-victim who exemplifies righteousness. This directly flips the archaic order in which the mob was the agent of violence and the victim was silenced and sacralized (in order to bring a kind of peace). Instead, in modernity, the victim is the primary agent, and according to the jihadist, the victim deserves vengeance and justice against his/her oppressors who have made a corrupt and immoral world. Bin Laden laid out this logic in a 1998 interview with John Miller:

> In today's wars, there are no morals, and it is clear that mankind has descended to the lowest degrees of decadence and oppression. They rip us of our wealth and of our resources and of our oil. Our religion is under attack. They kill and murder our brothers. They compromise our honor and our dignity and dare we utter a single word of protest against the injustice, we are called terrorists. This is compounded injustice. And the United Nations insistence to convict the victims and support the aggressors constitutes a serious precedence which shows the extent of injustice that has been allowed to take root in this land …
>
> The truth is that the whole Muslim world is the victim of international terrorism, engineered by America at the United Nations. We are a nation whose sacred symbols have been looted and whose wealth and resources have been plundered. It is normal for us to react against the forces that invade our land and occupy it.[49]

This type of justification of violence with regard to the victim has effected a radical transformation of the logic of violence. According to Jean-Pierre Dupuy, instead of a victim (or scapegoat) who is killed to contain violence (as according to the traditional sacrificial mode), jihadists label combatants such as suicide bombers as the real "victims" or "martyrs" (as declared by their group).[50] By virtue of their superior moral status, these "victims" are justified in destroying the enemy (whether combatant or civilian) with righteous violence. In this way, jihadists take the modern sympathy for the victim to a violent extreme, in order to re-justify and re-sacralize violence. Dupuy calls this "the revenge of the scapegoating logic" or revenge of the scapegoat mechanism "against the revelation that uncovered it."[51]

The logic of the terrorist distorts the modern consciousness of the victim by claiming that the victim-martyr dies "righteously" in opposing an enemy. The enemy has supposedly forced the victimized group to defend itself through indiscriminate violence, so that such violence is morally justified. In this way, the suicide bomber is "innocent" because he/she is killed opposing the unjust mob in the only way possible. By doing so, these so-called martyrs are self-sacrificial in that they bring to light the unjust conditions of the "victimized" group. In undertaking suicide missions or military campaigns against their oppressors, they believe themselves to be publicly revealing the conditions of their own victimization and the "real" violence of the oppressor. The jihadist mentality distorts the Abrahamic traditions' concern for victims—whose innocence is conventionally identified because the victim is targeted and killed by a mob—by purposefully creating victims. It does so by justifying jihadist violence within a "moralization" and "theologization" that hides the unjust, persecutory nature of such violence.

For the jihadist, then, the innocence of the victim-martyr is directly connected to the righteousness of the violent crusade against the enemy. In this way, suicide bombers or jihadist fighters seek to catalyze what they believe to be "good violence" (that of their own side) against the oppressive and persecutory enemy (broadly conceived). This "good violence" will wipe out the enemy and its "bad violence" which is being inflicted on their victimized or oppressed group. Thus, jihadists actually seek to provoke an escalating and indiscriminate cycle of violence by claiming to be victims, until they are victors.

In this way, jihadism is characterized by the revenge of the victim against the desacralized collective—by the one against the many—in which a new type of sacralization of the victim occurs: "Suicide attacks are from this point of view a monstrous inversion of primitive sacrifices: instead of killing victims to save others, terrorists kill themselves to kill others. It is more than ever a world turned upside down."[52] Because the jihadist suicide bomber is undertaking a "sacred" duty against the oppressive collective/enemy, their defiance of conventional Islamic injunctions against suicide and murder is justified. Such violent action is justified because the jihadist "martyr" is said to have an intention to protect Islam against an overwhelming and oppressive enemy rather than an intention to kill themselves or others.[53] This intention absolves the suicide bomber of the breaking of Islamic law.

In making this justification, jihadists draw on the category of the innocent victim—distorting their own tradition—and redirect it for violent purposes. In this way, jihadists are modern: they intentionally undertake violence, as self-identified victims, against the oppressive mob, in a way that exploits the only sacred category left by a modernity formed and influenced by the Abrahamic traditions. Thus, mimetic violence is seeking to re-constitute itself as the absolute center of human society by using the position of the victim as justification for unanimous, sacred violence. The logic remains sacrificial, but much more destructive: violence is done to institute a larger project of sacred order which either controls or destroys everything in its path. Adherents willingly sacrifice themselves and others—entering into the new "violent sacred" by explicitly embracing violence aimed against the "demonic" enemy.[54] Violence becomes more explicitly the heart of worship in order to re-create a sacred world (though this world is more frenzied, unstable, and disordered than traditional cultures).

Moreover, the action of the suicide bomber or the jihadist combatant actualizes and entrenches the belief and imagination of the jihadist group. It is, in fact, the foundation of their sacred mythology. Violence brings glory and everlasting reward to "the victim-martyr-warrior" because he/she has promoted the divine will and his attendant sacred order on earth, over against the oppressive collective of enemies arrayed against them. A powerful transcendent unanimity is created by undertaking violence over against the oppressive enemy that is centered on the victim-martyr-warrior. This unanimity effects a sacralization or externalization of violence that forms and drives jihadism. The jihadist collective who, as righteous victims themselves, fight a divinely-commissioned war, like the martyrs, over against the oppressive, "demonic" enemies, are part of a sacred order founded on transcendent violence. This new sacred collective of jihadists actually mirrors the one that is violently fought against: a violent jihadist mob is created to fight the supposedly oppressive enemy. In this way, the jihadist mob is covertly sacralized by their own violence as agents of the divinity. This sacralization makes the actions of the jihadist group absolutely right and good in their own eyes. Because of this, they are said to be commissioned by God.

Thus, jihadists use the privileged category of persecuted and innocent victims to re-justify absolute violence and create new unrecognized victims. As part of this justification, jihadists develop complex conspiracy theories. In these theories, any action is construed as part of a narrative in which jihadists (and their allies) are oppressed by monstrous state regimes supported by Western and Israeli imperialists. Bin Laden exemplifies this conspiratorial mentality in his public statements, in which he claims the "true victims" (Muslims) have been censured, injustice prevails, and violence demands a retaliatory response:[55] "Your forces occupy our countries; you spread your military bases throughout them; you corrupt our lands, and you besiege our sanctities, to protect the security of the Jews and to ensure the continuity of your pillage of our treasures."[56] This conspiratorial attitude emerges out of an exaggerated victim identity, which enables the violent jihadist to justify violence and sacralize it as the legitimate action of the "righteous" victims.

The response of the jihadist in defense of the victimized and as a result of the jihadist mob's sacralization is increasingly indiscriminate (not discriminating between civilian and combatant). This indiscriminate violence is justified by jihadists in various ways, which I examine in Chapter 6. In effect, the jihadist logic of violence leads to a complete breakdown in the combatant–civilian distinction and so toward total warfare and destruction. The aim of the jihadist is revealed, not as the pursuit of a general condition of peace (in which a group kills or expels one person to bring order), but rather as a highly partisan order that comes about through total, "apocalyptic" warfare against the enemies of Islam.

Righteous Violence

At the center of the response of militant jihadists to their perceived state of victimhood, and the perceived victimhood of the whole Islamic civilization, is "righteous" and "defensive" forms of violence. The jihadist response to modernity is focused on the impulse toward violence, including to destroy anything—in the name of God—that is opposed to the "divine law" and which is regarded as impure or threatening. Khosrokhavar argues that one of the defining traits of jihadism "is the major place that violence occupies in their undertakings, and their attempt to justify it, not only in terms of expediency and strategy, but also in a theological and juridical sense."[57] This commitment to violence is inextricably linked to jihad, as the "almost exclusive"[58] answer to Muslim problems and the essential and exalted virtue of Muslim identity. This commitment to violent jihad is connected to a rigid dichotomous mentality, a utopian vision of a Caliphate, the use of *takfir* (to exclude and kill), an emphasis on heroism and martyrdom, and for some, an "utter disregard for life (their own as well as that of others) and their 'ardent desire' to die and to kill others."[59] Khosrokhavar argues that militant jihadism is different from reformist and fundamentalist currents in contemporary Islam because of its violent rejection of democracy.[60] This rejection reflects a determination to bring about a "total" Islamic system constructed in an absolutist and ahistorical manner that draws on and distorts the Islamic tradition.

The violence of jihadism is, in many ways, the most primitive of all forms of violence, in the sense that it seeks to reproduce the unity around human sacrifice found in some archaic cultures. Laurent Murawiec comments that jihadism looks like a return to the system of human sacrifice:

> The suicide-killing manual ("Suicide Note") left by Muhammad Atta, leader of the September 11, 2001, killing squads, included this revealing comment: "13.

> Check your weapon before you leave [for the mission] and long before you leave. (You must make your knife sharp and you must not discomfort your animal during the slaughter.)" The victim is thus degraded to the status of an animal slated for sacrifice. Terror killing is a resumption of the practice of human sacrifice. The power of the victim, which flows out of its body with his (*sic*) blood, enters the sacrificator's system. The victims, animal-like human beings, are a sacrificial offering to God … Islamic terror, in its use of human sacrifice, has strayed farther and farther away from this pivotal event in the history of mankind, the prohibition of human sacrifice enshrined in the biblical story of Abraham and Isaac on Mount Horeb (Genesis 22:19) … The terrorist draws power from the fear he inspires, from the terror he instills in his victims. It is as though he drew sustenance from the flight of the prey.[61]

Thus, jihadism looks more like the worst kind of archaic religion—that dehumanizes and kills its victims as animals or monsters in offering to the gods—than an Abrahamic one that prohibits human sacrifice. The sacrifice of enemies in jihadism parallels the archaic form of sacrifice, in terms of its scapegoating dynamics and cathartic effects. However, jihadist violence is not resolved and placated with individual sacrifices. More and more sacrifices are needed until the utopian vision is realized. In this sense, jihadism contrasts to archaic cultures in that violence is intentionally instituted and explicitly celebrated at the heart of jihadist activity in defense of select victims to bring about an Islamist order. For traditional cultures, violence was not usually the object of motivation or worship, though it was the cause of their mythical projections. Rather, sacrificial violence was only a means to order. It was spontaneously discovered by these groups, employed out of necessity with limited and ritualized violence, and was justified by subsequent dehumanization and divinization of the victims. For archaic peoples, the survival of the group-mob was of the utmost importance and the unspoken necessity. Traditional cultures had little choice but to deploy violence for their survival (it was a choice between sacrifice and chaos).

For jihadists, by contrast, violence is more honestly, openly and "freely" embraced as a "defense" of victimized peoples. Though violence is professed to be a necessity, it is *chosen* by jihadists—shown by the explicit rejection of nonviolent means and alternatives. Violence is done with a premeditated and absolute antipathy toward the jihadists' enemies. It is modern in the sense that it targets enemies in the defense of select victims—persecuting the perceived persecutors—thereby creating new victims and scapegoats.

As an example of the embrace of violence in modernity by jihadists (and their enemies), Khosrokhavar notes there is a consciousness of violence in the conflict between Palestinians and Israelis, from which they choose not to extricate themselves: "René Girard's theses notwithstanding, the vicious circle of rising extremism has not completely blinded the actors involved."[62] Khosrokhavar is referring to Girard's notion that as humans engage in violence, their awareness recedes, and they enter into a state of *méconnaissance* (misrecognition). In this state, the rivals don't recognize the arbitrary, unjust, and reciprocal nature of their own violence. By contrast, Khosrokhavar points to the way in which some awareness remains in modern violence. Girard actually argues that there is a level of awareness among any violent actors, but at a point they repress such awareness in favor of their "righteous" rivalry and the need to be victorious. In modern violence, this awareness is heightened because most people have some sense of the arbitrary nature of violence against scapegoat-enemies (even though this sense may take some time to manifest). In order to repress such an awareness, violence must be more intentionally embraced and justified. The actors may retain some sense of the reciprocal nature of their violence (as bin Laden clearly does[63]), but they choose to embrace it as morally justified: their violence is still superior and must win.

This is not to argue that jihadists are always completely aware of the hurt and destruction they cause to others, how evil it is, and that their victims are innocent. However, there is some sense that jihadists are aware of the scandalous and transgressive quality of their violence and seek to justify it through exaggerated, though often revealing, rationales. They intentionally deploy violence to maximum effect as a form of terror and worship, despite the fact that their victims are often defenseless or tangentially connected to the crimes they are accused of having committed. Of course, jihadists are not alone in intentionally embracing violence in modernity (as Khosrokhavar indicates). They are the most extreme symptom of a larger problem in modernity—namely, that violence is done in spite of some knowledge that it is wrong or that one's victims do not really deserve the violence being done to them. Jihadists will claim that their victims are absolutely guilty and often show no remorse for their actions—protesting their own innocence (often too much). However, there is a continual stream of deradicalized persons who realize the evil of their jihadist violence, eventually defect, and change their behavior (e.g., during a conflict or while in prison).[64] They represent the consciousness of violence that is possible in modernity, which active jihadists seek to repress. Jihadists are not alone in this repression, but as I show in more detail in Chapter 6, they are extreme perpetrators of it. They become both perpetrators and slaves to a rivalrous dynamic that is appropriated with such ferocity that to let it go is to risk existential and cultural breakdown.

The mimetic relationships of violence in which jihadists situate themselves are so constitutive of their identity that they (and their enemies) fear recognition:

> René Girard's theses notwithstanding, the vicious circle of rising extremism has not completely blinded the actors involved. The tragedy lies in their inability to reject an action-logic in which passions have the upper hand. Palestinian martyrs fuel Israeli extremism, which in its turn corroborates the deadly premises based upon Israel's refusal to accept the Palestinians' right to existence and to political and territorial independence in a viable state. The outcome is a spiral of death in which both sides discover their identity in their ability to annihilate the other. At times, one or other of the protagonists may have a flash of insight, perhaps simply out of weariness. The confrontation then takes on a cyclical nature. The fascination with self-destruction and the destruction of the Other takes the form of an increasingly tragic crescendo, with each side accusing the other of having broken its word or the moral contract to restrict the violence. It is not only the restricted groups who are always killing each other that are attracted to death. Each side tries to neutralise the other so as to exorcise its own demons.[65]

Thus, there is a conscious element in modern violence that purposefully embraces violence against a rival—knowing, prior to its deployment, its destructive consequences. The adherent understands on some level the moral evil of violence but still undertakes it in order to conquer his/her rival and intentionally gives oneself over to the power of violence. This choice for violence obscures, to some degree, the mimetic and reciprocal nature of violence, so that the violent actor can believe in the righteousness of their cause in wiping out their enemy. Militant jihadism exemplifies this choice in an extreme manner to the extent that it regards its "righteous violence" as totally justified, no matter its indiscriminate nature.

Moreover, like other totalitarianisms, the jihadist's deployment of total violence seeks to terrorize those who resist jihadist violence into accepting its absolute power and legitimacy. Rather than being able to spontaneously draw all people into the unanimity of violent transcendence (as archaic religions did), jihadists use a mixture of attraction and force, which is common in modern forms of totalitarian violence.[66] Jihadists do this through encouraging fascination with violence or through enforcing acquiescence in terror and fear, as this statement from an Algerian jihadist group indicates: "Islam has ordered us to terrorize our enemies and whoever denies that is an infidel himself. Terrorizing our infidel enemies is a legal obligation. Whoever says that Islam is not related to terrorism has committed an infidel act—terror comes from Islam."[67]

This statement exemplifies the rigid dichotomous attitude that Khosrokhavar identifies as a defining trait of jihadism. It justifies the desire for violence and death as part of a righteous-victim mentality. This righteous violence enacts a false type of atonement for jihadists in which persecuting the persecutors acts as a way to serve God and expiate one's own guilt before God, particularly with regard to the jihadist's own personal involvement in immorality in the past.[68] This guilt is evident among violent jihadists, especially those converted and radicalized after a formerly "dissolute" or "immoral" life, often involving petty forms of violent crime or domestic abuse.[69] This category includes the infamous Abu Musab Zarqawi (whose real name was Ahmad Fadil Nazal al-Khalayleh), who became a notorious jihadist in Iraq after a period in prison.[70]

Alongside guilt, jihadism encourages a belief that one can completely break from one's "bloody past" and become "pure." This purity is defined over against other apostates and infidels—all those who live a sinful, impure, and evil life, especially those unjustly persecuting the innocent (e.g., the Muslim world).[71] This belief is characteristic of the jihadist-terrorist mentality, according to Charles Taylor, and prevents the jihadist from recognizing his/her own on-going inclination toward and involvement in evil and violence.[72] This kind of false moralism is an effective way to bring about group unity and scapegoat nonconformists as moral deviants, persecutors, or evil.

Conclusion

In militant jihadism, the agents of violence regard themselves as defenders of victims, who must be protected against the threatening collective. This oppressive collective—comprised of apostate states, Western imperialists, and infidels—is the enemy that must be wiped out. Jihadists perceive their own brutal and indiscriminate violence as justifiably defensive. As I have argued, jihadist violence is a modern form that seeks to twist and repress the consciousness of the victim in order to bring about a new sacred order. Like other totalitarianisms, jihadism sacralizes itself through its morally and theologically justified violence, which creates new victims. The victims of jihadism are not recognized as innocent but as guilty and so deserving of punishment and death. Though it functions like other totalitarianisms in re-sacralizing violence in the name of victims, jihadism has distinctive features, particularly in its reference to God, its theological rationales, and its explicit use of and commitment to violence in the form of jihad (struggle). In subsequent chapters, I focus on these features. In Chapter 5, I examine in detail violent jihad as the distinctive answer of jihadists to modernity and the essential means by which they promote true Islamic society.

5

The Globalization of Violent Jihad

Essential to achieving the aim of the Islamic modernity and being a true Muslim, according to militant Islamists, is undertaking violent jihad. Jihad is regarded as the necessary means for overcoming the obstacles that prevent the proper worship of God by enabling the construction of a truly Islamic state. This state is meant to address the problem suffered by "righteous Muslims": victimhood by the enemies of Islam. As discussed in the previous chapter, the identification with victimhood has become for militant jihadists a violent "victim identity" that justifies extreme rivalry and violence. From the vantage of this victim identity, Islam is reinterpreted theologically and ideologically to motivate a violent revolutionary response to modernity that defines militant jihad. This response relies on an intellectual approach that brings together a literalist, utopian, and apocalyptic interpretation of the Islamic tradition with a clear revolutionary vision for its achievement. This revolutionary vision of violence encompasses and channels the various grievances, tensions, frustrated desires, and identity issues of disaffected radical Muslims into jihadist campaigns.

This chapter traces key aspects in the history and doctrinal development of jihad within militant Islamism in order to understand jihad as a violent revolutionary response to modernity that has become global. The chapter begins by exploring the "neglected duty" of jihad and then moves on to examine the successes and failures of militant jihadists in order to show how violence has both structured and undermined the jihadist movement. The chapter then examines the particular targets or enemies of jihad as intrinsic to its logic and global expansion. Jihadist groups in the twentieth century initially focused on the "near enemy" and later moved to focus on the "far enemy" (through the influence of al-Qaeda). In the twenty-first century, they shifted to an amalgam of both (with the growth of ISIS and similar groups). The expansion of violent action against Islam's so-called enemies has resulted in a global approach to jihad, which has gone beyond resistance to local regimes and defense of so-called Islamic lands.

This global approach, spearheaded by Osama bin Laden and AQ, is distinctive of jihadism as a movement and resulted in it becoming the preeminent geopolitical threat of the twenty-first century. In its global revolutionary reach, militant jihadism exemplifies the escalating mimetic dynamics of rivalry in modernity (which were discussed in Chapter 2) and has resulted in a radical embrace of violence and death that defines jihadism as a global response to modernity.

The Duty of Violent Jihad

Throughout the twentieth century, violent jihad became central to the vision of the militant Islamist movement. According to such militants, violent jihad is an absolute imperative for Muslims because it defines the very identity of the Muslim and is necessary for the renewal and dominance of Islam in modernity. According to al-Zarqawi, the infamous leader of AQ in Iraq (later ISIS), "jihad is the identity of the Muslim in his existence."[1] In this view, violent jihad is not just one righteous act among many in Islam but is the quintessential act that defines and reveals the *being* of the true Muslim. In this way, according to militant Islamists, violent jihad guarantees the greatest eternal reward and is believed to continue until the day of judgment.[2]

In this sense, jihad has an eschatological purpose guided by God's plan for the world, which is intrinsically bound up with the realization of a utopian political regime.[3] Connected to its individual and eschatological benefits, violent jihad is an absolute imperative for militants because it enables the reestablishment of proper Islamic rule and practice in the form of a universal caliphate. In the view of militant jihadists, a caliphate stands for a "total system" that is claimed to bring about God's rule on earth—effected by jihadists themselves in accordance with God's plan—through defensive and offensive forms of jihad that overcome the alienation and injustice of modernity.[4]

Despite its centrality to Islam, the Egyptian Islamist theorist and al-Jihad activist, Muhammad abd-al-Salam Faraj called violent jihad the "neglected duty" among Muslims in the twentieth century.[5] This neglect helped to explain the Islamic world's malaise: "Jihad ... for God's cause [in the way of Allah], in spite of its importance for the future of religion, has been neglected by the ulama ... of this age. ... There is no doubt that the idols of this world can only disappear through the power of the sword."[6] Faraj argued that jihad was part of a hidden or repressed tradition in Islam, which had to be restored for Islam to realize its true dominance.[7] He claimed that mainstream Muslim scholars and leaders had neglected and repressed jihad because they were subjected to apostate authorities, and so, too afraid to implement a true Islamic vision.[8] According to Faraj, Islam was prophesized as being triumphant and it was incumbent on Muslims to bring about this prophecy.[9] Jihad would rectify the weakness of Muslim peoples and nations, and the problems caused by intermingling with apostates and non-Muslims, as Muslims recovered the lost essence of their faith. For militants, this "lost essence" would serve to more strictly define Muslim identity and draw clear boundaries around the Islamic world. In this view, the secular political realm in Muslim lands would no longer have any autonomy outside Islam, which would reassert control in the face of oppressive, apostate rulers.[10]

Faraj's line of thinking greatly influenced the militant Islamist movement in the 1970s and after by emphasizing jihad as a neglected activity necessary for the achievement of Islam's universal political goals. While Qutb thought of jihad as liberation for all people and resistance against apostate regimes, Faraj developed jihad as the means to revitalize Islam and reestablish the caliphate, so that Muslims could properly rule the world.[11] Moreover, the duty of jihad that Faraj identified has been used by militants to construct a heroic model of the jihadist who selflessly undertakes "true" jihad through violence. This model jihadist—who rejects love of the world and does not fear death—is contrasted to Muslims who are downtrodden, because they have submitted to cowardice and fear in the face of opposition (which is argued to be a sign of the unbeliever). Jihad is necessary, then, for reinvigorating the faith and righteousness of Muslims and reinforces the connection between God's providence and political success.[12]

Intrinsic to Faraj's view is the rejection of jihad as anything other than violent. He argued that the tradition of "greater jihad" as a spiritual struggle was false.[13] Jihad was inherently a violent struggle and the highest duty of the Muslim (in contrast to engaging in nonviolent charitable and pietistic activities). Taking up jihad was the only way to bring about a truly Islamic state rather than preaching or nonviolent means, which had already failed in Faraj's opinion.[14] Such jihad, according to Faraj, had to be directed against the "near enemy," the "infidel" ruler and state, which was the most immediate and oppressive arm of imperialism. Fighting the "far enemy" was, for Faraj, a waste of time, unless the near enemy was dealt with.[15]

Building on Qutb's claim that the individual Muslim has an obligation to undertake jihad, Faraj argued that all individual Muslims should undertake violent jihad against the near enemy (the "pagan state").[16] Traditionally Muslims have relied on a competent authority (e.g., caliph) to proclaim jihad, supported by Islamic legal authorities. However, according to Faraj, because such authorities were largely corrupt and Islam had lost its dominant position in its own lands (which it supposedly required to show the truth), jihad was declared an individual's Muslim's duty. In undertaking this duty, Muslims could defend and restore Islam to its previous dominance during a time of great ignorance and barbarism.[17]

In the 1980s, Abdallah Azzam (a member of the Muslim Brotherhood) infamously, too, emphasized the individual Muslim's duty to undertake jihad, particularly in defense of Muslim lands. Azzam's thought became influential particularly because of its effect in recruiting for and providing ideological justification for the Afghan campaign against the USSR.[18] This influence extended to mentoring jihadists such as Osama bin Laden. Bin Laden later drew on Azzam's arguments when justifying the jihad against the United States following the Gulf War.[19] While Azzam drew on the authority of existing fatwas from certain ulemas (including the future mufti of Saudi Arabia), he, like Faraj, argued that the authorization of the "Commander of the Faithful" was not necessary for the Afghan jihad (and similar campaigns). According to Azzam, violent jihad to reclaim Muslim lands was every Muslim's individual duty (morally and financially).[20] While Faraj primarily focused on what he called "the near enemy," Azzam emphasized fighting in those areas which could be most effective in defending and promoting Islam, like in Afghanistan.

The Successes and Failures of Violent Jihad

The intensification of jihad as an individual duty to undertake violence against certain enemies was vital for the growth and vitality of the militant jihadist movement in the latter part of the twentieth century. Militants used this duty to fuel violent activity against both apostate regimes and non-Muslim powers/populations ("the far enemy").[21] "The idea that violence is justified as the duty of individuals has proved to be an invaluable recruiting tool. For years now, it has been attracting fighters from across the globe to places as diverse as Afghanistan, Bosnia, Chechnya and elsewhere. In this sense, then, the individualistic 'jihadi' strategies and practices on display in recent attacks in Europe are far from new."[22]

The potency for global jihad to renew the Muslim world was particularly exemplified for militant Islamists by the military successes in Afghanistan in the 1980s and 1990s, as well as the Iranian Revolution of 1979. For Sunni groups, the Afghan campaign was a watershed moment. It was the first major gathering of, and victory for, a pan-Islamic jihadist movement. The Afghan campaign focused the attention of militant jihadists, with the support of Saudi Arabia and the United States, and was pivotal in the formation of a generation of jihadists. For jihadists like Osama bin Laden, the Afghan campaign came at a crucial stage of life in which he, like many others, "discovered religious devotion and a militant commitment that gave his life meaning."[23]

Most importantly, the Afghan campaign forged disparate national groups of Islamist fighters into a common cause against a much larger enemy and demonstrated the power and potency of jihad. For jihadists disillusioned by unsuccessful campaigns in their own countries, Afghanistan demonstrated the success of a militant effort under the umbrella of jihad (even though the victory was accomplished by multiple factors). It was even more significant since the fight occurred against a superpower, the USSR. Following the USSR's retreat from Afghanistan in 1989, it was claimed by jihadists that a successful jihad had defeated a superpower and had been pivotal in the USSR's later dissolution in 1991.

The victory in Afghanistan, however, was somewhat short-lived as the United States and Saudi Arabia withdrew support from the *mujahideen* and local Afghani groups engaged in a civil war (which lasted until the ascendency of the Taliban in 1996). The jihadist movement was, then, at a crossroads.[24] The extreme radicalization of the *mujahideen* had caused tension with their former allies, Saudi Arabia and the United States. This withdrawal of support alienated the militant jihadists who were without a clear enemy after the USSR's defeat and without wealthy supporters who could provide money, weapons, and logistics for their next campaigns.

Nevertheless, the inspiration of the Afghan campaign, as well as its ambiguous result, provoked jihadists from multiple countries to intensify their violent campaigns beyond Afghanistan in a new, narrowly defined international movement:

> The international brigade of jihad veterans, being outside the control of any state, was suddenly available to serve radical Islamist causes anywhere in the world. Since they were no longer bound by local political contingencies, they had no responsibilities to any social group either. … They became the free electrons of jihad, professional Islamists trained to fight and to train others to do likewise…
>
> This milieu was cut off from social reality; its inhabitants perceived the world in the light of religious doctrine and armed violence. It bred a new, hybrid Islamist ideology whose first doctrinal principle was to rationalize the existence and behavior of militants. This was jihadist-salafism. In academic parlance, the

> term *salafism* denotes a school of thought that surfaced in the second half of the nineteenth century as a reaction to the spread of European ideas. It advocated a return to the traditions of the devout ancestors (*salaf* in Arabic). Exemplified by the Persian Afghani, the Egyptian Abduh, and the Syrian Rida, it sought to expose the roots of modernity within Muslim civilization—and in the process resorted to a somewhat freewheeling interpretation of the sacred texts. In the eyes of militants, the definition of the term was quite different: salafists were those who understood the injunctions of the sacred text in their most literal, traditional sense.[25]

As Kepel identifies, Salafism became the dominant jihadist philosophy within Sunni contexts, heavily promoted by Saudi Wahhabism. Salafists sought to revive the practices of the "pious predecessors" (the first three generations of Muslims following the Prophet Muhammad) within "a redemptive philosophy based around an idealised version of Islam that enshrines both authenticity and purity."[26] Significantly, Salafi-Jihadists, according to Maher, violently reject the state in order to bring about revolutionary change that protects and promotes Islam.[27] Maher claims that these jihadists consistently deploy five key concepts, revolving around violent resistance and revolution: "The doctrine of *al-wala' wa-l-bara'* establishes lines of loyalty and disavowal; *takfir* delineates Islam against everything else and protects it against insidious corruption from within; *tawhid* and *hakimiyya* explain what legitimate authority should look like and who it should serve; and jihad prescribes the method for this particular revolution."[28] On this basis, "the jihadist-salafists … took the view that the Muslim world was ready to go on the offensive and wage the great jihad that would ultimately lead to the proclamation of the Islamic state."[29]

Following the dispersal of jihadist veterans from the Afghan campaign in the 1980s and 1990s, violent attacks against "apostate" governments and their "godless" Western allies increased in service of catalyzing the jihadist revolution. Attacks against the "far enemy" included the 1993 bombing of the World Trade Center, violent campaigns in Egypt against foreigners, the targeting of French people and interests in Algeria and France, the repulsion of US troops in Somalia in 1993, the 1998 attacks against US embassies in Kenya and Tanzania, and the 9/11 attacks.[30] Despite these attacks, the jihadist revolution was not sparked in the way militants hoped, not until the short-lived success of ISIS in Iraq and Syria in 2014–19.

Jihadists have arguably had their greatest successes since the US invasion of Iraq in 2003, when they were able to exploit the turmoil following the invasion. Reflecting on jihadist thought prior to 2003, Maher argues that Salafi-jihadism particularly clarified and defined itself in more depth in the Iraq War or Second Gulf War (2003–11). It did so in order to justify its violent actions to an uncertain Muslim audience.[31] Ever more brutal attacks occurred in Iraq by jihadist militants under the banner of jihad, which resulted in many Muslims and non-Muslims questioning what kind of Islam these militants were committed to.

For this reason, Khosrokhavar calls jihadism a "death culture" in which death and martyrdom are glorified and sought as the greatest service to Islam and a means to paradise.[32] Roy states that the embrace of death is distinctive in Islamist jihadism: "What is unprecedented is the way that terrorists now deliberately pursue their own deaths."[33] Reversing the Islamic injunction against suicide by distorting the traditional rules around warfare and jihad, jihadists glorify death: "We love death as you love life."[34] The success of violent jihad relies on the embrace of death, which becomes the way to prove oneself as a true Muslim and to destroy Islam's enemies, including those regarded as false or apostate Muslims:[35]

> Both Shi'ism and Sunnism, in different ways, have developed a subculture of death within the framework of the traditional subculture of violence that has always existed, as a minority phenomenon, in Islam. "Perverse modernization" has induced the transformation of the subculture of violence into a subculture of death. The latter has four main components: first, the only way to surpass the West is to let it see that Muslims not only die voluntarily but also aspire to die; second, the values of life are monopolized by the enemy (the West or the Muslim governments at large), and therefore only the values of death are available, superior to those of life; third, death is not only a second-best solution in dire situations requiring the ultimate sacrifice but the ideal to be achieved through violence; fourth, death is the realization of the self as an individual, in total contempt for reality and its requirements. All these ingredients are incorporated by Jihadists in their vision of life.[36]

This "death culture" is a perverse reaction to modernity that seeks to rival the West in producing more faithful and authentic adherents. Jihadists seek to outdo an enemy who seems powerful, decadent, and uncertain all at the same time (reflecting the different trends of Western global dominance, modernity, and postmodernity). Combined with a victim identity, the jihadist cult of death becomes all-encompassing in addressing those disaffected by modernity and binding them to an extreme use of violence.

In particular, young people have been radicalized to engage in these extreme forms of violence in the service of militant jihadism. Jihad addresses and redirects personal resentments, inadequacies, guilt, and frustrations through highly charged cathartic experiences and forms of heroism undertaken for high moral and religious purposes, in defense of victimized Muslims and Islam. Though a violent culture of death, jihad gives these young people meaning, camaraderie, and deep purpose through a violent victim identity. This purpose has a number of distinct features including: a commitment to jihad and fighting the infidel, an aim to give back what is due to the Islamic world and to return the suffering done by the enemy to the enemy (retaliatory justice), and actions of service (usually violent acts) to protect the religion of Allah and Muslims against its enemies to the point of self-sacrifice and martyrdom. Jihadi groups, moreover, give legal and theological justification for Muslims, especially young people, to undertake a total break from their previous lives. According to militants, these young people are encouraged to disassociate themselves from their previous lives and networks, especially family, to undertake violent jihad against Islam's so-called oppressors.[37] In their view, jihad is the absolute priority: anyone who prevents a Muslim from undertaking it is not a true Muslim. According to Khosrokhavar, this emphasis on jihad, within a very narrow worldview, has two aims:

> The purpose is twofold: to win the war of conviction (the defense of the Jihadist version of Islam against the Reformist and even Fundamentalist versions) and to push the youth to join the Jihadist ranks so as to wage a total war against the enemies. Jihadist discourse is Manichean. It is based on accusing others of not being true Muslims, as being apostates or unbelievers (*takfir*, whose legal punishment is death).[38]

This discourse aims at cultivating sacrifice in service of an agenda of total warfare. In this sense, jihadism is the modern inheritor of the revolutionary mode and model, seeking to remake the world in the image of its distorted form of justice for victims. Yet, according to Kepel, militant jihadism has failed to gain widespread popular support in much of the Muslim-majority world, such as Egypt and Saudi Arabia. However, despite failures, militant jihadist groups have been able to adapt, learn, and reinvigorate their jihadist objectives and campaigns. For example, according to Kilcullen, the Arab Spring challenged the claims of jihadists such as AQ because a nonviolent movement had achieved more in six months for Muslim citizens than violent jihadism had in years.[39] Yet, in the wake of this, violence was not renounced by jihadist groups like AQ. Rather, they intensified their violence, facilitated by botched political efforts to maintain and restore peace in Syria and Iraq. Despite alternatives, the professed faith of these groups in their violent mission was undisturbed and remained unabated. In fact, their violence seems to have escalated in brutality and fanaticism. In this regard, the Egyptian experience is indicative.

For example, in the 1990s, the militant jihadist groups declared war on the Egyptian government, perpetrating violent campaigns of terror that targeted secularists, Muslim "apostates," Christians, and foreigners.[40] This extreme violence, combined with armed robbery and killings of collaborators and informants, alienated much public sentiment, caused divisions in the Islamist movement, and hardened state repression.[41] The Islamist terror campaign culminated in the massacre of a group of foreign tourists at Luxor in 1997. This was the last major act of violence by the most extreme group, Gamaa Islamiya, who had lost almost all popular support.[42] Rather than turning public feeling against the government and foreigners, the militant jihadist movement in Egypt was blamed for the rivalry between the state and militant Islamists. Because of the failure of and popular disaffection with Islamist violence, some Islamists were even willing to give up violence in Egypt or become part of the democratic process. They did so, according to Kepel, to "escape the trap of their [jihadist] political logic."[43] These jihadists eventually recognized the trajectory of this logic in Egypt. It is the same logic that led to the 9/11 attacks: an escalating trajectory of extreme violence. When such violence failed to bring about an Islamic state, jihadists sought more violence, even if it brought repression. Violence was the answer to all problems. Thus, some Egyptian jihadists, including the leader of Egyptian Islamic Jihad (and the current leader of AQ), Ayman al-Zawahiri, turned their primary attention to other theaters of violence—to the "far enemy"—following the failure with regard to the "near enemy."[44]

Similar events occurred in Algeria during its civil war in the 1990s. Beginning with a majority of public support against the military dictatorship, militant Islamist groups alienated this support with the use of extreme violence. The most extreme jihadist violence was primarily perpetrated by the Armed Islamic Group (GIA). It targeted other Muslims and foreign civilians (including in France) and was involved in racketeering and other repressive measures. The spiraling of violence, which grew out of the moderate Islamists' control, "caused ordinary people to shrink from an ideology that had turned into a blood-drenched nightmare."[45] The rejection of extreme violence allowed the Algerian government to recapture popular support and elicit Western aid, especially from France, in the civil war.[46]

The alienation of the Egyptian and Algerian populaces from Islamist-jihadist violence resulted, at least in part, from the damage to their own interests that such violence was causing. At the same time, there was a deeper alienation from such violence than just material self-interest. In both Egypt and Algeria, popular sentiment turned against the jihadists in the 1990s because the victims they chose, and the associated violence they used, were not acceptable to much of the public, most of whom were Muslim.[47] The jihadist violence came to be seen as purely destructive, aggressive, and chaotic rather than as constructive or morally righteous. As discussed, Girard argues that violence is culturally acceptable when it provides unity against enemies or scapegoats. In other words, violence is acceptable when it is constructive of social order rather than arbitrary and indiscriminate, and so, potentially dangerous to all. The jihadists were regarded as using their military power in an exploitative, indiscriminate, and frenetic way for personal benefit or revenge rather than for the social good or according to Islamic notions of justice.

Thus, instead of the jihadists being seen as victims exacting righteous violence against their enemies, they came to be regarded as targeting innocent noncombatants in increasingly brutal, indiscriminate, and unjust ways. Their victims were seen to be innocent, and as such, a symptom of the brutal rivalistic logic of the jihadists. The jihadist narrative of claiming victimhood (over against the government and the West) transformed into a perception of them as the worst kind of victimizers who only seemed interested in fomenting chaos and destruction. This resulted in a dramatic shift in popular sentiment in Egypt and Algeria in which militant Islamists lost much of their support to the government which justified repressive action.[48] A similar alienation of public opinion has occurred regarding al-Qaeda and ISIS, because their violence was regarded as too destructive and indiscriminate. In al-Qaeda's case, this alienation occurred following the 9/11 attacks, which earned them repression from the United States and its allies in the West and Muslim-majority world.[49] In ISIS's case, this occurred in Iraq and Syria when brutal and extreme violence alienated much of the Shia and Sunni populations (both in 2006–8 and 2014–19).[50]

A shift in popular sentiment like that seen in Egypt and Algeria gives justification for one group (usually the state) to target and triumph over the other (the jihadists). This ascendency occurs because of the dynamics of scapegoating: the unpopular group is blamed for the disorder and destructiveness of rivalrous violence, and so, can be targeted. In each case, the government's rivalistic logic mirrored the jihadists in many ways, however there was one crucial difference: the government claimed its violence as being for the purpose of order, and so, was structured by the "logic of order," in contrast to the perception of jihadist violence as chaotic and indiscriminately destructive. Therefore, government violence could be construed as positive (acting for the population according to a traditional sacrificial logic) and the jihadist violence as negative and destructive.

Thus, jihadist groups have usually failed to catalyze revolution because they have been regarded by widespread popular opinion as being too violent.[51] In this sense, jihadists confront an internal contradiction: they need to do more violence in the name of jihad according to their ideology/theology (and to channel their frustrations/desires), but more violence has generally caused more alienation because jihadist violence has been perceived as destructive rather than constructive.[52] Because of this contradiction, it is characteristic of jihadist action that state-based violence has been mobilized against it, supported by local and foreign allies. This mobilization against militant jihadists occurs because they are labelled as a "violent" enemy, and so made into an appropriate target for state violence. It is for this reason that prominent jihadists such as Abu Musab al-Suri opposed the 9/11 attacks because he argued that they would bring state-based repressive actions against a jihadist movement that was too weak to repel them.[53]

Moreover, when jihadists have lost popular support, they have tended to use more extreme violent tactics to punish the populace, cause chaos, and enforce loyalty. They do so in order to project themselves as the only group that can stop or save people from violence (in order to recover their position of power with a brutally violent form of sacrificial logic).[54] The GIA attempted such tactics in the late 1990s in Algeria and AQI/ISIS undertook similar tactics during the tribal uprisings before the 2007–8 Surge in Iraq.[55] However, such violence has usually backfired on jihadist groups as it becomes too indiscriminate and damages those who jihadists profess to protect. Thus, when a credible governmental alternative to the jihadists arises, most populations are willing to side with such alternatives.

Significantly, when jihadist groups have lost popular support, even the populace, along with the state, have come to be seen as the enemy by hard-line jihadists—labelled as Muslim "traitors" to jihad. Because they no longer support, acquiesce to, and imitate the jihadists, they become obstacles in the way of achieving victory.[56] In Algeria, for example, the whole populace was labelled as *takfir* by the GIA leadership headed by Zouabri because of their lack of support. This occurred just as the GIA became more indiscriminate in its violence as well as more isolated and divided, even alienating Salafi-Jihadist allies internationally.[57] The disintegration of the GIA as a (semi-)coherent ideological and military force resulted in victory for the state as well as the fragmentation of the movement into smaller groups that continued to terrorize local populations.[58]

Thus, as they lose popular support because of the rivalrous and unstable nature of their violence, jihadists are susceptible to internal dissensions and rivalries. Internal dissensions and competition caused a split in the Islamist opposition to the Algerian state, with devastating consequences as violence escalated to brutal extremes. Similarly, in Afghanistan after the *mujahideen* came to control much of the country by the early 1990s, internal divisions appeared between local and foreign fighters battling for power. Thus, while the Afghan campaign forged a global movement, it also presented the consequence and violent nature of the jihadist movement: "The spectacle of triumphant militants on attack, massacring one another, was painfully eloquent: it crippled the moral authority to which they laid claim and 'rendered meaningless the years and centuries of campaigns for the propagation of the faith' [Abdel Wahab al-Effendi]."[59] The history of the relationship between ISIS and AQ presents the same dynamics: characterized by a rivalry for supremacy, forged by disputes over strategy and power, and veneered with principle, the split between the two groups has caused intense competition, resentment, and violence.[60]

In fact, according to Kepel, the major failure of Sunni jihadist groups (up until ISIS's so-called caliphate) has been the inability to build and maintain a broad-based revolutionary movement, like that which occurred in Shiite-majority Iran in 1979.[61] Their failures have been due to local state action as well as their own narrow ideology, internal divisions, extreme violence, and their provocation of conflict with local states or Western powers which they have been unable to win. Because of these factors, they have largely struggled to transform popular alienation from modernity into a broad-based political movement and revolution, except under conditions of conflict. Even then, their rule has been relatively short-lived (such as in Afghanistan and Iraq–Syria). The mixture of success and failure experienced by the international Sunni jihadist movement by the 1990s, as well as international political events, precipitated a major change in focus toward a new enemy: the United States and the West. This change in focus—beyond the traditional lands of Islam—resulted in militant jihadism catapulting to the forefront of geopolitical concern, as jihadism followed the path of modernity into a phase of intense globalization.

The Turn to the Far Enemy

The failures of the militant jihadist movement in local operations against state authorities, as well as the need to reignite popular support in the Muslim world following the Afghan campaign, propelled key parts of the movement to consider a change in its focus to the "far enemy" at the end of the twentieth century. This change culminated in the 9/11 attacks, which exploited antipathies toward the West in Muslim-majority nations. For example, Kepel argues that for many Muslims "the planes that crashed into the twin towers and the Pentagon were perceived ... as a fitting response to the Israeli (and Western) military challenge."[62]

Thus, rather than giving up on extremist violence after failing to bring about revolutionary change in the Muslim-majority world, a significant section of the jihadist movement turned to even more spectacular terrorist activity directed against the West. Building on the Afghan campaign of the 1980s, this change in the primary enemy reflected a fundamental globalization of the movement in seeking to attack targets beyond a local sphere of operations within the so-called lands of Islam. One of the important organizational changes that contributed to this globalization was the merger of Egyptian Islamic Jihad (EIJ) with AQ, after EIJ's failure and suppression in Egypt following its extreme use of violence. Furthermore, the perceived success of the Afghan campaign (against a "far enemy"), the continuing tensions over Israel and Palestine (leading to the First Intifada), and dissatisfaction with the Gulf War among many Muslim groups led militant jihadists to focus on the United States and its Western allies (especially Israel) as the primary adversary.

For these reasons, leaders such as Osama bin Laden and Ayman Al-Zawahiri wished to expand jihad beyond Islamic lands such as Afghanistan. Thus, this phase of jihad went beyond local resistance to a foreign power (like in Afghanistan or Iraq) to striking targets in Western nations themselves, including civilians. The closest precedent to this activity was the Algerian GIA's campaign against the French. The GIA in Algeria had combined fighting a local war against the Algerian government, while also targeting its Western ally, France, with terrorist operations.[63] While AQ wished to end the Western support of apostate governments (as the GIA did with the Algerian government), they effectively expanded jihad globally. In so doing, they justified their violent action as legitimately encompassing almost any enemy target—civilian or combatant.[64]

This global focus reflected the new mentality of battled-hardened jihadists from the Afghan campaign. There were many veterans from the Afghan campaign who thirsted for more combat, were formed and ready to be deployed as a multinational force, and were alienated from the United States and Saudi Arabia.[65] These jihadists had forged links across national boundaries and were inspired by the vision and possibility of an Islamist state. Though they had failed to bring about an Islamic state in the immediate aftermath of the USSR's defeat in Afghanistan, the disparate national groups of jihadist fighters had been formed into the beginnings of a global movement, which also had gained vital military experience and training, including from the Central Intelligence Agency (CIA). This training and experience "combined ultra-religious ideological brainwashing and fascination with violence."[66] The Afghan veterans had a taste for both violence and victory, and bin Laden and the leaders of al-Qaeda believed that they could achieve such victory against a new and even greater enemy, with more violence. In this way, they were ready to bring jihad to the world and try to replicate the success in Afghanistan of a united Islamic army fighting for the *ummah*.

The particular catalyst for the turn to the far enemy occurred following Iraq's invasion of Kuwait in 1990. Political and activist groups across the Muslim world were divided in their stance toward the invasion by Saddam Hussein's Iraq, as well as the UN-mandated intervention.[67] The involvement of the United States and other Western nations in the Middle East, however, catalyzed virulent anti-Western sentiment among many Islamist leaders and groups. The Arab-Islamic alliance with the United States and the West against Iraq represented a major setback for international jihadists. To Osama bin Laden and his allies, it represented another failure of the Muslim world to rectify its own problems and confront an authoritarian ruler (Saddam Hussein), who had begun as a secularist and was now claiming to be a leader in the anti-imperialist Islamist movement.

The divisiveness of the Gulf War among Islamists (and across the Muslim-majority world) was particularly felt because of the request by Saudi Arabia for US military assistance in the defense of Islam's own lands. Even more embarrassingly, Saudi Arabia had rejected the overtures of bin Laden and his jihadist followers to fight in support of Saudi Arabia and against Iraq, in place of the United States. This rejection led to great scandal among jihadists at their Western allies-turned-rivals. It was incomprehensible to these jihadists that self-professed Muslim nations such as Saudi Arabia had subjected themselves to the West and allowed themselves to be "occupied" by a foreign army, especially one that had abandoned the jihadists in Afghanistan and sought to repress them.[68] Most scandalous of all to bin Laden and his allies, the US now "occupied" a Muslim land with the holiest Islamic sites.[69] Such action by the United States was decried by bin Laden in 1996 as the "biggest mistake," "reckless," and "arbitrary," as a non-Muslim nation has never entered the territory of the "two holy mosques area."[70] This action was a particular outrage for bin Laden and his associates because, for them, it showed how far the so-called Muslim nations had betrayed Islam. In particular, this choice transgressed the jihadist understanding of *al-wala' wa-l-bara'* (loyalty to Allah/Islam and disavowal of those opposed to Islam or non-Muslim). This doctrine has become crucial in jihadist ideology and licensed resistance to treacherous Islamic regimes. Thus, they used the Gulf War as a rallying cry for true Muslims to rally for a renewed conflict—against the West and its apostate allies.

Thus, the US military presence undermined Saudi Arabia's carefully built leadership and reputation in the Islamic world and provoked fears of Western imperialism.[71] While initially opposed to Iraq's actions, many Islamists (of different militant stances) came to question US and Saudi actions and regard them in conspiratorial terms. For some Islamists (especially in Palestine, Pakistan, and Afghanistan), the Gulf War came to be regarded "as an American–Israeli plot to dominate the Middle East".[72] This conspiratorial mentality labelled Iraq as an innocent victim of American plots and aggression, which aimed to trick Islamic regimes to allow US troops to occupy Muslim lands. Most significantly, then, the Muslim world was again the victim of Western colonialism and domination according to radical Islamists. This victim mentality allowed Iraq's leader Saddam Hussein to capture anti-Western sentiment and cause division among Muslims over who to support.[73]

However, despite jihadist efforts to blame the United States for invading Muslim lands, Maher shows that other Salafi scholars and activists recognized that Saudi Arabia had invited the United States into its own territory and that the Muslim regime was responsible for its own situation.[74] Thus, the hard-line position of militant jihadists like bin Laden suggests that the attribution of blame against the US (and Saudi Arabia) was a convenient means to re-catalyze and redirect jihadist efforts. It grew out of their own bias, scandal, and rivalrous mentality, especially in being rejected by Saudi Arabia in favor of the United States to defend Muslim lands.

However, before reconstituting their focus against the far enemy, jihadist groups, especially those based around bin Laden, faced some major setbacks and failures in the 1990s. Bin Laden and his allies confronted increasing marginalization and repression in the Muslim-majority world, especially because of actions taken by the United States and conservative Islamic regimes such as Saudi Arabia to target these revolutionary jihadists. In the face of such repression, instead of choosing political normalization, these jihadists became more hard-line. As Roy argues, they intensified their commitment to "a closed, scripturalist and conservative view of Islam that rejects the national and statist dimension in favour of the *ummah*, the universal community of all Muslims, based on *sharia* (Islamic law)."[75] In line with this view, groups like al-Qaeda argued that the *ummah* could only be secured globally over against the West, who possessed the real power and were propping up satellite regimes in the Muslim-majority world. Moreover, targets such as the United States and Israel could potentially arrest declining public support and gain more sympathy for the jihadist movement among Muslim populations by exploiting anti-Western sentiment, especially against US and Israeli foreign policies.[76]

Thus, seeking to harness what was left of jihadist momentum from Afghanistan, al-Qaeda focused its efforts on an international jihad against the United States and the West. This was aimed to also undermine the West's "apostate" client regimes in the Muslim-majority world. In this regard, militant jihadists have found most success when they have undertaken actions that capitalize on modernist alienation and harness anti-regime or anti-Western popular sentiment. This has occurred most effectively in conditions of political or social unrest or conflict, such as in Iraq after the US invasion. In these circumstances, jihadists have been able to mobilize a critical mass of public support in opposition to the West (as scapegoats for modernist alienation) and so find legitimacy for their violent revolutionary campaigns. These tactics have also enabled jihadists to divide Sunni Muslims from Western allies or other "apostate" Muslim groups (such as the Shia) and put them in opposition to each other. This strategy worked at different points in the Iraq War following the US invasion in 2003 (though indiscriminate jihadist violence eventually alienated local tribes), as well as in other contexts such as in Algeria before the civil war and in contemporary Nigeria and the Philippines.

By violently directing modernist Muslim alienation through anti-Western sentiment, this strategy has also helped to justify the position of jihadists to reject the democratic pathway in favor of an Islamist theocracy. They have argued that a democratic pathway results in adopting a Western model of politics and accepting Western benevolence and favor.[77] In this way, jihadists seek to outmaneuver and embarrass their moderate Islamist competitors by proclaiming that they hold to a "pure" form of Islam that would properly and fully institute sharia law. By capturing public support in favor of a "pure" form of Islam, jihad becomes more palatable. This undemocratic pathway relies on unrelenting campaigns of violent jihad, which are professed by jihadists to be essential to the faith and vitality of Islam and attract recruits interested in revolution.[78] For example, regular jihadist campaigns were characteristic of the Taliban rule in Afghanistan (1996–2001) and of ISIS in Iraq and Syria.[79] Alongside externally directed violence, jihadists rely on brutally repressive internal violence against the populations under their control to maintain the "pure" form of Islam they profess. This violence is usually legitimized under the cover of a radical interpretation of sharia law and involves public spectacles of violence against targeted victims to maintain public support, such as that occurred under the Taliban and ISIS.[80]

Justifying Jihad against the Far Enemy

The transition from the near to the far enemy as the primary adversary required new ideological, exegetical, and theological justifications. This was because the jihad against the West looked like offensive action beyond the lands of Islam rather than just defensive actions inside the lands of Islam against perceived aggressors. Thus, justifications for aggressive and offensive action were required, which also involved justifying the killing of Muslim and non-Muslim civilians. First, the call to jihad and the defensive rationales provided for the Afghanistan campaign against the USSR in the 1980s were applied analogously to defending Muslims globally against Western imperialism. Second, Muslims were argued to be justified in retaliating to the perceived attacks and oppression of the West which resulted in Muslim deaths, occupation of Muslim lands, and the stealing of Muslim resources and wealth.[81] Osama bin Laden states,

> These tragedies and calamities are only a few examples of your oppression and aggression against us. It is commanded by our religion and intellect that the oppressed have a right to return the aggression. Do not await anything from us but Jihad, resistance and revenge. Is it in any way rational to expect that after America has attacked us for more than half a century, that we will then leave her to live in security and peace?!![82]

This retaliatory jihad was built on a deep and abiding sense of the victim identity discussed in Chapter 4, which was redirected against Western "oppression" rather than the local state. In contrast to Faraj, jihadists like those in al-Qaeda came to believe that resistance to Muslim-majority regimes was futile unless the Western aggressor and "puppet-master" was removed. Direct offensive action by jihadists against the West, as well as against Israel and Russia, was justified as a legitimate, reciprocal measure on behalf of the victimized Muslim peoples.

Moreover, according to jihadists like bin Laden, the identity of the "puppet-master" of the apostate regimes in the Muslim-majority world was clearer after the fall of the USSR and communism. These events left the United States as the only superpower and representative of the "imperialist" international order, which had abandoned and repressed the international jihadist movement in the 1990s.[83] The United States, then, became the focus of scandal and animosity on the part of jihadists whose attention, according to Kepel, was no longer directed against the USSR "as their principal scapegoat":[84] "Under your supervision, consent and orders, the governments of our countries which act as your agents, attack us on a daily basis."[85]

Violent campaigns against the US and West accentuated and weaponized historical suspicion of and opposition to the West which had characterized major streams of modern Islamist thought. Earlier Islamist intellectuals such as Maududi, Qutb, and Nadwi had viewed the rise of the "godless" West, which was corrupted by its scientific materialism, as linked to the decline of the Islamic East. In their view, the Islamic world had fallen under the influence of the West like that of a false model.[86] To escape this negative mimetic relationship, Nadwi placed responsibility on Muslims themselves. Moreover, Qutb and Maududi argued for stricter separation from Western influences by "creating an environment of separation and confrontation."[87] These ideas were developed by later Islamist thinkers to license a strict Islamic practice supported by an Islamic state that (violently) eliminated non-Islamic influences (through the application of doctrines such as *al-wala' wa-l-bara'*).

The hardening attitudes toward non-Muslims also led jihadists to harsher treatment of outsiders. While Islamic scholars have generally treated compulsion in conversion to Islam as anathema, militant jihadists have obscured this prohibition. They have forcefully argued that both defensive and offensive jihad are obligatory for Muslims to ensure Islamic dominance and to eliminate the obstacles and lies that prevent conversion[88]: "For Jihadists either non-Muslims convert to Islam, or otherwise they must choose between two solutions: they pay tribute to Muslims (*jizyah*), or they are at war with them."[89] For jihadist groups like al-Qaeda and ISIS, the choice often has effectively been reduced even further (such as during ISIS's campaigns in Iraq and Syria): convert or die.[90] Moreover, the traditional protections for Jews and Christians are disregarded in service to the violent vision of jihad.

Furthermore, widespread historical tropes and conspiracy theories among Muslim populations have also been used to justify offensive jihad against the West. These theories and tropes centered on Western, Israeli, and Russian political dominance and military intervention in the Muslim world, both in historic and contemporary terms. Earlier I gave an example of one such conspiracy theory regarding how the United States was said to have manufactured the Gulf War (1990–1) to justify its invasion and occupation of Muslim lands. This theory was popular among militant jihadist groups.[91] Such conspiracy theories have become the lens through which history has been interpreted by many Muslims (not only jihadists). Anti-Western sentiment, however, has deep roots and a long history in the Muslim world, according to Khosrokhavar.[92] It is grounded in stereotypes such as "of the 'ugly Westerner,' domineering and moved by a deep aspiration to destroy Islam."[93] Jihadists have used such stereotypes and developed contemporary conspiracy theories to claim there is a permanent fight against Islam propagated by "crusaders," Jews, and infidels (including Shia Muslims). On this basis, they justify and incite a violent response.[94]

Khosrokhavar argues that conspiratorial interpretations of history among jihadists are characterized by a sense "that Islam is the religion of the oppressed" that has been mistreated, distorted, and caricatured by the West.[95] The jihadist discourse is based on the belief that the West hates Islam and has continually sought to destroy it, with the crusades, colonialism, and imperialist wars held up as examples.[96] Muslims are claimed to be the ongoing victims of the West's violence, from Spain's treatment of Muslims in the fifteenth and sixteenth centuries (with expulsions, torture, forced conversion, and killings) to the contemporary US policies in the Middle East (e.g., Guantanamo Bay and Abu Ghraib prisons).[97] Significantly, the US military intervention in the Gulf on the side of Kuwait in 1990 and its establishment of military bases at the invitation of Saudi Arabia were seen as proof of the "Western conspiracy to contain Islam and keep Muslims in check."[98] In this way, any American action—whether directly or indirectly—is interpreted according to a conspiratorial victim mentality. Jihadists argue that the Islamic world has been unjustly dominated by the modern West, which has morally corrupted Muslim civilization and displaced Islamic law from its rightful place for the first time. *Jahiliyya* is said to reign as Western culture permeates all aspects of life and undermines Islamic civilizations, leading Muslims to neglect the essential duty of jihad.[99]

Thus, by cultivating a victim identity and blaming the West for many of the ills previously attributed to local apostate states and despots, groups like al-Qaeda shifted the jihadist discourse to focus on a new primary enemy. This change globalized jihadism in a fundamental way by focusing on the leading superpower of the world order. In this regard, the brutal and indiscriminate violence of jihadists is claimed to only defensively mirror or reciprocate the violence of the United States and the West, which has the destruction of Islam as its "true" aim. Thus, as the mimetic logic goes, because the US violence is global, so jihadist violence must be global. Despite jihadists projecting a view of Islam as anti-imperialist and anti-colonist, their ultimate aim is to gain their own world empire over against the Western and apostate states. Thus, in the mind of jihadists, the reciprocal or mimetic nature of the conflict is clear: the West and Islam are fighting for the same object, namely, world domination and power. In constructing the conflict in this way, jihadists believe they are fully justified in undertaking any means to win. This is especially because, according to the jihadists, the Islamic nations won't take up the fight with the United States. The preference for US support over jihadist assistance in the Gulf War made it clear to jihadists like bin Laden that the Muslim-majority world was subject to the United States and the West. It was argued, then, that jihadists must lead the fight in the place of Muslim nations because only the jihadists understand what is at stake and who is the real enemy. In this view, the US and the West have become rivals with the jihadists for the loyalty of Muslim peoples and rulers, and for the ascendency in Muslim lands and across the globe. Thus, jihadism became a global phenomenon focused on supplanting the world's superpower and leader. This globalization of jihadism mimics the mimetic nature of the conflict that has escalated beyond the bounds of the Muslim-majority world.

Like any party to an escalating rivalry, the jihadists believe that only they are justified in their fight, and that their rival is completely illegitimate. To justify their stance, they point to the mimetic and rivalrous nature of their enemies, who must be resisted. However, they do not recognize their own mimeticism. Rather, they only see their own self-righteous cause supported by Allah. They regard themselves as in no way dependent on the United States for identity or motivation. Rather, they argue they are only motivated by faith and justice. For this reason, Muslim "victims" now have the time and opportunity to reassert the true justice and supremacy of Islam through jihad. Victory is guaranteed in their eyes because of Allah's will and support of the righteous victims undertaking jihad (which was supposedly demonstrated in Afghanistan).[100] In this way, rather than recognizing their mimetic rivalry with the United States over common objects of desire, the mimetic nature of the conflict is used to justify more violence. For most jihadists, the awareness of their rival only heightens their desire to achieve victory rather than desist from violence. The moral and theological dubiousness of the jihadist violence is suppressed by jihadists in favor of a violent-mythical interpretation of theology and history, grounded in a view of Muslims as righteous victims defending themselves in holy war.

As discussed, the change in enemy and the globalization of jihadist operations has had political and theological benefits as popular resentment and mainstream scholarly opinions against the West and Israel have been harnessed. Thus, jihadists became like the "accusing finger" against the West, harnessing popular sentiment in a way that the "apostate" regimes wouldn't or couldn't. In this regard, Sunni radicals learned from their Shia counterparts to use popular opinion in their favor rather than stick to a purely theological mission. For example, Osama bin Laden's declaration on October 7, 2001 (with his al-Qaeda counterparts) not only justified the 9/11 attacks on the basis of the US "occupying the territory of the Two Holy Places" (referring to the US military bases in Saudi Arabia) but also as vengeance for the children dead or dying in Iraq (from sanctions and war) and Israel's actions in regard to Palestine. According to Kepel, the latter justifications were a new ploy to broaden the appeal of the Islamist movement to include popular grievances, especially against US policies in the Middle East.[101] On this basis, bin Laden and al-Qaeda could claim to be more Islamic than the bastion of Sunni Islam, Saudi Arabia, which had shown its true nature when it aligned with the United States and had rejected the "true" Islamic faithful.[102]

Furthermore, these accusations against the West are, as discussed, usually made in the name of defending Islam against an overwhelming threat. This stance coincides with Girard's contention that defensive posturing can be the most potent veneer for aggressive intent. According to Girard, defensive justifications are used as moral cover in modernity to legitimize aggression against an enemy. Girard argues that even clearly identifiable aggressors, such as Nazi Germany, generally argue for a "defensive" position when they undertake acts of aggression. Claiming "to defend" is an effective way to catalyze and focus mimetic dynamics against an enemy, who is morally condemned as an aggressive victimizer.[103] In this way, defensiveness gives moral weight to one's own claims in modernity, especially because one can claim victim-status. It also provides a convenient means to channel underlying resentments against one's rivals.[104]

Thus, the turn to the far enemy presents how the targeting of specific enemies is constitutive of the jihadist movement and ideology. Over the course of the twentieth century, the focus on different enemies by militant jihadists has led to doctrinal and strategic changes that have restructured the identity of jihadism as a revolutionary movement. These changes usually occurred as a result of the dynamics of rivalry, which shifted under changing political conditions. With regard to the far enemy, jihadists could redirect the resentment and modernist alienation experienced by many Muslims toward a morally reprehensible enemy, particularly by claiming victim status. It also had the benefit of redirecting the blame and ostracism that the jihadists had experienced in Egypt, Saudi Arabia, and in other Muslim-majority nations toward the United States and the West.[105] Most significantly, the change in enemy focus reflected how jihadism is a symptom of modernity: it became increasingly globalized under the momentum of escalating mimetic dynamics of competition and rivalry. In this regard, by expanding the "defensive" jihad (which Azzam had theologically spearheaded) to cover the whole globe, al-Qaeda justified a global rivalry and war with the United States in which any enemy location or person could be targeted (which I explore in more detail in the next chapter). ISIS expanded this war even further to justify any attack against Muslims or non-Muslims in the fight for a caliphate.

However, high profile terrorist actions against the world's leading superpower involve high risk, with the possibility of swift repression and popular alienation.[106] For these reasons, the turn toward direct warfare with the United States and its Western allies was disputed inside the jihadist movement. There was even debate within al-Qaeda whether the appropriate conditions existed for large-scale attacks, like the 9/11 attacks, to catalyze mass mobilization and jihad against the West. For example, al-Suri and al-Zarqawi believed jihad was in a "phase of weakness" rather than a "phase of consolidation," in contrast to Zawahiri and bin Laden who believed the time was right for a jihad against the "puppet-master." Al-Suri's view was that large-scale attacks would not provoke widespread Islamic revolution among Muslims but would rather provoke a repressive Western military response. Instead, he advocated for the use and training of decentralized terrorist cells to cause disruption and mobilize Muslims to side with jihad, which has become the recent tactic of jihadist groups in the West following the repression that al-Suri predicted.[107]

Despite the chance for repression, Kepel argues that bin Laden and AQ resorted to the 9/11 attacks because of the failures and weakness of the Islamist-jihadist movement to mobilize the Muslim masses in their favor. They required action to put jihad in the spotlight. Thus, they resorted to isolated, public terrorist actions to reassert their influence and show that they could attack the very epicenter of the United States.[108] Yet, more than the strategic need for a major operational success, I have sought to show in this chapter how the expansion of the militant jihadist movement has been structured according to its own internal logic of rivalry, scandal, and victimhood. Combined with strategic desperation, jihadism's expanding violent logic, built on rivalry with the near enemy and far enemy, has led to globally destructive consequences (what Girard calls an "apocalyptic" scale). Unless such logic is rejected—as some Egyptian jihadists did in the late 1990s while others intensified their commitment to it, resulting in the formation of al-Qaeda—it escalates to ever greater extremes, as 9/11 starkly shows. In the next chapter, I present how this escalating logic of violence is intrinsic to the jihadist movement. It has manifested itself in escalating and indiscriminate forms of violence which have become characteristic of the jihadist movement over the course of late twentieth and early twenty-first centuries, both in terms of action and doctrine. This indiscriminate violence has occurred even in circumstances where militant jihadists have had territorial success, such as in Syria and Iraq.

Before moving to examine the intrinsic connection between jihadism and violence in the next chapter, I conclude this chapter by examining the other major impetus to global jihad which occurred in the latter half of the twentieth century: the Iranian Revolution of 1979. This revolution presented the radicalization of the other major branch of Islam, Shiism. In the remainder of the chapter, I provide a brief analysis of the key elements of revolutionary jihad in Shia Islam, especially to trace the dramatic transformation of this passive and quietist tradition, and identify areas that are shared with Sunni radicalism. Revolutionary jihadism had to be justified within a minority tradition, which was aware of the victimization of its founding leader and generally distanced itself from political power and violence. While Shia Islam seemed an even less likely vehicle for militant jihadism than Sunni Islam, the Iranian Revolution united people around a message of victimization in which the oppressed were empowered to fight back against perceived oppression (much like Sunni jihadist discourse). Ayatollah Ruhollah Khomeini was particularly responsible for this feat, especially by weaponizing and radicalizing the Shia remembrance of and solidarity with the victim.

Violent Jihad and Martyrdom in Shia Islam

Despite their differences, Shia and Sunni traditions have both undergone violent radicalization in the modern period that has resulted in groups in both traditions seeking global impacts for their revolutionary form of Islam. These groups have been characterized by strong antidemocratic and anti-modern features. Moreover, they share a common vision of a leader and state that is able to promote jihad and Islamic law and orthodoxy.[109] In fact, there were meetings between Shia and Sunni radicals in the early stages of Islamism's development, including some pioneered by al-Banna and the Muslim Brotherhood, which Murawiec called "an Islamic ecumenism based on radicalism."[110] However, Shia jihadism differs from Sunni jihadism in its particular theology and minority position in the Muslim world. The revolutionary transformation of Shia thought—which was largely passive, quietist, and wary of the state—in the latter part of the twentieth century is perhaps the greatest and most unlikely achievement of militant Islamists.

In the late 1970s, the success of a faction of Shia Muslims in bringing about a revolution in Iran was unprecedented and rocked geopolitical relationships and logic. This revolution relied on a mass Shiite uprising, combined with the support of secular elites and other minorities alienated from the government of the Iranian Shah. Kepel argues that Ayatollah Khomeini was able to politically, theologically, and ideologically maneuver revolutionary Shia Islamic thought to capture the grievances of multiple classes and groups. His support included the urban working class and poor, devout bourgeoise, and secular elites and middle class.[111] He rallied the masses, including even secularized Muslims, who felt marginalized and oppressed by the Iranian Shah, economic problems, and other forces of modernity. He did so under the banner of the "disinherited" (*mustadafeen*) and so, was able to broaden the appeal of his Islamic revolution in a way that Sunni radical groups had not been able to do up to that point.[112] In this way, he unified secular and religious groups and classes against the Shah and his government, and provided a cultural and religious vision which each group could accept. He also allowed each group to invest their aspirations in the movement, until he gained power and purged those elements which were no longer necessary for the maintenance of power.[113]

Khomeini's theological vision, encompassing a violent view of jihad, reinterpreted the Shia tradition into a violent revolutionary uprising in the context of social crisis. Khomeini's approach stood in contrast to the conventional passivism and quietism of the Shia clergy. Due to Shia history and theology, the clergy traditionally separated themselves from political power (in contrast to Sunni clergy which had a closer relationship with political leaders). This traditional stance drew on the founding identity of the Shia who trace their origins to the defeat of the "rightful Caliph," Imam Al-Ḥusayn/Hussein, by opposing Muslim forces allied with Yasid I (from which Sunnis derive their origins). Shia identity and hierarchy are particularly symbolized by what they regard as the martyrdom of Imam Hussein. His commemoration is characterized by mourning and lamentation, climaxing in the self-flagellation of the *Ashura* ritual which expresses the guilt and pain of the failure to defend the rightful Caliph.[114] This identity generally led to an avoidance of political activism and entanglements, with the Shia clergy able to maintain political and financial independence from the state through *zakat* (alms). In modern Iran, they were also able to conduct their own schooling system (though this was curtailed by the regime of the Shah).[115]

Ayatollah Khomeini transformed Shia identity by advocating for more political engagement, and eventually, revolution. He wished to replace the regime of the Shah with a theocracy (*velayat-e faqih*) in which ultimate power was held by a cleric who was expert in Islamic law.[116] This approach initially marginalized him among the Iranian clergy. However, from his exile outside Iran, Khomeini was able to provide a political–theological framework that captured and led the mood for change in Iran. In particular, he was able to appeal to and ally himself with a range of groups, including the disenfranchised poor and middle classes.

One of the most potent symbols of the transformation of Shia practice and theology centered on the commemoration of Imam Hussein's martyrdom. Beginning with Ali Shariati and developed by Khomeini for mass mobilization, the commemoration of Imam Hussein's martyrdom at Karbala was used to symbolize the struggle against a modern oppressor-caliph who was wrongfully in power (the Shah). It became a symbol to mobilize people into political action, which stood in contrast to the traditional way in which this martyrdom was ritualized and understood.[117] The identification with the victim-martyr through mourning and guilt was used to justify a rivalrous logic against the oppressor, as part of which revolution and an ethic of martyrdom were promoted in the name of Islam.[118]

Thus, Shia theology and practice were transformed to legitimize a revolutionary political theology. This transformation centered on the commemoration and symbolism of the victimized martyr (*shahid*) at the heart of Shia Islam. Like in Sunni radicalism, the victim became the impetus for rivalry and justice, and so, the site for the re-sacralization of violence. In the name of defending victims against the oppressor, mass political mobilization occurred that justified forms of sacred violence and self-sacrifice in the name of God and Islam. In this way, Khomeini was able to offer a powerful Shia theological program to justify political activism and revolution based on righteous jihad. This program was determined in its pursuit, maintenance, and expansion of an Islamic regime that fought on behalf of the Iranian people against the "oppressor-caliph" and the corrupting encroachments of modernity:

> Islam's *jihad* is a struggle against idolatry, sexual deviation, plunder, repression and cruelty. The war waged by [non-Islamic] conquerors, however, aims at promoting lust and animal pleasures. They care not if whole countries are wiped out and many families left homeless. But those who study *jihad* will understand

> why Islam wants to conquer the whole world. All the countries conquered by Islam or to be conquered in the future will be marked for everlasting salvation. For they shall live under [God's law]. … Those who know nothing of Islam pretend that Islam counsels against war. Those are witless. Islam says: "Kill the unbelievers just as they would kill you all!" Does this mean that Muslims sit back until they are devoured by [the unbelievers]? … People cannot be made obedient except with the sword. The sword is the key to Paradise which can be opened only for Holy warriors! There are thousands of other [Quranic] verses and hadiths urging Muslims to value war and to fight. Does all that mean Islam is a religion that prevents men from waging war? I spit upon those foolish souls who make such a claim.[119]

Though the Iranian Revolution contained a mixture of nonviolent and violent tactics, it was increasingly violent in the consolidation of state power and later in the effort to spread the revolution. Alongside the early purges of political enemies and unwanted allies, Khomeini encouraged and justified the mass sacrifice of Iranians in defense of the Revolution in the Iran–Iraq War (1980–8). This sacrifice most infamously was expressed in the "human wave attacks" which helped Iran repel Iraq's invasion. These attacks were justified as a way of righteously standing against the Iraqi and Western "oppressors."[120] In this way, Shia Muslim adherents (mostly young men) could undertake the meritorious path of Imam Hussein to martyrdom. Yet, this "meritorious" path of martyrdom marked out by Khomeini in defense of the victimized nation entailed the slaughter and sacrifice of thousands of young men, as well as the deaths of Iran's enemies, consistent with his revolutionary, jihadist theology. It exploited the Shia sense of victimization and the sense of self-recrimination at failing Imam Hussein:

> Historically, Shi'ism, as the religion of a mostly persecuted minority (mainly repressed by the Sunni rulers) found refuge in a culture of self-recrimination and quietism that could find solace only at the end of times, by the Islamic Messiah, the Twelfth Imam. This subculture of internalized violence was transformed, through the modernization of the twentieth century, into a culture of death in which dying as a martyr became of the utmost importance. At the same time, quietism was transformed into revolutionary activism. The Sunni culture of death is close to the Algerian case, in which killing the enemy of Islam is the aim, the death of the Muslim being subordinated to that goal. In Shi'ism, dying as a martyr is more important than inflicting death on the enemy, although achieving the latter through one's sacred death is the most desirable.[121]

The desire for a sacred death resulted in hordes of Iranians (primarily young men) running to their deaths and so becoming immortalized by the Iranian regime as martyrs.[122] Thus, Iranian martyrdom in the 1980s became what some have called a "death wish." Death was sought, resulting in the sacrifice of the masses, supposedly in the struggle for justice, revolution, and righteousness before God.[123] The Iranian government encouraged this mentality, based on the traditional Shia "mournful" culture (which tended towards self-recrimination at times).[124] The consciousness of the victim—exemplified by the Shia commemorative culture based on Imam Hussein—became the catalyst for self-sacrifice, which resulted in the sacralization of these "martyrs" in the Iranian public memory: "Khomeini's regime celebrated the martyrdom of the nation's young by cloaking itself in the legitimacy their sacrifice conferred."[125] It led to the semi-divinization of these martyrs whose sacred aura legitimized the semi-divine Islamic Republic. Moreover, such sacrifice had the practical effect of directing and controlling the youthful masses toward warfare, where their political value would be turned in favor of the regime.[126]

The way in which the martyrs were semi-divinized by the regime allowed it to overcome what Girard calls the lack of divinization of the victim in modernity. Instead of the scapegoats of violence being sacralized like in archaic cultures, the victims of war were sacralized by taking advantage of the victim consciousness. It did so by moralizing and theologizing the conflict as a fight of divinely ordained martyr-victims against the unjust persecutors, as Khomeini had done for the revolution. This type of moralization of conflict is typical of modernity, as I discussed in Chapter 2. The perversion of the victim consciousness was used in Iran to support waves of violence and death. This is not to claim that Iran did not have a right to defend itself but rather to reflect on how such defense was justified: the victim consciousness in Shia Islam was turned into a new form of sacred violence. This sacred transcendence allowed Iranian leaders to claim almost divine-like powers to inflict widespread violence and death on their enemies (both internal and external):

> The self-inflicted subculture of death became, at the hands of the Islamic theocracy, an awesome instrument of inflicting death on others, in the name of the purity of the power holders, who thought Islam needed to assert its potency against those whom they held to be inauthentic Muslims or Hypocrites (fake Muslims sowing the seeds of dissension in the Islamic community). In other words, a subculture of death, even turned towards the self, easily becomes a gruesome instrument of death against others, once it is applied to them in the name of a transcendent principle by the Powers that Be.[127]

The most successful export of Iran's victimary–revolutionary approach has been in the form of the Hezbollah militia in Lebanon. The radicalization of the Lebanese population along Khomeinist lines was attempted with success: "For example, instead of using the celebrations of Hussein's martyrdom as a vehicle for heightened community awareness, the movement transformed them into violent demonstrations against the 'enemies of Islam.'"[128] Based on this weaponization of the Shia tradition, Hezbollah used suicide attacks to great effect in the civil war in Lebanon. By labelling such bombers as martyrs (*shahid*) who undertook defense of Islam against its enemies, they could circumvent the traditional prohibition on suicide. The success of the tactic in forcing Western forces to leave Lebanon (after the West sought to protect the Palestinian minority from Christian militia and prevent further escalation in violence) gave Hezbollah even greater legitimacy among Shia groups.[129] The discourse of martyrdom, again, aided in sacralizing the violence and conflict undertaken in the name of Allah and Islam.

The Shia approach to martyrdom and jihad has had implications for Sunni militancy, particularly in its pioneering use of "martyr" suicide bombers. Moreover, in their mutual influence on each other, Shia and Sunni forms of militancy present aspects of a common identity, though with different underlying theologies. Violent forms of martyrdom and jihad characterize both Shia and Sunni extremism and have acted as two major signposts for groups in these traditions to attempt to reclaim modernity. They address a modern crisis of identity and transcendence with powerful forms of sacred violence based on the modern consciousness of the victim, which is weaponized through a rivalistic logic. In this regard, Khosrokhavar argues that in Islam, martyrdom and jihad are the basis of a violent globalized response to modernity, which has manifested itself in both major branches of Islam:

> Martyrdom and jihad are not just aspects of an Islamic tradition that has become mythologised and radicalised; they are also a way of appropriating and using Western modernity, and of exploiting the technological resources of a society that relies heavily upon communications. … Martyrdom takes on a new form, combines Islamic notions and a modern content of self-expression. It gambles with life and death because its deadly sense of the sacred has been concocted inside a purely imaginary but warlike neo-umma. Killing oneself and one's enemy in a generalized Apocalypse is a way of fighting the injustice of the Crusaders from a Judaeo-Christian West who are supposedly oppressing Muslims. But the death that is inflicted in the name of a jihadist concept of Islam is also a way of avoiding the implications of a modernity that distributes

> economic opportunities and political relations on an unequal basis. Jihadism is a typically incoherent product of the globalisation of the last world-religion to have a social and cultural utopia that still has credibility in the eyes of some believers. It is one of the avatars of the globalisation of the world.[130]

Thus, jihadism has become a global phenomenon, tracing itself along modern lines while seeking to reject and transform modernity in an extreme and violent fashion. In the next chapter, I turn to examine how jihadism takes this rejection of modernity to a terrifying extreme in the justification and use of indiscriminate violence. I show how militant jihadism has mythologized and re-sacralized the Islamic tradition through jihadism's intrinsic connection to violence. In being so bound up in violence, I then present in Chapter 7 how jihadism seeks to address issues of mimetic identity and resentment through a rigid and brutal logic of rivalry against its model-rival.

6

Jihadism and Violence

In Chapter 3, I discussed how the Islamist-jihadist vision for an Islamic modernity seeks to answer the crisis faced by the Muslim-majority world. It aims to create a new Islamic modernity that is fuelled by a jihadist-apocalyptic vision actualized by sacred violence. In Chapters 4 and 5, I showed how jihadism takes possession of the consciousness of the victim and uses it for violent, rivalrous purposes. This violent rivalry becomes identified with the struggle of Muslims in jihad. In so doing, jihadism builds a "total system" that is reliant on the sacralization of violence in the defense of the victimized. In this view, for example, suicide bombers are transformed to become semi-divine martyr-victims who fight unjust persecutors and give legitimacy to a semi-divine Islamic state and ideology. In this chapter, I analyze in more detail how the jihadist vision and energy are intrinsically connected to the fascination with and the deployment of "total violence" against its enemies. This fascination with violence is identified with the worship of God and even becomes a kind of worship of violence itself. I, then, go onto show how the intrinsic connection between jihadism and violence means that Islamic concepts are consistently applied by jihadists to justify extreme and indiscriminate violence.

The Intrinsic Connection between Jihadism and Violence

In the previous chapter, I showed how violent jihad is integral to the ideology of militant Islamist groups. Jihadist groups such as al-Qaeda and ISIS are enthusiastic combatants and exploit opportunities to fight where there are acute political and cultural crises, particularly in Muslim-majority countries. For example, according to Kilcullen, ISIS attacks whichever rivals it feels will help it to gain territory and expand its righteous violence using a "twin strategy of manipulating others' grievances and exploiting sectarian conflict."[1] Further, jihadists have been willing to mount local terror and guerrilla campaigns as well as deploy almost anywhere in the world that they regard as an efficacious part of the fight against the infidels and apostates. They have done so as clandestine terror cells as well as regular armed forces. These groups are willing to act in extreme ways with indiscriminate violence, exemplified by al-Qaeda's dramatic acts of terrorism against Western targets and Islamic State's massacres and public beheadings of both Muslims and non-Muslims. In his book *The Blood Year*, David Kilcullen comments on how extreme and intentional were the use of violence by ISIS in Iraq, which sought to provoke violent Shia reactions and terrorized the local Sunni population. Though he is an expert in counter-insurgency who formerly served in Iraq, Kilcullen was personally not able to fully describe the extent of ISIS brutality in his own work.[2]

Nevertheless, jihadist groups also act in conventional ways: they have rivals for power and land (e.g., the Alawhite/Baathist Syrian government, the US military, or the Shia-dominated Iraqi government), and as they defeat these rivals, they seek to establish supremacy over territory. However, they do so in order to institute their brand of totalitarian or puritanical rule. Sunni jihadists (especially ISIS) seek total victory—one Islamic state to dominate the whole world—and they do so at almost any cost. In its treatment of enemies and almost total disregard for civilians, jihadist violence is consistent with totalitarian forms of violence. However, militant jihadism is different in the way that violence is explicitly sacralized with reference to God rather than implicitly or covertly sacralized in regard to a political ideology, nationalism, or state. Violence is publicly and formally a form of worship. It is not hidden but rejoiced in, as service to the one God. It is apocalyptic in that it will risk total and mutual destruction in order to achieve what is believed to be certain victory. Violence is intensified, then, in a way that justifies its indiscriminate and apocalyptic nature in jihadism.

While militant jihadists are capable of terrible violence, the tactics used by jihadists are, in part, strategic to cause the most damage and gain the most attention and fear, as is typical of small insurgency movements who feel threatened by a more powerful foe. Yet, the way in which jihadists like ISIS put their violence on public display even goes beyond some guerrilla movements who become desperate in the face of defeat. Their extreme violence, such as suicide bombing and public massacres, is not just made out of desperation or because of asymmetrical warfare. It is always justified in the name of jihad because God wants the violent, imperialist "crusaders," infidels, apostates, and enemies wiped out.

Though violent jihadists use tactics that are common to asymmetrical warfare, their indiscriminate violence is more commensurate with their ideology rather than primarily or only with their situation in battle. For example, as ISIS became more territorially dominant in Iraq and Syria, the tactics of asymmetrical warfare changed into those of conventional warfare, however their engagement in conventional warfare was in an extremist or "total manner." It involved using ethnic cleansing, genocide, widespread slavery and rape, and civilians as human shields. Thus, the range of violent tactics—from suicide bombing to genocide—is consistent with their extremist ideology that condones indiscriminate violence.

Moreover, groups like ISIS and al-Qaeda don't try to hide their violence from the media or stay silent about their responsibility for such violence (like some insurgency movements). Nor do these groups undertake their primary violence in secret (like many totalitarian regimes). Instead, they purposefully and publicly display their violence and happily claim responsibility. In particular, the public display of violence is the means by which jihadists use and manipulate media for their own means. Their spectacular, indiscriminate violence is suited to a mass media age.[3] ISIS has been particularly adept at producing these violent spectacles. Jihadist groups have used such spectacles for the edification of militant Islamists and for those who resist them, as part of their tactics to encourage fascination with violence or acquiescence and fear. Thus, extreme violence allows jihadist groups to cause widespread terror and fascination, as well as publicly celebrate violence in the face of their enemies:

> Not only were many terrorist atrocities filmed, they were publicized, reproduced on videotapes, and aired around the clock by al-Jazeera and other Middle Eastern television channels. This was not just bragging: it was flaunting one's exhilarating sense of total power and offering the viewing public a chance vicariously to partake in it. The killing of Westerners gave viewers, as it gave perpetrators, a sense of identity.[4]

This sense of identity is mimetically formed and provided by jihad being a form of violent worship. Jihadists regard violence as a form of worship, and in many cases appear to be worshipping violence itself. Maher discusses how for jihadists, violent jihad itself is the highest act of "worship," and so, "the lifeblood of Islam":[5] "jihad in the path of God is *'ibada*, an act of worship akin to ritualistic acts such as prayer (*salaa*), pilgrimage (*'umra*), or fasting (*sawm*)."[6] For militants, jihad is "the most excellent form of worship," as it rests on the divine command to establish and spread the religion of God/Allah in the face of unbelievers.[7] It is an individual duty commissioned by God (not reliant on individuals or even Islamic authorities) that begins as a defensive act of Muslim peoples and lands. However, as I discussed in the previous chapter, defense has been broadly interpreted by jihadist leaders to justify indiscriminate violence and masks a retaliatory, aggressive intent. For militants, jihad even overrides the closest social obligations, such as to family, in favor of a society of true Muslims who fight for the ascendency of Islam.[8]

Murawiec identifies that among jihadists there exists "the exceptional prevalence of a cult of violence, of a glee to inflict suffering, in short, a bloodlust that had little if any counterpart."[9] This bloodlust is fuelled by a revolutionary mentality, like that of the Bolsheviks, Nazis, Fascists, and Maoists, in which a permanent campaign is necessary to cleanse a "filthy society."[10] As part of this, the blood of victim-martyrs is literally regarded as purifying. As Murawiec comments, the blood of the victim in modern jihadism can be regarded as powerful and sweet in its offering, much like a primitive sacrifice.[11]

As part of the campaign to cleanse society, the jihadist sacrifice of enemies is undertaken to symbolize a larger threat in which the potency of the revenge of the victimized—who are privileged by God—is put on public display. The individual attack or sacrifice represents the larger aim of collective destruction: that all enemies will be targeted, including civilians, to the extent that those who are not jihadists—the non-victimized group or the collective mob—do not acquiesce to jihadist violence.[12] Thus, instead of saving the social body (as sacrifice was used in the archaic mode), the sacrifice of people in jihadism is intended to destroy all those who do not conform to the jihadist mob's will and rules. In this sense, it is a form of modern totalitarianism that takes sacred violence to a new level: the sacrifice of all or the domination/acquiescence of all. In this regard, the attacks against civilians, such as the GIA's hijacking of an Air France flight in 1994 and the Paris bombings in 1995, are premonitions of future apocalyptic violence, like that of 9/11, that seek such domination.

God, death, and violence become inseparable in the worship that is jihad. The correlation is clear: the divine is worshipped primarily with violence and death, which are imperative for jihadists in the achievement of an Islamic utopia. Girard explains this correlation between religion and violence as being motivated by the transcendent effects of violence. He points to the way violence is externalized and projected by its protagonists onto the sacred—which is the transcendent repository of violence—in order to maintain its efficacy over time. Thus, in a similar way, violence maintains the sacrality of the jihadist cause and belief system. It makes the protagonists content and unified as it answers the need for mimetic transcendence and direction, while providing a structure of meaning in ritual to justify and repeat sacred violence. However, while archaic cultures stumbled upon the power of violence and held it in sacred fear and reverence, jihadism has taken violence to a new level by explicitly and intentionally instituting it at the center of its activity in a totalitarian and apocalyptic fashion.

Yet, for the jihadist movement, violence and death not only produce the transcendent effects of worship, but they are increasingly glorified in themselves. Jihadists commonly rejoice in their violence: "They chillingly boast about the pleasure they take in killing their enemies. One claims to have beheaded at least 70 people."[13] For some adherents this becomes repulsive (leading them to try to defect[14]), while for those who remain and fight, they joyously embrace it:

> Wherever jihadis operate in the world, their delight at killing and displaying the slaughter is pervasive. Stories and reports, films and pictures, all testify to the ubiquity of the practice and the sentiments that go with it. Some of the material that documents the sentiment reveals far more than the explicit content: It brings to light the underlying motivation and the belief structure that enable this behaviour. Zarqawi and his fellow jihadis "have chosen a slow, torturous method to terrorize the Western audience."[15]

This rejoicing in violence seems to corroborate Girard's work that shows violence produces very powerful affective experiences and bonding for the group undertaking it when such violence is effective (in producing unanimity and victory). Human groups conventionally try to replicate this transcendent and affective experience in ritual. Militant jihadists seek this replication through their constant jihad campaigns. However, they cannot ritualize their violence in the same way as traditional peoples who divinized their victims. Jihadist violence seems to be a reaction to the undermining of the efficacy and sacredness of violence in the way it heightens and escalates violence. Moreover, the jihadist explicitly sacralizes violence as part of a holy war commissioned by God against the "enemies of Islam" to bring about true justice and peace. Like in the archaic sacred, violence is externalized by projecting it onto the deity. In this way, violence has transcendent justification and the transcendent effects of violence can be projected onto God. However, God and violence become so entwined that the distinction between the two is practically lost: violence is the means of worship and becomes a kind of object of worship.

The externalization of violence as "holy war" for God also effects a powerful theologization and moralization of war, which I discussed in the previous chapter. As part of this "holy war," enemy people and groups are construed by militant jihadists as morally defective and less than human, such as being animals or monsters.[16] These enemies usually represent a rival sectarian, cultural, or religious tradition condemned for their apostasy or paganism. Furthermore, this holy war is usually put in defensive terms by the jihadist groups, though with universal implications. As discussed in Chapter 5, Girard argues that in modern war the defensive party has the strategic and moral advantage because it is claiming to be responding to aggression.[17] Yet, this defensive status can hide a more aggressive intent and provide a façade to justify aggressive violence. For example, in the conflict in Iraq (2014–17), ISIS fighters claimed to be defending the Muslim population against an unjust and sectarian government, which was supported by the "imperialist," the US. In this way, they claimed to be protecting the lives and rights of faithful Muslims to Islamic rule (a caliphate).[18] However, these kinds of defensive claims distort real claims to victim-status (and just cause) in order to justify rivalry for power and victory, which escalated to ugly extremes in Iraq and Syria.

The centrality of violence to jihadism is evident, moreover, in the testimony of jihadist fighters, especially those who leave groups like ISIS out of disgust for its violence. In one study of fifty-eight defectors from ISIS (also known as IS), the following narratives were identified as key:

1. IS is more interested in fighting fellow (Sunni) Muslims than the Assad [Syrian] government.
2. IS is involved in brutality and atrocities against (Sunni) Muslims.
3. IS is corrupt and un-Islamic.
4. Life under IS is harsh and disappointing.[19]

In a different study an ex-ISIS fighter, Hamza, recounted the intense military training and initiation techniques explicitly involving executions and rapes. Hamza joined ISIS for religious reasons and rejoiced in destroying the boundary between Iraq and Syria for the caliphate. However, he became disillusioned with the extreme violence and dissolute lifestyle of the ISIS fighters: "The executions, or more horribly the beheadings, as well as the raping of the non-Muslim girls. These scenes terrified me. I imagined myself being caught up in these shootings, executions, beheadings and raping, if I stayed where I was."[20] Hamza feared that, despite his will, he could be caught up in the contagion and power of violence, forced to participate, and have his conscience dulled by the experience:

> At the beginning I thought they were fighting for Allah, but later I discovered they are far from the principles of Islam. I know that some fighters were taking hallucinatory drugs; others were obsessed with sex. As for the raping, and the

> way different men marry by turn the same woman over a period of time, this is not humane.
>
> I left them because I was afraid and deeply troubled by this horrible situation. The justice they were calling for when they first arrived in Fallujah turned out to be only words.[21]

For Hamza, the transcendent allure of an Islamic state founded on righteous violence—including against innocent civilians and woman—was stripped away. The reality that was left was an ugly world of brute power, disordered desires, petty identities, and totalitarian evil. For many ISIS fighters, the sacralization of violence works (at least for a time) in providing identity and channeling desire and resentment, but for some, the illusion bursts to reveal a reality of brutality and confused identities. Even as violence is purposefully sacralized by groups like ISIS, it shows itself to be unstable and, for some, increasingly ineffective in maintaining its own rationale. For Hamza, jihadism bore little resemblance to Islam and was fed by constant fighting (with other groups, militants, or governments). In this fighting, the object of desire was increasingly forgotten in the imperative to defeat enemies.

The repetitive and extreme nature of jihadist violence is aimed at overcoming the problems of conscience by habituating fighters to the mimetic "highs" of violence. Moreover, despite its delusional qualities, ISIS ideology has a powerful effect over its fighting force in justifying such violence, to the degree that fighters will commit terrible atrocities in the name of God and Islam. On this basis, the Islamic State (like other militant jihadist groups) expects total loyalty, over and above any other allegiance, and a full appropriation of its jihadist agenda. This goes so far as to institutionalize military training in its education system (such as when it controlled parts of Syria and Iraq), so that children can become soldiers of ISIS, purveyors of jihad, and defenders of Islam.[22] In this way, it is made clear that the jihadist ideology/theology is the only model for the true Muslim—only it enables its members to properly imitate the first generation of righteous Muslims.

In institutionalizing its violence and ideology, jihadist groups like ISIS mirror and extend the modern nation-state in its operations and dynamics to become a "total," self-sufficient system. This total system claims to be "Islamic" and in the service of Allah but is fundamentally statist in its outlook and aims. As a rival who seeks to attain the violence of the state, jihadists are absolute, totalitarian mirrors of the state. The violence they do and the territorial gains they make are made in imitation of what they believe other states—their enemies—do, though in a total and absolute manner. They seek to become better than any state by constructing the *one* world state, which would dominate all forms of violence. This involves the absolute monopolization of violence, justified in a moralized and theologized cause of defending the victimized (as a form of worship of the divine).[23]

Though mainstream Islamic thought focuses on the possibility of an Islamically inspired state, jihadist groups appropriate and exaggerate this theological position to justify their totalitarian pretensions. In this sense, they do not respond to modernity in an authentically Muslim way but rather construct a totalitarian response modelled on the Western nation-state, in which jihadist violence is totally absolute and integrated into the system. Violent jihad is expected of all members/citizens as part of the Islamic state's commissioning and direction, and violence is threatened on any who do not comply to the laws and norms of the Islamic state. Furthermore, it is totalitarian in its aims: groups such as ISIS seek to universalize their system as the *only* legitimate state and global authority. They also seek to be the *only* brand of Islam—the only legitimate religious authority (over against its sectarian and religious rivals), defined and built on jihad.

In this way, jihadists seek to become the antidote to the problems of the Muslim experience of modernity by becoming the dominating state and the divinely commissioned authority. Moreover, they regard themselves as the best arbiters of technology and science, the most transcendent and effective system of law and order, and the most successful culture—all over and above the West. Jihadists essentially want to become the victorious model—one that even the West must bow to—as their propaganda demonstrates. Alarmingly, for a period in 2014–18, it looked as if ISIS was achieving this project in Iraq and Syria.

As discussed in Chapter 1, Girard shows how violence increasingly takes over from the original desire or motivation. As a rivalry becomes increasingly intense, and scandal at the other increases, violence takes on a life of its own. The original goal recedes in importance and defeating the other in violence becomes primary. Similar dynamics can be seen within militant Islamism, as increasingly brutal tactics—many of which are contrary to the mainstream Islamic tradition—are used and justified to defeat sectarian or Western rivals. Jihadism manages to use and twist Islamic frameworks to justify this escalating violence. These justifications suggest that violence is not only undertaken by jihadists in the name of a just cause and intentionally embraced as the highest duty and explicit means to achieve its vision. Their logic shows that they wish to justify any form of indiscriminate violence that they regard as necessary for victory against their rivals, as part of which violence is almost glorified in itself.

The Logic of Violence in Jihadism

While the intrinsic connection between jihadism and violence can be shown in the practice of militant jihadists, it is also evident in the jihadist use and distortion of Islamic thought. In regard to specific acts of violence, jihadists have been able to claim a range of justifications. These justifications particularly center on the status of civilians and why it is justified to kill them. On some level, jihadists are concerned about critiques of their indiscriminate violence, especially in regard to the killing of Muslim civilians. They are particularly concerned about criticism from Muslim clerics, leaders, peoples, or former jihadists, which they vehemently and extensively reject. Their detailed treatises and public statements reject any criticism in order to legitimize their indiscriminate violence and the lack of protection for civilians.

Among Salafi-jihadists, arguments have been made for the most violent positions, particularly as these jihadists became a global focus with spectacular attacks and insurgency movements in the twenty-first century. In particular, an erosion of Islamic legal protections for civilians has occurred in militant jihadist thought, as a development and, in some ways, a distortion of mainstream Islamic thought. Shiraz Maher, an expert in Salafi-jihadist thought, comments in this regard,

> The exigencies of war have proved to be a driver and catalyst of theological change. This has given rise to revisionist theories which both develop and expand Islamic principles relating to *jus in bello*. … [F]ollowing the 2003 invasion of Iraq it appeared as if al-Qaeda was prepared to develop its own understanding of the rules relating to jihad in such a way that they could license almost anything at all.[24]

As an example of the al-Qaeda logic, civilians in countries like the United States (especially democratic countries) are argued to be culpable for their government's actions and so can be fairly killed.[25] Furthermore, it is argued that civilians can be killed as collateral damage, or what are known as "human shields" in Islamic thought. This is justified because of the practicalities of modern warfare in which civilians and combatants cannot be easily separated.[26] Examples from the Prophet Muhammad's life are used to justify this stance (though these examples are contested).[27] Significantly, Muslim civilians can even be killed under the category of "human shields," according to militant jihadists, because of the necessity to wage jihad in the contemporary context, which involves collateral damage. Thus, civilians can be killed because of their moral responsibility or their proximity to conflict.

The actions of jihadists against civilians, especially Muslim civilians, have required extensive justifications because of their extreme and unconventional nature. Sunni jihadists often target places that are primarily civilian in nature and that include large numbers of Sunni and Shia civilians, such as marketplaces. They have also assassinated Sunni heads of state, such as President Sadat in Egypt, or government and tribal leaders, such as Sunni and Shia leaders during the Iraq War.[28] The fact that Salafi-jihadist justifications for killing even go so far as to include Muslim civilians, including Sunni civilians, is a revealing position. It shows that jihadists are willing to countenance forms of violence that kills anyone in pursuit of their Islamic utopia. Four reasons in particular stand out in Salafi-jihadist thought to justify civilian, especially Muslim civilian, casualties, including Sunni casualties. I have briefly described above a couple of reasons for such violence, but I now give a fuller account of jihadist reasoning to show how it seeks to license indiscriminate violence.

First, jihadists are able to strictly define who deserves protection (usually members of the jihadist group) and who is an enemy, which can include numerous people belonging to multiple groups. For example, they argue that opposition or minority Muslim groups, such as the Shia or Ahmadis, are not real Muslims. They have even argued that some fellow Sunnis who oppose or do not support them are not worthy of protection as Muslims. To do this, they have popularized the use of *takfir* to label some Muslims, especially those to whom jihadists are opposed, as apostates, including in conflicts in Syria, Iraq, Egypt, and Algeria.[29] Maher argues this has been an effective way for jihadists to define what it means to be Muslim, police the borders of Islam, and expel those who do not meet the jihadist definition of being Muslim and so are thought to be subverting Islam. It has particularly fuelled sectarian Muslim violence.[30] It also acts as a way to construct an Islamic ideal and motivate certain actions, particularly violent ones, because faith alone is not sufficient to claim to be a true Muslim, according to jihadists.[31] Thus, *takfir* acts as a coercive doctrine to impose conformity, suppress dissent, and motivate jihad. Most importantly, it licenses jihadists to target and kill other Muslims.[32]

Alongside the use of *takfir*, the doctrine of *al-wala' wa-l-bara'* in particular grew in importance during the Afghan campaign, especially through the writings of Abu Muhammad al-Maqdisi (who wrote, in part, during his time in Afghanistan and Pakistan). Like *takfir*, this idea has been used to strictly define the boundaries of Islamic belief and practice for jihadists and license active violent resistance to those regarded as outsiders or enemies, especially other Muslims. It refers to a double action—loyalty and disavowal or love and hate for Allah's sake—that defines the active loyalty of true Muslims and the violent disavowal of those not regarded as true Muslims. It has been a resilient and widely used doctrine among militant jihadists to define Islam on jihadists' terms. It has produced active dissent and violent action against jihadists' enemies, including governments, rulers, and scholars in Muslim-majority nations that do not conform to the Islamic system that jihadists believe to be absolute. Based on this principle, violent jihad becomes "a personal religious duty" according to militants "until the time when non-Muslims and Muslims alike submit to their warrior version of Islam."[33]

Maher traces how the concept of *al-wala' wa-l-bara'* has grown as a response to crisis and conflict, deriving from a Saudi context that used it as a passive doctrine of disassociation and was later weaponized by militants like Maqdisi.[34]Interestingly, Maqdisi particularly pointed to the Prophet Ibrahim (Abraham) as the basis for his more radical interpretation of *al-wala' wa-l-bara.'* Maqdisi argues that Ibrahim spread the message of the monotheistic God and reconstructed the *Ka'ba* in Mecca (as loyalty and love of God), while destroying the idols surrounding the *Ka'ba* (disavowal of that which is against Islam and God).[35] On this basis, Maqdisi argues for a series of responsibilities and obligations connected to *al-wala' wa-l-bara'* that require the Muslim to undertake active forms of resistance and disavowal of unbelievers (or those declared as such), rather than just passive disassociation or omission. According to Maher, Maqdisi transformed *al-wala' wa-l-bara'* from a passive Wahhabist concept into "a muscular and aggressive one, requiring an offensive approach," including against an unjust ruler who must be actively disavowed and opposed.[36]

This aggressive approach to *al-wala' wa-l-bara'* became a tool of violent political mobilization among subsequent jihadists. It was applied in more extreme ways, especially after they became increasingly isolated by regimes in Muslim-majority states following the Afghan campaign. Ayman al-Zawahiri and Osama bin Laden particularly deployed this doctrine in seeking to undermine the legitimacy of Muslim regimes and justify violence against their enemies. In this way, it helped to establish groups like al-Qaeda as proper and alternative sources of authority to these regimes. Zawahiri particularly argued that *bara'* (disavowal) required confrontation with those who had offended God, especially against those who collaborated with unbelievers.[37] This confrontation took the form of violent jihad, and combined with *takfir*, supported the jihadist effort to define Islam in pure and exclusive terms, delegitimize their opponents, and license violent action. Maher argues that the development of *al-wala' wa-l-bara'* "has been driven and shaped principally by conflict," as it has become defined in more narrow terms to strictly define insider–outsider distinctions and license violence against enemies.[38]

Furthermore, while jihadists on occasion might argue that they would like to avoid civilian casualties, once someone is named an enemy or is in proximity to an enemy, including Muslims, they are a fair target of violence. Labelling someone as an enemy can be done for various reasons, even for as little as not joining the jihad: "According to the Jihadists, the Other must suffer because he is guilty of the most heinous crimes, namely not getting involved in Jihad. The most striking feature is the dehumanization of the adversary, but the notion of 'enemy' itself undergoes a notable change."[39] This broad definition of enemies and the dehumanization of them, consistent with scapegoating practices, sets the preconditions for indiscriminate violence, which includes targeting Muslim and non-Muslim civilians. As Khosrokhavar argues, jihadism is defined inherently over against others, and as such, it has become one of the worst examples of how people can be dehumanized and persecuted *en masse*:

> Jihadist discourse is full of polemical, dichotomist, Manichean, incriminating, agonistic, warmongering, and resentment-laden words. Jihad is waged against the Shi'ites, quietist Muslims, the West, and all Muslim rulers. The fight against the disbelievers and the 'fake Muslims' obsesses jihadist discourse. Those who are called Hypocrites (*munafiq*) are only Muslims by name; their major crime is to disagree with Jihadists on the necessity of holy war. Their obsession makes the Jihadist version of Islam almost entirely devoted to violence and its justification. … Jihadist ideology is not in fact traditional. … Jihadists hold the reactionary attitude of those who would fight against a manifold enemy. … Religious feeling is defined not as a peaceful, spiritual, self-centred aspiration to salvation (as is the case with many Islamic Reformists, mystics, Sufis, or Urafa) but a defying and confrontational attitude towards others, in order to assert one's own righteousness.[40]

For example, al-Qaeda in Iraq (AQI, which later became ISIS) under al-Zarqawi became infamous for the indiscriminate targeting of civilians and dehumanization of enemies in Iraq in 2006–7. Al-Qaeda in Iraq was ostensibly fighting against Shia Iraqis and the US "occupier," but their victims even included assassinating Sunni leaders and civilians who were said to oppose, or potentially could oppose, AQI. All these victims were construed as enemies of Islam.[41] Similarly, during the brutal Algerian civil war, jihadists killed indiscriminately (often in response to brutal government action), which included killing Muslim civilians from villages as well as rape and enslavement of women.[42]

Second, there is a practical reason given to justify killing Muslim civilians, which applies to all civilian casualties. Asymmetrical warfare is claimed to be the primary or only option for jihadists to use against the military power of the West. This type of warfare often involves imprecise forms of attacks, such as suicide attacks or bombings of civilian areas and so usually results in widespread civilian casualties, including Muslims. According to al-Qaeda, civilian casualties, including Muslims, are permissible if distinguishing between the enemy and Muslims is too difficult and the intention of the attacker is right (in seeking to institute God's law and will in an Islamic state).[43] Maher argues that what AQ did in this regard was to produce "a more aggressive and deadly doctrine borne of pragmatism and necessity."[44] These types of tactics and justifications would not be permissible under most mainstream Islamic scholarship, including the killing of non-Muslim civilians, though some Salafist scholars endorsed attacks against the United States and Israel (based on the notion of reciprocity).[45]

Yet, the claim that indiscriminate attacks are the only or primary way to conduct a jihadist campaign is questionable. Jihadists could easily choose more strategic targets, with less civilian casualties, and avoid areas where most or all those who are killed are civilians, including Muslims. However, indiscriminate violence is intrinsic to the jihadist logic: their aim is to destroy, cause chaos and division, and conquer. Jihadists prefer tactics that inflict maximum and widespread civilian casualties, often sending suicide bombers to the most crowded places, such as markets, airports, and train systems. This also includes inciting and directing "random" attacks against civilians. These tactics are preferred as jihadists seek to cause chaos within enemy states. They believe such tactics will divide civil society, especially dividing non-Muslims from Muslims, and decrease the will of democratic peoples to fight the War on Terror. The indiscriminate nature of the jihadist attacks, nevertheless, undermines their claim that this kind of violence is their only way to wage war against their more powerful oppressors.

Third, there is an ideological reason for targeting civilians. Since jihad is of the upmost priority for militants, it is argued that the likelihood of civilian casualties should not deter this aim. Zawahiri states that, while civilian casualties should be minimized, the propagation and maintenance of Islam is more important: "Forfeiting the faith is a much greater harm than forfeiting money or lives."[46] As mentioned, civilian deaths could be more easily avoided in AQ or ISIS operations, but destructive jihad is ultimately more important than concerns about civilians. What is conventionally prohibited in Islam, such as suicide and murder, can be justified if the intention is to promote jihad.[47] Whether civilians die during jihadist operations or because resources are directed away from the needy to the conduct of jihad, it does not matter for hard-line jihadists.[48] Muslim civilians can be justifiably killed in the name of jihad, if a suicide bomber or militant has the right intention to propagate the dominance of Islam.[49] This is because jihad is regarded as an absolute—as *the* way for Islam to achieve its "true" place and dominance.

Thus, in this view, even traditional Islamic restrictions are overridden in favor of jihad, which Kazimi stated demonstrated "the triumph of battlefield logic over theology."[50] Jihadists, then, become the mirror image of their constructed enemies: imitating and escalating the indiscriminate uses of violence and oppression of which they accuse their enemies. In order to avoid this realization, jihadists place ultimate responsibility for their actions on God, who supposedly commissions their acts. This means that despite all their heinous and traditionally forbidden actions, jihadist violence ultimately remains in God's hands. According to Zawahiri, "we can kill Muslims used as human shields ('collateral damage') to safeguard jihad. When we let the hungry die or the human shields die in this case, they die by God's hand."[51] Jihadists do not recognize the symmetry between their own actions and what they accuse their enemies of, because they externalize their violence and justify it in regard to the deity, much like archaic cultures.

Finally, a fourth reason that civilians can be killed, according to jihadists, is because of the legitimacy of defensive retaliation. Jihadists have particularly justified this stance by applying and reinterpreting the law of equal measures or retaliation (*qisas*).[52] This justification is primarily aimed at justifying the deaths of non-Muslim civilians of enemy states or groups but it can include Muslim civilians. Salafi scholars have applied *qisas*—which was developed for regulating the relationships of private individuals—to international affairs.[53] This move has allowed militant jihadists to justify their violence in a broad, indiscriminate manner as part of a "defensive jihad": "We kill the kings of infidels, kings of the crusaders, and civilian infidels in exchange for those of our children they kill. This is permissible in law and intellectually."[54]

Jihadist violence against an "oppressor" is argued to be a form of just retaliation for similar or worse forms of violence and destruction undertaken by the enemy, which they deem to have been aimed against Islam.[55] Bin Laden exemplifies this logic in justifying the 9/11 attacks: "That which you are singled out for in the history of mankind, is that you [the US] have used your force to destroy mankind more than any other nation in history; not to defend principles and values, but to hasten to secure your interests and profits."[56] Moreover, bin Laden made these statements to justify jihadist terrorism against civilians in the 1990s:

> The Americans started it and retaliation and punishment should be carried out following the principle of reciprocity, especially when women and children are involved. Through history, American [sic] has not been known to differentiate between the military and the civilians or between men and women or adults and children. Those who threw atomic bombs and used the weapons of mass destruction against Nagasaki and Hiroshima were the Americans. Can the bombs differentiate between military and women and infants and children? America has no religion that can deter her from exterminating whole peoples. Your position against Muslims in Palestine is despicable and disgraceful. America has no shame … We believe that the worst thieves in the world today and the worst terrorists are the Americans. Nothing could stop you except perhaps retaliation in kind. We do not have to differentiate between military or civilian. As far as we are concerned, they are all targets, and this is what the fatwah says … The fatwah is general (comprehensive) and it includes all those who participate in, or help the Jewish occupiers in killing Muslims.[57]

Thus, the indiscriminate violence of the United States—which purportedly included targeting women and children—justifies retaliatory violence of the same kind. To support this claim, *qisas* is also combined with other arguments, such as the culpability of citizens for their democratic-elected government's actions or the labelling of the enemy as a "military society" (which Hamas has attributed to Israel).[58] In this regard, bin Laden references democratic voting mechanisms and taxation to show that civilians are culpable for their government's action and so can be legitimately targeted.[59] Moreover, bin Laden argues that the American army comes from the civilian population, and thus in his eyes, the military is identified with such a population. Thus, the application of *qisas* allows jihadists to target civilians indiscriminately, even Muslim citizens of a Western state who are killed as part of jihadist operations or who implicitly support and acquiesce to their government.

Jihadists like bin Laden, then, identify American society and democracy as implicating all civilians in the actions of their governments. In this way, bin Laden completely collapses the civilian–combatant distinction to allow for indiscriminate attacks on civilian populations.[60] According to Maher, this was a novel development in Salafi-jihadist circles which allowed jihadists to move beyond fighting their own governments (in "rebellions") to target Western military and civilian populations.[61] These views became more popular among Salafi-jihadists, including clerics, who used a monolithic view of democratic structures (neglecting their contested nature) to justify turning civilians into "fighters" who could be legitimately targeted.[62] Thus, the distinction between civilian and combatant was eliminated, allowing for indiscriminate violence.

Furthermore, as part of the application of the principle of *qisas*, grievances and accusations are central. Maher argues that *qisas* is generally applied to blame someone and identify a grievance, usually against a foreign government, which justifies violence. Jihadist grievances include the US military involvement in Muslim lands, US support of authoritarian regimes, US targeting of jihadi groups, and unfair trade agreements.[63] The scope and method of violent retaliation, then, is justified as a defensive response to other, primary violent acts perpetrated by the enemy:[64]

> Allah, the Almighty, legislated the permission and the option to take revenge. Thus, if we are attacked, then we have the right to attack back. Whoever has destroyed our villages and towns, then we have the right to destroy their villages and towns. Whoever has stolen our wealth, then we have the right to destroy their economy. And whoever has killed our civilians, then we have the right to kill theirs.[65]

Thus, jihadism acts according to a mimetic mentality that reciprocates and escalates violence perceived to be done to them. It sacralizes such violence in monotheistic terms. The identification with the victimized is usually expansive (to maximize grievances), while the protection accorded to civilians who are associated with the enemy that jihadists are aggrieved with, such as Muslim civilians, is much more restrictive or nonexistent. In this way, jihadists rely on exaggerated claims to fuel their escalating forms of vengeance. Moreover, the retaliatory or retributive "justice" of jihadists is usually not proportionate but involves escalating forms of violence. The following statement demonstrates the logical outcome of the jihadist use of *qisas*, which escalates to genocidal proportions in order to retaliate against perceived Muslim sufferings supposedly caused by the United States and its allies: "It would be perfectly permissible for us (al-Qaeda) to kill around 10 million Americans."[66]

The destructive potential of jihadist apocalyptic violence is further demonstrated by the way the principle of *qisas* has been used to justify the use of

WMDs. Radical Islamists, including the Saudi cleric Nasir ibn Hamad al-Fahd, have written in support of their use. This stance has subsequently been adopted by al-Zawahiri and al-Qaeda.[67] Any means are justified as part of the retaliatory schema, even total destruction of the world. Thus, while jihadists may use the terms of combatants and civilians, they essentially undermine their own use of these terms with a kind of apocalyptic logic.[68] This apocalyptic logic is connected to an apocalyptic worldview, in which violence predominates: "Jihad plays a major role in Muslim apocalyptic literature as well. Since the early Muslims' existence was largely dominated by fighting and conquest, it is hardly surprising to find that their vision of the future just before the end of the world, as well as their vision of the messianic future, was characterized by a state of continuous war."[69]

This apocalyptic worldview displays the logic of jihadist violence and its mimetic drivers: the violence of the other, interpreted in an escalating fashion, is imitated until it leads to the total destruction of the enemy (and even the self). This indicates that jihadists are not really guided by principles or rules but rather have been overtaken by the dynamics of mimetic rivalry and resentment—in other words, by "battlefield logic."[70] Moreover, the claims of militant jihadists to be the subject of "absolute victimization" by the forces of the West and modernity means that reform and compromise are impossible: only victory or destruction are possible.[71] Thus, the jihadist groups become the mirror image of their "arrogant," "decadent," and "intransigent" secular or apostate rivals.

Other Salafi scholars and even a former al-Qaeda scholar have complained of the misuse of *qisas* by radical and militant groups. They have critiqued jihadist theorists for applying it out of its context in service to their indiscriminate violent logic, particularly with respect to civilians and children.[72] Ayman al-Zawahiri was compelled to write a lengthy response to this critique on behalf of the al-Qaeda leadership to maintain the Islamic justification for their actions.[73] This shows that for the jihadists it is crucial to claim the Islamic "high ground" in order to maintain the appearance of orthodoxy and rationality, especially among their Muslim supporters. Yet, it is an edifice meant to provide a cover for jihadist delusions and violence. This edifice is shown in that the most radical claims about jihad made by militant Salafists expand and even distort the historical orthodox tradition that restricted and regulated jihad and related concepts of warfare, particularly with regard to civilians.[74]

Despite the trajectory of jihadist thought in justifying more extreme forms of violence, there have been instances where jihadist leaders have counselled that violence be restricted. For example, in Iraq, many Muslims were repelled by the actions of AQI because of their brutality and because al-Zarqawi targeted fellow Muslims. Even though his Shia victims were seen by Sunni jihadists as heretics, there was a general sentiment among many Sunnis that they shouldn't be targeted for killing. The sectarian violence of AQI became so extreme that the AQ leadership, including bin Laden and Zawahiri, became concerned and counselled Zarqawi against such brutal violence against Shia Muslims. In writing to Zarqawi, Zawahiri expressed concern that AQI was sacrificing the global jihad for the interests of Iraqi Sunnis to make gains against their sectarian rivals. Even though they may be wrong in identifying Shia Muslims as part of the *ummah*, Zawahiri argued that many Muslims were appalled at AQI's tactics, which were alienating Muslims from the jihadist cause.[75] Such restraint on the part of the AQ leadership demonstrated a strategical calculation according to the logic of violent rivalry, in the sense of Girard's analysis, that some violence needed to be deferred to ensure ultimate victory. This deferral of violence would ensure that the larger community of Muslim sympathizers of AQ were not alienated. Zarqawi rejected such advice and AQI eventually split from AQ to focus on building an Islamic state through its brand of brutal and extreme violence.

It is important to note the concern among the wider Muslim world about AQI/ISIS: that those identified as Muslim civilians were being killed by a Muslim group as unworthy or innocent victims of violence. It shows an identification with Shia Muslim civilians as both victims and fellow Muslims. This identification gave them protections in the popular mind among most Muslims and generated a disgust at AQI's violence, especially at the suicide bombings and massacres of civilians. This connected with a concern at the increasingly indiscriminate nature of AQI violence, which was also aimed at Sunnis, especially those who rejected AQI rule or dominance. Such concern at extremist violence, and for the victims of it, was also expressed in the late 1990s in Egypt when militant Islamist violence escalated, resulting in the massacre of non-Muslim tourists and civilians. Like in Egypt in the 1990s, AQI's violence in Iraq was becoming more indiscriminate (extending to Sunnis), generating a primal fear that violence was escalating out of control to threaten the social order. It was potentially leading to unending cycles of mimetic violence or to a totalitarian brutalism that characterized AQI's supremacy when they defeated their enemies. It also showed that in popular opinion in Iraq and across the Muslim world, the Shia (like the Western tourists in Egypt in the 1990s) had not been shown to be enemies such that they deserved a violent death. The protections of the Islamic tradition and people's conscience had not been deformed in such a way to provide legitimation for such jihadist violence. Rather, they showed sympathy for the innocent victims of violence and wanted the chaotic and escalating cycles of violence to end.

The End Game of Militant Jihadist Logic

Despite being willing to make strategic qualifications, jihadist groups have generally been willing to license more extreme and indiscriminate forms of violence as the movement developed in twentieth century and into twenty-first century. It is important to note that while jihadists are unrepentant about their aims for total victory and their use of extreme violence to achieve it, they have deployed arguments to rationalize and justify such violence (as was the case for Nazism and Soviet Communism). This rationalization presents a double-sided phenomenon: that jihadists realize they must own and justify their actions (showing a degree of intentionality) while also needing to repress any contrary Islamic arguments or broader questions about their motivations, including from themselves. This hiding of real desires and motivations parallels the role of mythology in traditional cultures, though the jihadists construct arguments more consciously and methodically.

Thus, while jihadists have clear (altruistic) aims and realize to some degree the choices they are making, they also must avoid realizing how they are being driven by the dynamics of violence, identity, and mimetic rivalry. Such a realization would undermine their own whole enterprise as idolatrous, expose their motives as undergirded by brutal mimetic dynamics, and highlight all the innocent victims of their violence. This would leave the jihadist (in madness or despair) to realize that he/she has been subject to the basest human desires—stimulated and distorted by violent delusions and forces—rather than the most transcendent ones. Instead of this recognition, violence is rejoiced in and defines the jihadist movement. In the worst cases, violence is sought for itself—for its own destructive quality.

Thus, rather than containing violence in proportionate forms of retaliation, the justification of violence by jihadists results in mimetic escalation and ever-worsening forms of violence. The resentment and scandal of the jihadist is expended in justified violence against the enemy as scapegoat. The violent response of the jihadists to their enemy-scapegoat (and the enemy's purported indiscriminate violence) is, then, justified with reference to Islamic principles.[76] The magnanimous and merciful responses of the Prophet Muhammad and later Muslims to attacks by enemies (including by the West), which even some fundamentalist Islamic authors recognize, are ignored by contemporary militant jihadists.[77] Instead, they prefer their mythic veneers to cover over the mimetic dynamics of violent resentment and scapegoating.

At the heart of these mythical justifications is the way in which any target, including civilians, has become legitimate, enabled by the minimization or elimination of the distinction between civilian and combatant. The loss of this distinction encourages the intentional and widespread use of suicide bombings, massacres, and missile or chemical weapon use in public locations where civilians congregate. While jihadist rationales are meant to cover up the mimetic reasons for violence, they show the intentionality of jihadists to use theological principle as "a tool of generalized and indiscriminate violence" including against women and children.[78] Instead of mythologies being constructed to cover up a limited use of violence (as was the case in traditional societies), jihadists rely on a "rational" discourse of principles and rules to justify ever-worsening forms of violence in pursuit of absolute victory.[79] The jihadist attitude degenerates into targeting anyone not deemed to be a true Muslim (usually defined by membership of the radical group) as an enemy worthy of being killed. In this way, ISIS, al-Qaeda, and other jihadist groups publicly rejoice and glory in their violence in a way that shows it to be constitutive of their identity.

The sign of some kind of legal and moral code among these terrorist groups, nevertheless, should not be glossed over or disregarded. It shows how the ritual and legal violence of jihadists is operating according to what they believe to be "rational" and "Islamic" criteria. However, as I have shown, these justifications serve as a type of myth to morally and theologically legitimize the impulse of the jihadists to do violence in a retributory and indiscriminate manner. This effort stands in contrast to the Islamic legal traditions that restrict violence and warfare. Instead, jihadists exclusively privilege violent and offensive notions of jihad that suit their agenda.

The violent logic of the jihadist movement is powerful and, moreover, effects an intrinsic connection between violence and being a true Muslim. One cannot live without the other: Islam is inherently defined as jihad, and jihad is violence and destruction, including of civilians. Girard's diagnosis of the trajectory of violence in modernity following the degradation of the distinction between combatant and civilian is on stark display. In fact, any means can be potentially legitimated, even one's own suicide, if it serves the will of God, promotes jihad, and brings about the transcendent utopian goal of an Islamic state.[80]

Because of the way jihadism distorts its own religious tradition, such as by allowing actions that were previously prohibited, Khosrokhavar argues that it undermines Islam in the frenetic search for identity and communion. By opposing modernity and secularization with a radical and distorted view of Islam, jihadists effect a kind of secularization that undermines Islam's own tenets.[81] With jihadism, the breakdown in tradition in service of a modern utopia is present. In justifying themselves, jihadists are conscious of their destructive logic and its consequences, though they do not realize the full extent to which they are beholden to violent mimetic dynamics which they externalize into an idolatrous notion of God. In seeking to repress this realization, jihadists draw on and distort Islamic thought, as well as modern Western political thought.[82] In these justifications and actions, jihadists show themselves to be thoroughly modern while also drawing on the ancient tradition of Islam to use and distort its justifications for violence.

Thus, as militant jihadists undertake increasingly extreme action, the place of violence is not only stripped away to become more transparent, but its intentional amalgam with a transcendent—though debased—vision of the world becomes clearer. Jihadists have embraced public and indiscriminate acts of violence as inherent to their motivation, faith, and vision of life. In the next chapter, I examine why they do so, in the context of a metaphysical and social crisis of identity.

7

Violence and Identity

For jihadists, the modern world and Islam are in deep crisis. Violence is the ultimate solution and the means by which the Islamic system can be maintained and grow. I've attempted to show that Girard's notions of mimesis and "the sacred" help to understand the dynamics of rivalry and violence in militant jihadism. The jihadists' narrative of deep crisis and their solution in sacred violence is a common pattern to the way humans seek order through scapegoating violence. I've also shown how such violence has escalated in modernity, and that jihadism is a reflection of this escalating, totalizing violence. Nevertheless, there remain questions: Why are jihadists *so* violent? What gives rise to such virulent and violent forms of mimesis? Why do they resort to violence to solve their problems? These questions concern the underlying dimension of mimesis: the yearning for being that Girard identifies as interacting with mimesis to form distinctly *human* types of identity. This chapter shows, then, that underlying the attraction to sacred violence in jihadism are metaphysical identity issues and resentments. These issues lead militant jihadists to grasp for violent differences around which identity can be defined over against enemies, who become victims of jihadism's totalitarian violence.

Identity and Difference

It has been previously argued that militant jihadism attempts counter the deep sense of alienation and dislocation in modernity, which has particularly influenced the Islamic revival and the rise of Islamism. Yet, the intrinsic connection between violence and militant jihadism, and the underlying motivations that help forge such a connection are not often well understood in the West, as Atran identifies:

> Despite our relentless propaganda campaign against the Islamic State as vicious, predatory and cruel—most of which might be right—there is little recognition of its genuine appeal, and even less of the joy it engenders. The mainly young people who volunteer to fight for it unto death feel a joy that comes from joining with comrades in a glorious cause, as well as a joy that comes from satiation of anger and the gratification of revenge (whose sweetness, says science, can be experienced by brain and body much like other forms of happiness).[1]

Atran suggests that jihadist violence encompasses the frustrated desires, emotions, and resentments of its members in a transcendent act of worship.[2] This act of worship brings both camaraderie and catharsis. It is an act of transcendence seeking identity, meaning, and communion. Moreover, the violence that drives jihadism reveals deep identity issues and relies on the construction of fundamental differences over against its enemies. The construction of these differences is projected onto God as sacredly commissioned violence.

With the onset of globalization, it is often commented that the modern world is characterized by a breakdown of difference as well as a "clash of civilizations." While it is unclear whether such a clash is occurring, the crisis of difference and the clash of competing groups and ideologies are widespread problems felt across an increasingly interconnected world, driven by capitalist, technological, and geopolitical forces. These issues manifest themselves in confusion regarding identity and frenzied efforts to create a sense of belonging, often over against others (both in reality and virtually). Echoing various studies, Shiraz Maher comments that these issues of identity and belonging are commonly identified as the underlying motivators for jihadist radicalization and extremism: "Strip away all the grievances and myriad individual triggers that might drive an individual to join an extremist group and you find underlying issues of identity and belonging. None of this is new."[3]

These issues of identity and belonging have arisen as traditional cultural forms have been challenged by changes brought about by various forces such as colonization, industrialization, urbanization, secularization, and globalization. In a particular way, traditional cultural structures have struggled, especially as the historic consensus around religion has been challenged or lost. Pankaj Mishra describes the situation as characterized by people with a "widely felt spiritual hunger"—"of men looking desperately for maps of meaning in a world they found opaque and uncontrollable"—for which various false cures have been proclaimed, often ending in various totalitarianisms.[4] While men generally make up the majority of the fighting force of militant groups such as ISIS and AQ, there has also been a significant and noticeable number of women joining such groups, even sacrificing what look to be freer lifestyles (e.g., in the West) to join the jihadist cause. Such women have fulfilled various roles, including as willing suicide bombers or as members of "al Khansaa Brigade, an all-female militia group of ISIS."[5] A fundamental crisis of identity, then, seems to be felt across the genders. The appeal of jihadism in its ideological vision, group cohesion, and violent action draws various people, especially young people and even whole families. Despite the danger of joining such a movement, it draws people in a way that seems to answer their deeper longings and frustrated desires, fill existential or social gaps, and enable a sense of pride and empowerment (especially to address guilt, trauma, or pain).

In particular, Scott Cowdell traces how jihadist terrorism is usually driven by a range of "frustrated aspirations":

> Drivers of terrorism include unequal access to the benefits of modernization (e.g., education but no jobs), a loss of traditional social controls, and globalization experienced as colonization, with religion providing a focus for dissent and the recovery of lost control.[6]

As is evident in the literature around radicalization, members of violent jihadist groups usually lack a solid identity, which they try to grasp through membership of an extremist group that is built on a strict ideology and acts of violence. Maher states that the same features recur in radicalization: "The underlying ingredients are always the same: righteous indignation, defiance, a sense of persecution and a refusal to conform."[7] Moreover, radicalized young people, especially in the West, have been often found to be socially or economically alienated, involved with petty crime, and regard (re-)conversion to Islam as a positive break with the past.[8] Connected to this is group membership, which is key for any jihadist, who never truly acts alone and who gains identity and solidarity from the group.[9] The group provides the defining points of difference for a firmly constructed identity, by means of the militant jihadist ideology/theology:

> If they [jihadists] are suffering from anything, it is from what they see as the emptiness, meaninglessness, materialism and narcissism of the contemporary West and the corruption of secular regimes in the Islamic world. As Eric Hoffer noted in *The True Believer* (1951) and as Scott Atran has shown in his study of suicide bombers, *Talking to the Enemy*, individuals join radical movements to alleviate the isolation of the lonely crowd and become, however briefly, part of an intense community engaged in the pursuit of something larger than the self. They are motivated by genuine ideals. They feel the suffering, the pain and

> the humiliation of their fellow believers. They seek to dedicate and if need be sacrifice their lives to end what they see as the injustice of the world and to honour the memory of those they see as its victims. As Michael Ignatieff wrote in *The Warrior's Honor*, the book he wrote in response to the Balkan wars, "Political terror is tenacious because it is an ethical practice. It is a cult of the dead, a dire and absolute expression of respect." Holy warriors are altruists, and what they commit is altruistic evil.[10]

Thus, the frustrated desires and aspirations of those who are radicalized are addressed by a sense of deep purpose and meaning given by jihadism. This purpose and meaning are, as discussed, reliant on intense and transcendent experiences of violence. This violence is invested with mimetic power and deep meaning as it is done in the name of the victimized Muslim masses of modernity and commissioned by God himself. Militant jihadists, including those who mount extremely violent terrorist attacks, have a deep sense of their own mission and purpose, in place of the marginalization and displacement otherwise present. Richardson argues that terrorists are generally driven by three factors: revenge (for a grievance or rivalry), the pursuit of renown (which terrorist groups provide through the martyrdom discourse), and the expectation of reaction (whether to inspire a revolution or repression).[11]

Similarly, Slavoj Žižek presents an account of how modernist alienation transforms itself into resentment and violence directed against the "Western infidel" or Muslim apostate. Žižek argues that the creation of enemies by the jihadist terrorist is an effort of internal projection that seeks to construct differences and barriers to the Western lifestyle, which is so culturally pervasive but from which they feel disaffected and profoundly marginalized. This feeling of discontent results in an effort to grasp desperately for any and all points of differentiation:

> The terrorist pseudo-fundamentalists are deeply bothered, intrigued, fascinated, by the sinful life of the non-believers [or one could add, the Muslim apostate]. One can feel that, in fighting the sinful other, they are fighting their own temptation.
>
> … the passionate intensity of the terrorists bears witness to a lack of true conviction. How fragile the belief of a Muslim must be if he feels threatened by a stupid caricature in a weekly satirical newspaper? The fundamentalist Islamic terror is *not* grounded in the terrorists' conviction of their superiority and in their desire to safeguard their cultural-religious identity from the onslaught of global consumerist civilization. The problem with fundamentalists is not

> that we consider them inferior to us, but, rather, that *they themselves* secretly consider themselves inferior. … The problem is not cultural difference (their effort to preserve their identity), but the opposite fact that the fundamentalists are already like us, that, secretly, they have already internalized our standards and measure themselves by them. Paradoxically, what the fundamentalists really lack is precisely a dose of that true "racist" conviction of their own superiority.[12]

At the heart, then, of militant jihadism is not strict differences but the fear of sameness and nothingness. As discussed in Chapter 1, Girard argues that it is this fear of sameness or identity with the rival, and of being nothing in comparison to the rival-model, that is at the heart of mimetic rivalry and violence. The subjects of rivalry try to avoid this fear and construct an identity built on definitive differences through victory and acquisition. Militant jihadists do this in an extreme, frenzied way through unrelenting and totalitarian forms of violence. As the agents of the state and modernity seemingly encroach upon them, jihadists are driven by disdain and hatred for their own condition projected onto the other. Thus, they need to reassert control in order to escape their inferior and confused state. Girard puts it in these terms:

> As the distance between mediator and subject decreases, the difference diminishes, the comprehension becomes more acute and the hatred more intense. It is always his own desire that the subject condemns in the Other without knowing it. Hatred is individualistic. It nourishes fiercely the illusion of an absolute difference between the Self and that Other from which nothing separates it. Indignant comprehension is therefore an imperfect comprehension—not nonexistent as some moralists claim, but imperfect, for the subject does not recognize in the Other the void gnawing at himself. He makes of him a monstrous divinity. The subject's indignant knowledge of the Other returns in a circle to strike him when he is least expecting it. This psychological circle is inscribed in the triangle of desire. Most of our ethical judgments are rooted in hatred of a mediator, a rival whom we copy.[13]

In a similar way to Žižek, then, Girard discusses the relational dimensions of the hatred and resentment experienced by militant jihadists toward their enemies, especially the West, which manifests in a sense of inferiority and rivalry.[14] This rivalry, at its core, represents a grasping for being—for divinity—from the other (which is fundamentally a form of idolatry): "What each is trying to snatch away from the other was the divinity [absolute being] that he claimed to have, and the more they fight, the nearer that divinity approaches, until it is tangible in the destruction threatening the group."[15] In fighting the enemy to the death, militant jihadists seek to project an absolute identity—a self-sufficiency ostensibly reliant on God. However, their identity and unity are fundamentally structured on a violent relation with their enemies. In this way, the jihadists are in a double bind: they seek to grasp at the being of the enemy—who is the real object of worship, terror, resentment, and disdain—but do so by rejecting the enemy. The jihadist is both attracted to and repelled by the rival.[16] In this relationship of attraction–repulsion, what is sought is the depth of being portrayed by the rival, who appears to be superior but who the jihadist wishes to make inferior.

The problem of identity is exacerbated because of the intermingling of West and East in modernity. Differences are receding, while identity becomes more confused. According to Roy: "Middle Eastern societies are Westernized. They are urban, modern societies. The problem is not with a traditional society; we have no problem with traditional people. We have problems with the people who have been Westernized. And under their hand, now, Islam is definitively rooted in the West."[17] Roy argues that militant jihadists are deeply influenced by Western political, economic, and cultural structures. They want to attain the goods of modernity which Westerners seem to possess with so much joy and abundance. Yet, according to Girard, the view of the model as complete and self-sufficient is a delusion of the subject in regard to the model. The model may not actually be satisfied with the objects he/she possesses but appears to be so from the subject's inferior and acquisitive perspective. As Girard warns, which seems apropos of the passionate jihadist: "Even the most passionate among us never feel they truly are the persons they want to be. To them the most wonderful being, the only semi-god, always is someone else whom they emulate and from whom they borrow their desires, thus ensuring for themselves lives of perpetual strife and rivalry with those whom they simultaneously hate and admire."[18]

In the jihadist view (as Žižek suggests), the West is the demonic model—admired and hated—who must be resisted, expelled, and eradicated but is also imitated and emulated. For this reason, jihadists are willing to adopt some Western forms, such as modern technology and science, but reject other Westernized forms of culture, economics, religion, and politics that they feel are imposed on them. Yet, they have no answer to this "imposition," except to violently reject it through what they feel is authentically their own, namely, Islam. The jihadists' aspirations and desires for modernity, then, become projected onto God and Islam. They seek a transcendent point of reference to assist them against their much larger model. However, even their construction of Islam is deeply imbued with Western and modern characteristics. It is totalitarian in form and is motivated by a distortion of the Abrahamic tradition that uses sympathy for the victimized to reassert ascendency and power.

The sense of inferiority that both Žižek and Girard identify as driving problems of identity and violence is evident in one of the most important turning points for the jihadist movement. In 1990, Osama bin Laden and his militant associates felt deeply scandalized after they were rejected by Saudi Arabia in favor of the United States following the Iraqi invasion of Kuwait. This rejection provoked a sense of their own inferiority and solidified their rivalry with the United States and the West.[19] This reaction emerged from a state of passionate "strife," as Girard suggests, because bin Laden and his followers were eager to fight the jihad (especially following the success in Afghanistan) but were reeling from one fight or refuge to the next. They sought refuge with friendly Muslim rulers and regimes but were being expelled even from them (e.g., Saudi Arabia and Sudan).

This rejection by Saudi Arabia during the Gulf War sparked deep resentment because it exposed the inferiority of the jihadist movement in comparison to the West, or at least the perception of it. To make matters worse, it revealed this inferiority through the eyes of a leading Muslim country. Despite being "righteous" and battle-hardened jihadists, they had been judged by their fellow Muslims to be less effective and trustworthy than the United States in warfare. This rejection led to outrage and provoked passionate, rivalrous rhetoric against the United States. Bin Laden and his followers were able to turn this rejection into a new focus and new mission against the United States, whose occupation of the "land of the two holy places"—the heart of Islam and the clearest sign of the jihadists' loss to the West—was said to be the "greatest of all these aggressions."[20] Moreover, despite being rejected by Muslim nations, it brought forth deep shame among Islamists, especially militant jihadists, that the Islamic world needed the help of the West to resolve their own internal disputes.[21] Again, projection seems to have been playing a role, as the jihadists protected their own identity by projecting the shame of rejection onto the Muslim nations. Rather than recognizing the shame of their own rejection, al-Qaeda focused on the perceived shame of Muslim nations seeking Western help. For the militant jihadist, this put on public display that the Muslim-majority states regarded themselves as inferior to the West because of their need for help from the superior militaries of the West. This public recognition of inferiority was shameful and embarrassing, according to bin Laden and his jihadist comrades.

Following this "occupation," bin Laden called for jihad as "every man's duty" (quoting Abdallah Azzam) to expel the Americans from Islamic lands and destroy apostate regimes such as that of the Al-Saud family in Saudi Arabia.[22] In 1998, this aim was escalated with a fatwa from bin Laden and other jihadist leaders in which Muslims had a "personal duty to kill Americans and their allies, whether civilians or military personnel, in every country where this is possible."[23] Thus, the rival's supremacy had to be challenged and destroyed.

In contrast to the perceived weakness of Muslim states, militant jihadists put forth their vision of a strong Islam—a "complete and total system"—which is achieved with violent jihad against the United States and its allies and that reasserts Islam's true superiority. According to bin Laden and his supporters, only a purely Islamic system could arrest the decline of the Islamic world (*dar-al-Islam*) and reassert itself over against the West. This system is to be universal, with an international appeal across Muslim-majority states and beyond:

> Contrary to the Islamists who wanted to build an Islamic State in a given country and thus became embroiled in nationalism, neo-fundamentalists are championing the transnational ummah, they address the universalist yearning of Muslims who cannot identify with any specific place or nation. The constructivist ummah therefore must span the globe, where it battles the Western political, economic and cultural uniformity that, ironically, it requires to sustain itself. Thus McDonald's and English-as-a-second-language is fought by neo-fundamentalists wearing white robes and beards who also speak English-as-a-second-language and go for halal fast food.[24]

Thus, the rivals become like each other, without recognizing it. In order to counter recognition of this inferior imitation of the West, jihadists assert the radical authenticity of their own mission and identity. Roy argues that Islamic neo-fundamentalism (like other contemporary religious movements) is strong on religious feeling and experience, revealing how religion has been individuated to secure identity.[25] In this way, Islamization parallels processes of modernization and Westernization.[26] The crisis of the self is part of the crisis of the social order, which is caused by various changes in modernity, most fundamentally among them being the breakdown of sacred violence. The human self-of-desire historically was reliant on a highly structured culture built on sacred transcendence and difference. Yet, almost all modern communities (especially those touched by the Abrahamic faiths) suffer from an inability to divinize victims and so bring about truly binding community and transcendence through unanimous violence. The breakdown of community, then, leads to the breakdown of the self, as unrestrained mimetic desire multiplies rivalries and fragments identities. The effort to grasp at identity in jihadism is a way to alleviate this breakdown. Yet, this effort is highly frenetic and unstable. At its worst, this crisis of identity can lead, as Girard shows in *Deceit, Desire, and the Novel*, to madness and violence, as one's identity and being are exposed as empty.

It is to this crisis of identity that jihadism attempts to provide an answer, albeit a temporary and violent one. It is one that is highly sadistic in that it seeks to acquire being by grasping from and dominating the horrible and dreaded rival-model that the jihadist has constructed. This construction leads to indiscriminate violence that jihadists justify and commit for mimetic reasons: because, for example, they are retaliating to the violence of the rival (e.g., the United States) in the name of the victimized and on behalf of God. They imitate the perceived violence of their rivals—seen through the lens of delusional, self-identified victims—in order to be better at it and so acquire the rival's being and identity. This violence is particularly shown when jihadists come to dominate others. Girard argues that masochists can turn into sadists when they come to dominate others. In other words, they imitate the rival-model they believe to be dominant and inflict the pain and oppressive conditions on others that they believe gives the rival his/her power and self-sufficiency.[27]

Girard identifies "metaphysical desire" as being at the heart of the grasping of humans for identity, and charts its course in *Deceit, Desire, and the Novel*. He shows how distorted human desire leads into emptiness and despair when the interplay of mimetic desires becomes hollow, that is, lacking true and good objects and relationships. In order to counter this hollowness, mimetic desire intensifies, as does the metaphysical desire for being. In this state, rivalry becomes more likely between desiring subjects, because humans tend to irrationally regard victory in rivalry as the answer to their metaphysical problems. Girard claims that this rivalrous search for being is common to modern ideologies.

Despite professing a righteous cause, these modern revolutionary ideologies, like communism or jihadism, are not really interested, according to Girard, in achieving liberation for the oppressed. On the contrary, they are fixated on continual fighting against an overwhelming enemy in order to achieve a metaphysical victory. Yet, these ideologies cannot really achieve victory—the working class is never truly in ascendency, nor are jihadists ever going to dominate the world in an Islamic state. In this way, the purveyors of these ideologies, like the militant jihadist, are really masochists—they prefer the pain of absolute rivalry to the uncertainty of being in modernity. They prefer their sense of inferiority to the rival-model, rather than to live and struggle in the ambiguity and richness of modernity. It is easy in a sense to keep fighting. The rival-model supposedly prevents the achievement of desire—for example, for the goods of modernity—and so the subject fights endlessly against the rival in the name of those the rival supposedly victimizes. Rather than examining their sense of alienation and inferiority or struggling with the tensions of modernity, they rush toward the simplistic pain and brutality of conflict against the "wicked" and "monstrous" rival-enemy:

> The masochist is at once more lucid and more blind than other victims of metaphysical desire. He is more lucid in that he possesses that lucidity, increasingly prevalent in our time, which permits him alone among all desiring subjects to perceive the connection between internal mediation and the obstacle; he is more blind because, instead of following out the implications of this awareness to their necessary conclusion, instead of giving up misdirected transcendency, he tries paradoxically to satisfy his desire by rushing toward the obstacle, thus making his destiny one of misery and failure.
>
> The source of this ill-starred lucidity which characterizes the last stages of ontological sickness is not difficult to discover. It is the increased proximity of the mediator. Enslavement is always the final result of desire, but at first it is very distant and the desiring subject cannot perceive it. The eventual result becomes increasingly clear as the distance between mediator and subject decreases and the phases of the metaphysical process are accelerated. ... When the desiring subject perceives the abyss that desire has hollowed out beneath his feet, he voluntarily hurls himself into it, hoping against hope to discover in it what the less acute stages of metaphysical sickness have not brought him.[28]

Thus, the jihadist is both aware and not aware of his/her predicament. I explored this dynamic of awareness and repression in regard to violence in Chapter 4. Here Girard is providing insight into this predicament: rather than facing it, the subject rushes into the obstacles supposedly standing in their way of true being. The mediator is so close, yet never really able to be challenged. Rivalry only leads to an abyss—an emptiness that must be fueled by more violence. This seems to precisely describe the metaphysical and mimetic dynamics of the jihadist's predicament and actions.

Girard's identification of the lucidity of the masochist seems present in this pronouncement from bin Laden: "If Sharon [former prime minister of Israel] is a man of peace in the eyes of Bush, then we are also men of peace!!!"[29] Bin Laden seems to be able to recognize the violence in himself and his rival. However, earlier in the same letter, bin Laden derided the United States for enabling Sharon to enter the Al-Aqsa Mosque in order "to pollute it as a preparation to capture and destroy it."[30] Sharon and his US allies were clearly powerful rivals, whose violence was transgressive and unjust in the eyes of bin Laden. In this way, bin Laden rejected any real insight into his relationship with his rivals. Instead, he continued to condemn and oppose them, though to little avail. While the "enemy" had drawn ever closer through the intense and multiple mediations of modernity, bin Laden was only really interested in rivalry with his overwhelmingly powerful enemies, which he could never really defeat. Rather than seeing identity with his rival, bin Laden focused on the Muslim's enslavement to Westernized modernity and politics, and to the obstacles that it produces in the way of an Islamic utopia (*jahiliyya*).

Thus, despite the glimmers of awareness, militant jihadists gravitate to the abyss of rivalry—to the intense rivalry that aims to provide some antidote to modernity and re-create the strict bonds of traditional solidarity. Ex-jihadists particularly recognize the misdiagnosis of their own alienated condition, once they are removed from radicalized thought patterns and violence. Unfortunately, for the jihadists who never defect or escape, they struggle with their own enslavement by projecting it onto others. In struggling against their mimetic and metaphysical problems violently and rivalrously, they deepen them. In seeking to strengthen social bonds over against the "infidel" and "apostate," they enslave themselves to distorted desire and rivalry.

The jihadist, then, projects the plight of confused identity and intensifying desire—that is, to growing enslavement to modernity—onto the enemy and onto a reinvented "sacred." This projection provides an alternative point of transcendence to the pervasiveness of the Western model of modernity. However, this transcendence is just another projection of rivalry—another idolatry. While their identity is built on rivalry, militant jihadists cannot abide—nor do they wish to, if they remain in fixed rivalry with the West. The double bind is manifest again: jihadist identity is structured by rivalry but their deepest aspirations are fixated on victory—a victory that not only they cannot achieve, but which would lead to the disintegration of their identity. Thus, they face a fundamental contradiction, which they attempt to keep repressed with ever-worsening forms of violence. Yet, their own desire for being—for victory—will win out: they must defeat their rival—which is ultimately a projection of themselves—by destroying themselves in useless conflicts.

Thus, absolute rivalry is the resort of those, like the jihadist or totalitarian actor, who see violence as an antidote to the modern, desacralized condition. Yet, absolute rivalry is a self-fulfilling prophecy: it lives out its own victimization and defeat over and over again. Even if one enslaved to absolute rivalry gains victories or territories, the subject can never gain the being it wants because one is always defined over against the (superior) other. This solution responds to the problem of modern human desire which cannot find a unanimous or effective scapegoating outlet and so tends to lack the passionate intensity of a unified community. Jihadists try to re-create this intensity through "altruistic evil" in defense of the victimized over against the infidel West and its apostate allies. However, it is inherently unstable as no victory ultimately provides true peace and communion.[31] This instability, instead, leads toward more intense and indiscriminate forms of jihadist violence, built on a false pride and frenzied internal mediation. In this sense, holy war is only ever a grasping onto an empty transcendence which temporarily reinvigorates personal and social identity but invariably results in death or nothingness: "Beneath the modern phantasmagoria, beneath the whirl of events and ideas which lies at the end of the ever more rapid development of internal mediation, lies nothingness."[32]

Resentment and Difference

In addition to the personal problems of identity/being that influence militant jihadists and their radicalization, there are issues of a collective nature, particularly regarding collective difference and resentment, that demonstrate the manner in which jihadists seek to define their communal identity (over against their enemy). The way in which jihadists attempt to construct a self-enclosed system is often argued to be driven by fundamental differences between the West and Islam. Jihadists themselves point to these differences in terms of culture, mores, and behavior. For example, bin Laden accuses the United States and the West of deluding themselves regarding the decadent and immoral nature of their society:

> It is saddening to tell you that you are the worst civilization witnessed by the history of mankind. ... Let us not forget one of your major characteristics: your duality in both manners and values; your hypocrisy in manners and principles. All manners, principles and values have two scales: one for you and one for the others.[33]

Of course, the implication of bin Laden's diatribe is that the jihadist movement represents a contrary type of civilization compared to the West. The attempt to define clear differences by bin Laden is part of his effort to provide a sense of collective identity. Ultimately, this effort relies on violence, which constructs difference in an absolute way. The "us-and-them" becomes foundational to the identity of the movement as it is enacted with violence.

Girard argues that differences in human cultures are constructed based on scapegoating violence, which establishes the definitive difference between the mob and the victim. These differences are the foundation on which cultural groups can assert identity, power, and stability. Rather than difference driving violence (at least initially), the force or impetus for difference relies on the effectiveness of violence to suppress the condition of sameness that the human subject fears that he/she shares with one's model (or enemy). This condition of sameness or "undifferentiation" arises because of mimetic competition that moves rivals to desire the same objects:

> The error is always to reason within categories of "difference" when the root of all conflicts is rather "competition," mimetic rivalry between persons, countries, cultures. Competition is the desire to imitate the other in order to obtain the same thing he or she has, by violence if need be. No doubt terrorism is bound to a world "different" from ours, but what gives rise to terrorism does not lie in that "difference" that removes it further from us and make it inconceivable to us. On the contrary, it lies in the desire for convergence and resemblance. Human relations are essentially relations of imitation, of rivalry.[34]

Thus, differences are constructed to obscure mimetic conflict. This is not to argue that differences in modernity do not exist prior to particular acts of violence, but that differences gain their significance and power in particular conditions of social conflict. Violence is deployed to sharpen and solidify difference in order to bring about identity, power, and order.

Under the weight of modernity, there has been a breakdown of traditional cultural institutions, which channeled violence through hierarchical differences, requiring the construction of new identities. If this construction cannot be done peacefully (e.g., through solidarity among peoples), arbitrary points of difference are invoked in ever more violent ways to cover over a lack of difference and identity. The frenetic and indiscriminate violence of the jihadist can be understood in this context. It has a logic—rationalized in defense of oppressed Muslims—to reconstruct difference through the prism of victims and victimizers, oppressed and oppressors. It does so by twisting the revelation of the victim through re-sacralizing violence with reference to the God who defends victims:

> When I read the first documents of Bin Laden and verified his allusions to the American bombing of Japan, I felt at first that I was in a dimension that transcends Islam, a dimension of the entire planet. Under the label of Islam we find a will to rally and mobilize an entire third world of those frustrated and

> of victims in their relations of mimetic rivalry with the West. But the towers destroyed had as many foreigners as Americans. But their effectiveness, the sophistication of the means they employed, the knowledge that they had of the United States and their training, were not the authors of the attack in a sense at least partly American? Here we are in the middle of mimetic contagion.
>
> Far from turning away from the West, they cannot avoid imitating it and adopting its values, even if they don't avow it, and they are also consumed like us by the desire for individual and collective success.[35]

This effort at re-sacralizing violence emerges from the jihadists' fear that their lack of any sense of real identity over against others will be exposed. This sense of lack and inferiority, discussed earlier in the chapter, results in collective resentment. Resentment is one of the clearest markers of jihadist discourse. In his quantitative analysis of jihadist discourse, Khosrokhavar concludes that

> Jihadist discourse is resentment-laden. Muslims are from the Jihadist point of view suffering deep humiliation under the yoke of the enemies of Islam from within (inauthentic Muslim governments) and without (Western governments, in particular the United States). … Feelings of oppression, humiliation, frustration, and unease are common Jihadist traits. This reflects in part the situation of Muslims in their relation toward the United States, Israel, Russia (Chechnya), and the modern world in general. But the major difference between Jihadists and other Muslims is that this humiliation is only part of the latter's world perspective, whereas in the Jihadist discourse, it excludes all other aspects of life, creating an all-encompassing view that swallows up other considerations altogether and does not leave any possibility for openness and flexibility. Jihadism makes a restrictive, exclusive Muslim viewpoint the only base upon which to build up an Islamic identity. It makes violent Jihad (not the spiritual form, the Greater Jihad, *jihad al akbar*, promoted by the Reformists since the end of the nineteenth century) the central pillar of the religion, giving it a significance and a magnitude that go far beyond many Muslims' sentiments.[36]

Thus, the humiliation of the victimized is fuel for a closed, resentful discourse aimed at constructing strict and clear differences. Such differences lead to a violent, restrictive identity as the antidote to a fragmenting, desacralized modernity. This identity is constructed in an absolute way, built mimetically and affectively on the resentment of enemies, especially the West. Brighi notes that in the psychology of terrorism there is agreement that resentment provides one of major drivers of radicalization.[37] According to Brighi, this manifests in two forms: the resentment against oppression and the desire to reestablish justice; and *ressentiment* in which the subjects feel "a frustrated, misdirected and generalized sense of victimhood and envy."[38] These forms of resentment, moreover, have been increasingly individualized and globalized in modernity. According to Brighi, the individualization of late modernity has multiple causes, including the degradation of forms of social mediation and sacrality as well as a "romantic" notion of the autonomous "rational individual" that has become privileged in social, economic, and political affairs.[39]

Brighi calls for a fuller analysis in mimetic theory of the two states of resentment that she identifies with reference to jihadist terrorism, as she notes that the two states blend into each other in Girard's work.[40] Though this danger exists, there is a way to individually investigate these two types of resentment by utilizing Girard's work, while also showing how they connect to each other mimetically. The former state—the resentment caused by oppression and injustice—reflects a sense of the integrity of one's own being-in-relationship—that one's life, formed and engrained in relationships, has some intrinsic value. This value is actualized and concretized in relationships, in which values and virtues, such as justice, are culturally formed and directed. Violence can offend the standards of justice, which are ultimately based on the integrity of our relationships (which are structured by mimesis). Justice refers to the expectations and habits in our relationships, which are meant to be constructive and fair. Properly formed relationships will be just when they provide a long-lasting sense of integrity and contentment in one's being-in-relationship.

Yet, when injustice is committed, the standards of justice—that is, the standards we expect of our relationships—can be grounds for anger or hurt. When improperly directed toward violence, this sense of injustice can turn into resentment, in which injustice becomes a cause for scandal and rivalry against others. For example, jihadists claim that apostate regimes have transgressed basic Islamic principles making them totally illegitimate, and "crusader" nations have initiated illegitimate, aggressive violence against Muslims and so must be destroyed. In both cases, injustice leads to a total attribution of blame that justifies the disproportionate use of violence. The "enemy" is the transgressor who must be punished or resisted in to preserve justice and order. This sacrificial logic results in "bad" violence being met with an overwhelming and over-powering amount of "good" and self-righteous violence.

This overwhelming, disproportionate response from the jihadist turns violent sacrificial logic into an apocalyptic logic. In this situation, one's self or group feels so much resentment that they engage in total forms of violence that are primarily or exclusively destructive to resolve the perceived injustice. The claims of injustice in these cases usually reveal themselves to be fundamentally mimetic in nature (rather than based in objective values), for example, al-Qaeda's offence at the US assistance for and presence in Saudi Arabia during the Gulf War. It is important to note how the sense of injustice here was influenced by mimetic sensibilities: the feeling of resentment toward the US as a rival gave rise to the exaggerated claims of bin Laden and others that the United States was occupying Muslim lands as an "oppressor." Thus, the sense of injustice connects with victimhood, which characterizes Brighi's second type of resentment. Jihadist calls of injustice, while in places pointing to circumstances of alienation, combine with a rivalrous victim mentality to distort the jihadist worldview. Injustice comes to be colored by exaggerated and rivalrous claims of victim status that are increasingly arbitrary and conspiratorial.

The claims to victim status demonstrate Brighi's second type of resentment built around envy and a moralistic sense of victimhood. As I showed in Chapter 4, a violent victim mentality dominates jihadist thinking and is a powerful cause for increasing violence. Despite their noble aims, Islamic law and the discourse of human rights can be manipulated by those with a violent victim mentality to persecute a perceived persecutor and re-ignite a cycle of violence.[41] This victim mentality combines with forms of envy and inferiority, as I discussed earlier in the chapter, to become fixated on the rival-model. In this way, a sense of injustice and victimhood combines to justify violence, which is undergirded by envious and rivalrous forms of mimesis.

The outcome of the path of resentment is *ressentiment*. *Ressentiment* represents the descent of the subject into an abyss of distorted, rivalrous desire—as Girard so well describes in *Deceit, Desire, and the Novel*—while frenetically grasping for some solidity to their identity by claiming a sacred victim status. The status is sacred precisely because it seeks to create new victims by violently casting the distorted desires of oneself and others onto the "victimizer." For this reason, the creation of enemies is necessary for jihadists to maintain some sense of identity, but it is frenetic and unstable, and increasingly global as more victims are sought. An absolute "us-and-them" attitude develops in which almost anyone can be killed because they are not members of the righteous groups of Muslims. Murawiec describes this mentality as gnostic or Manichean in dividing the world absolutely between *dar-al-Islam* (realm of peace) and *dar al-Harb* (realm of war).[42]

On the basis of this absolute division, jihadism seeks a definitive difference in order to reconstitute a sacred social order. Jihadists forcefully impose such a difference through ever more frenetic forms of violent scapegoating of their enemies. For example, al-Qaeda in Iraq sought to brutally manufacture difference by deploying extreme violence against the occupying forces as well as Sunnis and Shia Muslims in 2006–7. This violence was aimed at repressing Sunni dissent and forcing them to support AQI against their "common enemy":

> For example, fighters from an AQI cell might establish a safe house in a Sunni neighbourhood, creating a hideout in an abandoned row of buildings, fortifying compounds and mouse-holing connecting walls so they could move freely. They'd assassinate a few local Sunnis in spectacularly brutal fashion to remind everyone else to keep their eyes down and their mouths shut. Once they'd created a base, AQI would scout the neighbouring Shi'a community, kidnap young boys, torture them to death and dump the bodies—eyes gouged out, ears, little limbs and genitals hacked off, cigarette and blowtorch burns all over them or (an AQI trademark) the tops of their heads sliced open and electric drills thrust into their brains—back on the street in front of their houses, hoping to trigger outrage and retaliation from the Shi'a. Their goal was to provoke a sectarian conflict that would force Sunnis to close ranks in an AQI-led proto-state which, by October 2006, they were already calling *Dawlat al-Iraq al-Islamiyyah*—the Islamic State of Iraq (ISI).[43]

These horrible and brutal tactics of AQI show the extremes that they were willing to countenance in order to violently construct a difference—between a manufactured "us-and-them"—that enables cultural identity to be stabilized and defined. The ultimate aim of AQI was to gain victory within a highly volatile and violent totalitarian order, in which neither Sunnis nor Shia were really safe. This order required redefining the community's differences and enemies, which could be either Sunni, Shia, or Western depending on the context.

Conclusion

For jihadists, then, sacred violence in service of a totalitarian system becomes the ultimate answer to personal and collective crisis—an answer that seeks to address the alienation from modernity in a modern mode. A totalitarian response is built around absolute rivalries and the scapegoating of the "enemy," in the search for a victory that can never really be achieved. By constructing personal and collective identity on such unstable differences, jihadism constantly returns to its own double bind—its internal contradiction. This contradiction is that jihadists attempt to build identity in an absolute way over against rivals whom they seek to totally dominate or destroy, but in achieving such a total victory, they would undermine their identity built on difference from their rivals. Thus, the identity of the jihadist group is built on illusive differences "whose opposition grows ever more exact." These differences are an effort to avoid the abyss of being through an empty totalitarianism built on a "relentless" and "senseless" struggle (jihad):

> Stendal, Flaubert, Tocqueville describe as "republican" or "democratic" an evolution which we today would call *totalitarian*. As the mediator comes nearer and the concrete differences between men grow smaller, abstract opposition plays an ever larger part in individual and collective existence. All the forces of being are gradually organized into twin structures whose opposition grows ever more exact. Thus every human force is braced in a struggle that is as relentless as it is senseless, since no concrete difference or positive value is involved. Totalitarianism is precisely this. The social and political aspects of this phenomenon cannot be distinguished from its personal and private aspects. Totalitarianism exists when all desires have been organized one by one into a general and permanent mobilization of being in service of nothingness.[44]

In this chapter, I have sought to investigate the personal and social aspects of jihadist totalitarianism. As the personal crisis of being, in which sameness is feared, merges with a collective crisis of difference, in which envy and resentment predominate, totalitarianism emerges. Jihadists have mobilized in service of a total system that purports to address all aspects of life and rectify all injustices against the victimized Muslim masses. In this, jihadism mirrors other totalitarianisms in putting absolute meaning in what Girard calls "a general and permanent mobilization of being in the service of nothingness."[45] It is to the nature of jihadist totalitarianism as a constructed sacred enterprise that I now turn in the last chapter of this section.

8

Sacred Jihadist Totalitarianism

In this chapter I examine how jihadist violence—done in the name of Allah and His Prophet in defense of select victims—seeks to institute a totalitarian system as the absolute manifestation of Islam's "total system." This totalitarian system is based on a modern form of "the violent sacred," which seeks to counteract the effects of desacralization in modernity. This modern form of the sacred involves the (semi-)conscious deployment of violence based on a violent victim identity that is a direct distortion of the Abrahamic traditions' sympathy for the victim. Rather than seeing solidarity with the victim as the means to be liberated from humanity's addiction to violence, militant jihadists use the Abrahamic God—who is believed to defend the victimized—to escalate and re-sacralize violence. This chapter, then, analyzes the totalitarian nature of jihadism that distorts the Abrahamic traditions in service of a new sacred order.

Furthermore, I show in this chapter that when jihadists sacralize their violence with reference to God, they construct a totalitarian system that privileges the agents of "divine" violence. These agents believe they are doing God's will (with God's support) when they employ their apocalyptic and destructive violence, in order to bring about the definitive reign of God's law and justice. Yet, this "divine" reign is based on scapegoats and violence, just like traditional cultures were, though in a more conscious form. In effect, these agents of jihadist violence are sacralized, to a degree, because they deploy sacred violence in a transcendent and unquestionable way. Thus, the mob covertly sacralizes itself, instead of the victim (which occurred in traditional cultures).

The Violent Character of Jihadist Totalitarianism

Jihadist groups such as al-Qaeda and ISIS have brutally displayed their violent, totalitarian nature in practice. The extreme violence they deploy and the type of rule that they institute when coming to power show characteristics of a totalitarian system. This system seeks total and absolute control according to an apocalyptic logic of victory or destruction:

> This is the purposeful plan of violence that Abu Bakr al-Baghdadi, the Islamic State's self-anointed Caliph, outlined in his call for "volcanoes of jihad": to create a globe-spanning jihadi archipelago that will eventually unite to destroy the present world and create a new-old world of universal justice and peace under the Prophet's banner. A key tactic in this strategy is to inspire sympathisers abroad to violence: do what you can, with whatever you have, wherever you are, whenever possible.[1]

Based on the identification of these aspirations, Kilcullen argues that a militant jihadist group like ISIS is more than a "death cult," though he affirms its brutality and the way in which it acts like a death cult. Instead, he identifies ISIS as fundamentally a "revolutionary totalitarian … state-building enterprise":[2]

> If ISIS is a state, then what kind of state is it? Pretty clearly, it's a revolutionary totalitarian state, which seeks to expand by military conquest, refuses to recognise the legitimacy of other states (specifically, those defined by the Sykes–Picot Agreement that created the modern Middle East, or Iran or Israel) and wants to redraw the map of the Middle East and North Africa. It's a state that claims extraterritorial jurisdiction (under the caliphate) over Muslims, wherever they may be, and propagates a totalitarian ideology based on a specific interpretation of Islam. It seeks overseas dependencies (the wilayat or provinces in Sinai, Khorasan, Libya, Sana'a and Algeria). … It's a state that sees itself in a world-historic struggle against Shi'a Islam and the West, and expects an apocalyptic showdown from which it will emerge victorious.[3]

The absolute vision of jihadism of victory or destruction underlines its totalitarian character. Those who do not gather with the jihadists are deeply mistrusted—"illegitimate, even 'enemies'"—and are labelled as outsiders in terms of "'apostasy' (*ridda*), polytheism (*shirk*), Unbelief or Disbelief (*kufr*) or more generally, godless ignorance (*Jahiliya*)."[4] This absolute and dichotomous worldview undergirds the closed and repressive totalitarian system of jihadists. Khosrokhavar describes jihadist totalitarianism in this way:

> Sunni radicalism is explicitly totalitarian; it leaves no room for any compromise, no loopholes in the ideology, nor in the envisaged political system. … In the past, radical Muslims existed, but the new version is deeply influenced by Western totalitarian thinking, by the globalized media phenomenon and by the

new technologies of communication (the Internet, among others). They give it a prominence it would otherwise not have wielded. The crisis of the Muslim world has added to their appeal as well as sometimes one-sided American policies towards Muslims. Jihadism is the only major totalitarian phenomenon in the post-communist world that shows no signs of weakening.[5]

In regard to its totalitarian nature, Murawiec argues that militant Islamism has been influenced by elements of communism in which terror is turned into a "system of power."[6] It acts like European models of totalitarianism that violently enforce acquiescence to what Khosrokhavar describes as a "closed system of thought that precludes any legitimacy to dissent, rejecting those in disagreement as traitors or enemies."[7] The difference, though, between jihadist and European totalitarianisms is that, despite the European ideologies having quasi-religious elements (especially in the sense of absolutes that became idols), Khosrokhavar argues that they did not present themselves as "religions."[8] This difference most importantly amounts to direct reference to God, who is conscripted into the jihadist scheme as its justifying center. The Islamic tradition is used, then, to support this absolute claim for God. This claim is based on a form of transcendent unanimity that seeks to resuscitate the violent sacred from the ashes of modern desacralization.

In this regard, Cowdell classifies jihadism as a "political religion" that resuscitates the archaic sacred as part of "a mimetic struggle within globalized modernity":[9]

> [Charles] Taylor's account is of reforming, mobilizing modernity disembedding many people from clan, family, and community, who then find a new identity with the help of religion (especially if it is sufficiently us vs. them). Hence what emerge are neo-Durkheimian identities akin to those found in modern nationalism. Militant Islam seems most clearly explicable along these lines, resembling one of the aforementioned "political religions."[10]

According to both Girard and Cowdell, this political religion exploits Islam (just as socialism was exploited by Lenin-Stalinist or Maoist communism) as a rallying call to all self-perceived victims of the current global order.[11]

By referencing God and the Islamic tradition, militant jihadism explicitly seeks to return to the violent sacred through an identifiable transcendent system that is based on unanimous forms of violence. Rather than a covert or "secular" path to sacred violence through nationalism or ideology, jihadism goes for the highest transcendent signifier, God (understood in Islamic terms), which still retains great currency in the Muslim world. On this basis, they overtly engage in and celebrate sacred violence.

In this sense, the claims of Olivier Roy, who regards radical Islam as a nihilistic movement resorting to violence as an end, and Scott Atran and Gilles Kepel, who regard radical Islam as pursuing transcendent goals as part of an Islamic vision that is violently pursued, may be reconciled to some degree. There is agreement between both sides that radical jihadism embraces death and violence as the essential fuel for their religiopolitical campaigns. Justifications for these jihad campaigns become increasingly extreme and nimble in their use of Islamic concepts to rationalize violence. Ideology is ultimately serving violence in the repulsion of enemies and the satisfaction of metaphysical desire for an absolute identity in a utopian vision. Nevertheless, the Islamic vision of militant groups is integral to their cohesion and actions. This vision is usually genuinely believed in and provides the contours and framework for jihadist violence, though it is constantly reinterpreted according to the exigencies of violent "battlefield logic."[12]

This sacred jihadist totalitarianism is, as I have discussed across this section in terms of its actions and ideology/beliefs, directly reliant on violence for its identity and unity. Violence is integral to radicalization and is inherent to the militant's vision of life, particularly in jihad. It remains integral to the enactment of this total vision of life, which justifies the jihadists' public enactment of sacred violence. Moreover, as the jihadist engages in sacred violence, it becomes difficult to distinguish whether it is the divine command (a transcendent goal) or addiction to violence (transcendent violence) motivating action. In fact, the two blend together in such a way that violence enlivens the divine command and vice versa. Each is dependent on the other, so that what results is a return to the violent sacred, though in a modern, malicious, and extreme form.

Khosrokhavar argues that violence for jihadists forms "a holistic view of the Self and Other that makes violence both a means to achieve the desired ends and a self-contained goal."[13] Jihadist violence provides an integrating point for the modern self with the other that is embraced in and for itself (though as discussed in the previous chapter, it is internally contradictory). As an integrating point, violence is the transcendent means to achieving sacred goals, such as defending Islamic peoples or building an Islamic state, and is an intrinsic part of the jihadist worldview in which perpetual war is fought against non-Muslims. This violence is motivated by grievances that are historical, cultural, and ontological: that the world is not aligned to the law of Allah and that its practices and systems are idolatrous.[14] Violent totalitarianism in the name of

God is the only answer to bring about the true rule, which imposes itself on the world through the agents of jihad. Furthermore, even when established (as ISIS showed in Iraq and Syria), such rule will continue to impose itself violently against criminals and infidels.

Thus, in its activity or performance, jihadist violence becomes integral to defining what is a "good Muslim": "In Islamist *jihad*, killing is not just a means to an end; means and end have merged. The samurai, or the feudal warrior in general, does not derive pleasure from the act of killing itself; the pleasure springs from the feeling of a job well done, according to the requirements of *bushido*. The Islamist does and broadcasts it."[15] This distinctive merging of the means and ends manifest the way the divinity and violence are merged in jihadism. Violence, God, and Islam are difficult to distinguish in jihadism: violence is worship and serves a larger divine plan, though it even sometimes appears as an object of worship. Militant apocalyptic thought is the exemplar of this phenomenon: violence is an inherent part of the divine plan to bring the divine reign. Violent jihad is worship—it enacts and provides fulfilment here on earth—and brings the divine plan to fulfilment. Yet, in doing so, violence is celebrated in such a way that appears to be rejoiced in for itself and its powerful transcendence.

Girard's anthropology helps to understand the connection between violence and Islam in militant jihadism. Girard shows that violence is such an overwhelmingly transcendent and transfixing experience for the mimetic human group that it becomes externalized. It is projected onto a third party as a sacred being and end in itself, which is explained and justified. The rationale for violence articulates a vision of life in which violence is externalized and perpetuated under the cover of the sacred. In archaic terms, the role of violence is never clear, because the group has sacralized and so not come to terms with its own violence. In the case of contemporary extremism, violence has become transparent and public. With the revelation of the victim exposing violence, it needs to be more consciously and "rationally" embraced. In this sense, jihadist violence is embraced as the manifestation of the divine will—as a form of externalization that is totally open and convinced of its righteous violence.

Furthermore, when violent acts are performed the vision of a jihadist paradise is enacted. Yet, this vision is always referring itself back to its foundational act: scapegoating violence. The ISIS regime in Syria and Iraq bears this out: it was characterized by daily violence enacted along strict lines of prohibition and exclusion. The lives of true Muslims must be "pure," according to the militant logic, requiring that jihadist regimes will always require violence to police itself. Such violence is enacted on others—enemies, traitors, or apostates—to sustain itself. Similarly, the rule of the Taliban in Afghanistan was characterized by regular violence, which was legally and theologically sanctioned, with public spectacles against "criminals" and regular jihadist warfare against rebels and enemies.[16] These campaigns were a way to expand territory, channel internal tension outward, and reinforce the sacred qualities of the regime. These regular jihads were required under the Taliban to ensure the destruction of enemies and to avoid a reversion to internal violence (which characterized Afghanistan before the Taliban rule).[17]

Sacred Totalitarianism in the Name of God, the Defender of Victims

At the heart of the jihadist's sacred violence is, as discussed in Chapter 4, a rationale that privileges the defense of select and constructed Muslim victims. Of course, in undertaking violence in the name of victims, new victims are created. This violence creates unanimity among jihadists that fuels a process of sacralization in which new, unrecognized victims/scapegoats are created (i.e., unrecognized as a scapegoat by the radical Islamists). This process parallels archaic religion in creating a scapegoat and externalizing the transcendent power of scapegoating onto a third party (namely, the victim). However, jihadism uses the revelation of the victim to do so, and projects violence onto God (as the third party) rather than the victim.

By taking the position of those who regard themselves as victimized and oppressed, jihadism parallels other modern totalitarianisms, such as Nazism and communism, in the effort to re-sacralize violence in the name of the state, ideology, the nation, or the divinity. As discussed, the process of sacralization transfers the transcendent power of violence from the victim to the divinity and the mob. The same process of violent sacralization that is witnessed in jihadism occurs in other forms of totalitarianism (e.g., Nazism or communism): an oppressed class is identified (the nation, race, or the working class), and ideological agents claim that they must violently set matters right. Their success is due to a transcendent power—for example, the Fatherland or the proletariat—which brings about a utopian world order. This new order strictly applies a vision of life through brutal violence. Moreover, the totalitarian regime claims to be surrounded by constant threats (e.g., dissidents or traitors) who are regarded as a monstrous and ever-threatening mob that will potentially overwhelm the group/state unless it responds with strong "defensive" violence. In this way, totalitarianism justifies its ongoing repressive violence that is institutionalized in the organs of the state.[18]

Jihadists, thus, deploy the same type of violence and sacred justifications as "secular" totalitarian regimes to reinvigorate their own violence. The use of violence in jihadism has become ever more brazen and explicit in a "hyper" form of sacralization. The sacralization that is sought by jihadists presents their desperation to bring about a new transcendent order through the scapegoating mechanism as well as the increasing ineffectiveness of this mechanism to bring about such a transcendent order. More and more "infidels" are sought out for sacrifice to an arbitrarily constructed system of sacralized violence (much like the Aztec system needed increasing numbers of victims to feed a failing sacrificial system). Yet, while there seems to be a return to archaic forms of religiosity in jihadism, there is an important difference: the victims of the jihadists are not divinized. They are condemned as "dogs" and monsters, but they are not revered as supernatural gods, like victims in traditional cultures were (or, in some rare cases, are).

As discussed in Chapter 1, Girard argues that cultural difference is established and sacralized by divinizing the victim. Instead of identifying the power of reconciliation in the mob's action, the victim is attributed with supernatural power to mediate and unify all desire as the agent of both chaos and order. This is a crucial attribution for traditional cultures, as Girard shows, because it allows them to distance themselves from the dangerous power of violence and to justify their own precarious relationship with it. The inversion of the victorious mob and the scapegoated victim in this sacralized manner as worshipper and divinity, according to Girard, is the foundational cultural difference.

In the case of modern violence, however, the victim is not divinized by the mob (though the scapegoat may be given qualities that are excessive or exaggerated). According to the jihadists, the scapegoat remains a monstrous enemy who needs to be eliminated for the promotion of God's sacred order. The cause of this lack of divinization is, as discussed, the growing awareness of the innocence of the victim and the desacralization of violence that results. The attempts to re-sacralize human violence and culture by jihadists are an effort to counter the effects of desacralization and the nonviolent implications of the revelation of the innocent victim. In this way, militant jihadism represents a new stage in the sacralization of violence by seeking to reclaim the Abrahamic God to undergird a violent totalitarian order. Jihadism, then, is a more direct assault on the Abrahamic traditions (than other totalitarian systems) because it seeks to distort God's position in solidarity with the victims for violent purposes. On this basis, militant jihadism attempts to bury any awareness of the injustice of scapegoating under even more extreme forms of violence.

This new foundation for violence is so efficacious that it institutes new forms of unanimous violent transcendence. Through this transcendence, the monotheistic God and God's mob are divinized (or sacralized), instead of the scapegoat of jihadist violence. God is sacralized because violence is done in God's name on behalf of the victimized, which gives the jihadist mob a powerful rationale and experience of unanimity, purpose, and order. The jihadist mob, moreover, shares in the sacralization of God because they are "his agents" (which I discuss in more depth in the next section of this chapter). In this way, they become semi-divinized in association with the divinity in whose name sacred violence is accomplished. Violence, then, becomes the center of a new sacred system by appropriating and distorting existing Islamic frameworks around God.

The claim for a transcendent source for jihadist violence is important because modern protagonists of violence need to not only explain the experience of mimetic transcendence (as the archaic cultures did) but also the *moral* purpose of violence. They need to do this because the violence at the heart of culture has been desacralized and exposed as unjust through the revelation of the scapegoat. Jihadism is able to exploit the moral position of the Abrahamic God, who defends victims, for the purposes of totalitarian violence. Jihadists theologize and moralize violence in order to show that their violence is rational, just, and divinely ordained rather than something that is undertaken because of an archaic fear or duty.

These moral and theological justifications for violence are powerful because they license jihadist totalitarianism to seek total domination for the victims of an encroaching modernity. Jihadists are commissioned by the transcendent source of violence—God—to construct a total Islamist system that is truly just and well-ordered. In this way, the mimetic mobilization of people through militant jihadism seeks a total unanimity aimed at nothing but domination. In pursuit of this total system, the jihadist violently and frenetically constructs absolute differences in order to fight a loss of cultural difference and to rebuild a desacralized world in the midst of a collapsing and fragmented identity. In this sense, they counter the forces of modernity through violence that has escalated to a new level: victims are clearly targeted and put on display rather than covered up and hidden (which even other totalitarian systems did); and violence is celebrated. Moreover, those who perpetrate jihadist violence—whether as combatants or suicide bombers—are counted as glorious warriors or martyrs who gain eternal renown.[19] This discourse exalts the self-of-acquisitive-desire, who is totalized in an intense communion embedded in absolute rivalry and inherently wedded to violence.

Though the jihadist directly attempts to subvert the Abrahamic traditions by appropriating God for the purposes sacred violence, jihadism mirrors other totalitarianisms in putting absolute meaning in what Girard calls "a general and permanent mobilization of being in the service of nothingness."[20] Like other totalitarianisms, jihadists seek a moral purpose in their transcendent source of violence—God and the Islamic law/state—to license and motivate their mobilization and violence. Instead of fascist or communist ideology, jihadists justify their violence through a radical interpretation of who God is and of Islam.

Yet, the force with which jihadists seek to construct their system indicates they are fighting a formidable opponent—both in themselves and in the ineffectiveness of their violence to bring personal and collective integration. This struggle, according to Girard, is a sign that violence is actually losing its potency to unite people and is increasingly seen as a futile way to construct identity and order (at least on its own).[21] The result is that resort to violence is becoming more deliberate and extreme:

> Once unbridled, the principle of reciprocity no longer plays the unconscious role it used to play. Do we not now destroy simply to destroy? Violence now seems deliberate, and the escalation to extremes is served by science and politics.
>
> Is this a principle of death that will finally wear itself out and open onto something else? Or is it destiny? I do not know. However, what I can say is that *we can see the growing futility of violence, which is now unable to fabricate the slightest myth to justify and hide itself.*[22]

Jihadism challenges "the growing futility of violence" by seeking to remythologize and re-sacralize violence in the name of the God. The unconscious mendacity of the traditional systems of violence is being replaced by conscious celebration of violence, meaning the perpetrators are more overt about what they do. Militant jihadism, then, is the resort of an extreme fringe to "push-back" against a disconcerting, pluralistic (post-)modernity, in which desacralization, or "secularization," is dominant. The "hyper-sacralizing" of violence—which is claimed to be morally and theologically upright—is regarded by the jihadists as their major point of differentiation from the "corrupt" secular world. Their violent pursuit of divinely ordained boundaries and laws is the only way to save the world from the threat of a baseless modernity:

> What the Muslim really sees is that religious prohibition rituals are a force that keeps the community together, which has totally disappeared or is on the way out in the West. People in the West are united only by consumerism, good salaries, etc. The Muslims say: "their weapons are terribly dangerous but as a people they are so weak that their civilization can easily be destroyed."[23]

The jihadist's "righteous" violence, then, seeks to bring about a stable cultural and religious system—a total system—that is fully orientated to and authorized by the divine. This system provides the true way of living in the midst of a confused and evil world led by the West and corrupt Muslim regimes. In this sense, jihadist violence is constitutive of the ordered reign of God—and is its most fundamental contradiction. As the Abrahamic traditions fundamentally show, sacred violence against victims cannot bring true order and peace but only ongoing strife. Therefore, as mimetic rivalry moves to extremes in the modern world, so the structures of sacred violence are taken to their extreme to attempt to address this instability. Yet, in doing so, violence reveals itself more clearly as the heart of worship, culture, and politics in totalitarian systems like that of the jihadists.

Hyper-Sacralizing Violence: Transferring Sacred Power to Totalitarian Agents

As discussed, rather than the transcendent power of violence being ascribed to the victim/scapegoat, it is ascribed to a third party—God—in jihadism. Yet, there is one further important step. Once God is violently sacralized, this "God" commissions the jihadist group in a sacred mission to bring about the domination of the true religion and society, Islam. Rather than seeing the victim-god in control (like in the archaic mode), the jihadist sees their construction of God—their idol and repository of transcendent violence—as in control, and so, by extension, they regard themselves as having been delegated power over violence because of their divine commission. The jihadist is, then, the agent of God, because God (ironically) does not act on his own behalf; rather the jihadist acts on God's behalf, supposedly with God's blessing and help, to deploy brutal forms of violence. God, in this schema, is really an idolatrous projection of the jihadists' own power, like a mob addicted to the transcendent power of indiscriminate violence.

In modern violence, then, the totalitarian mob is covertly sacralized along with "God." For this reason, the jihadist mob wishes to be seen to be in direct relationship with violence rather than to distance itself from it. For jihadists, moreover, God and violence become so entwined that the distinction between the two is almost lost: violence is the means of worship and becomes a kind of object of worship. For traditional cultures, violence was not usually the object of motivation or worship, though it was the cause of their sacred projections. Sacrificial violence was only a means to order. Jihadism, on the other hand, takes violence to an idolatrous and frightening extreme: total victory or destruction in the name of the ultimate power, God.

Thus, jihadists become divine agents of violence as a sacralized collective acting on behalf of God for victims. The jihadists are entitled to wield this violence on behalf of God because they are morally righteous in their supposed adherence to Islamic law and engagement with jihad to protect select victims and achieve an Islamic caliphate. This collective is led by a righteous leader (caliph) who is said to rule on behalf of Allah (who possesses true sovereignty).[24] The leader represents the full transference of violent divine authority to humanity (usually claimed with reference to the sharia and the Qur'an), which gives the leader and his group the ability to wield absolute power and violence. A totalitarian system is founded, then, with the mob as its sacred and semi-divine agents.

This transference of sacred violence onto a transcendent figure, such as the state or God, and then onto the human agents of violence, is paralleled in other forms of totalitarianism, including "secular" forms. For example, in East Timor during Indonesian occupation (1975–99), the state became the transcendent center from which agents of the state could inflict various and wide-ranging forms of violence on victims:

> For the purposes of the Indonesian state, the victim was not divinised as in archaic religions, though he or she was attributed with blame and the power to disrupt the social order. Instead of worshipping the victim, then, the state transferred the power of victimage onto itself by having the victim legitimate the state's monopolisation of violence and the rivalry the state had created [between the state/people and the victims/enemies], and by spreading propaganda about the victim as a deviant or subversive enemy. Rather than the victim being sacralised, the state became the depository of the violent sacred as it determined blame and order (which even the victim recognised).[25]

On this basis, the perpetrators of violence (the agents of the state) were willing to be explicitly identified with the power of violence through the mediation of the transcendent third party, the "sacred" nation-state. This situation was exemplified in torture where, if successful, the victim ascribed blame onto him—or herself (through confession) and so justified the violent actions of the state agents in forcing this confession. This confession, in turn, justified the omnipotent status of the state, and its total monopoly on violence, because the state had "protected" the populace and social order through righteous violence. This, then, further justified the state in deploying extreme violence against dissident populations or groups, so to create totalitarian "order."[26]

Both the totalitarian state and jihadist groups sacralize violence by attributing it to an external agent (the state or God) and by way of the external agent, to themselves. Accordingly, in the case of the religious agents, jihadists become the guardian of the divine will and order, meaning that they can target anyone for punishment or praise in the name of the Almighty (who is, ironically, also claimed to be all-merciful by jihadists[27]). Like the totalitarian state seeking enemies and dissidents, jihadist groups create rivalries and seek to justify them by reference to divinely commissioned violence that is structured around a discourse and imagination of enemies. These groups become like the archaic sacred by distributing disorder and order, though in a conscious and deliberate manner. For example, just like the Indonesian state in East Timor, AQI/ISIS perpetrated brutal violence to provoke rivalry and conflict in Iraq. This violence included sectarian violence against the Shia, as well as repressive violence directed against the Sunni. Both forms were indiscriminate, with victims often chosen at random. The sectarian violence was aimed to turn the Sunni population to the AQI so that they could become the saviors and protectors of the people "in a cycle of escalating violence and fear," while the repressive violence against the Sunni was meant to eliminate any potential dissent:

> For AQI's campaign was driven by a brutal political logic: in provoking the Shi'a, Zarqawi [AQI leader] hoped to back the Sunni community into a corner, so that his group would be all that stood between Sunnis and the Shi'a death squads, giving people no choice but to support AQI, whatever they thought of its ideology. This cynical strategy—founded on a tacit recognition that AQI's beliefs were so alien to most Iraqis that they'd never find many takers unless backed by trickery and force—meant that Shi'a killing Sunni was actually good for AQI, and so they'd go out of their way to provoke the most horrific violence against their own people. … Like gangsters running a protection racket, they themselves created the violence from which they offered to protect people. Why leave it to chance?[28]

This most extreme of "protection rackets" deployed a reprehensible form of strategic violence. It led the protagonists of violence to become increasingly attached and addicted to violence and to engage in more extreme uses of it to ensure their totalitarian rule was established. Yet, while perpetrating violence in order to save people seems to correlate with the archaic sacred, the intentionality behind the deployment of totalitarian violence differentiates it. In the archaic schema, the sacred is believed to inflict and save people from violence, though the discovery of the sacred's power, and its continued bestowal, is not believed to be in the group's exclusive control. In modern totalitarianism, the situation of chaos is purposefully created by the violent agents in order to bring about the conditions whereby God or the state "saves" people. This action results in the state or jihadist group being directly identified with sacred violence, whereas the ancients generally feared being in close proximity to sacred violence.

Furthermore, the jihadist violence is construed as a public service because it is supposedly revelatory of injustice, which I discussed in Chapter 4. Though totalitarian violence seeks to provoke conflict and crisis, such manipulations are justified in the eyes of the jihadists because they expose the cause of modern Islam's malaise, namely, the oppression of the infidel or apostate enemy. According to jihadists, these enemies will not give up power easily, so jihadists believe they are actually serving oppressed Muslims by provoking their enemies into violence. According to Kepel, this kind of logic is displayed in the 9/11 attacks:

> The terrorism of September 11 was above all a provocation—albeit a provocation of gigantic proportions. Its purpose was to provoke a similarly gigantic repression of the Afghan civilian population and to build universal solidarity among Muslims in reaction to the victimization and suffering of their Afghan brothers. In this second act of the terrorists' drama, the roles are reversed: the attacker becomes passive, and he himself is attacked, while the original victim of terrorism becomes the prime mover. ... The terrorist actor would then have attempted to become the catalyst of a mass movement of outrage, driven by the language of jihad against the "impious" invaders of Islamic land who massacre innocent Muslims.[29]

Thus, while 9/11 struck a major blow to the United States, it was ultimately aimed to manufacture a crisis in which the "real problem" of the modern world—the apostasy and idolatry of the jihadists' enemies—would be revealed. To reveal such apostasy and idolatry is a service to Islam, in the jihadist view. Nevertheless, it is an act of scapegoating in which jihadists wrongly attribute the cause of a cultural, theological, and metaphysical crisis to their enemies. Thus, just like the totalitarian nation-state, jihadists intentionally resort to sacred violence that seeks to define a global order around such violence.

In seeking to provoke conflict and bring about a totalitarian order, jihadism is apocalyptic. In provoking rivalry and crisis through violence, jihadists believe they will bring about a definitive conflict in which divine judgment will effect true cultural and cosmological harmony. This harmonious state is realized when the jihadist version of Islam gains its rightful place of domination in the religious and cultural pecking order. In order to bring this about, jihadists ritualistically sacrifice themselves as suicide bombers or combatants in service of their totalitarian vision, as part of which they establish a mimetic model and in so doing enforce individual and group identity. Ultimately, jihadist apocalypticism is a self-fulfilling prophecy that relies on a negative mimetic logic: violence to provoke violence.

Conclusion

In this chapter, I have contended that militant jihadism represents a totalitarian effort to re-sacralize violence, so to institute a new type of order that would be as effective as the archaic system but which is more intentionally violent. Jihadists undertake this task in a way that fetishizes and celebrates violence, moving beyond how traditional cultures imitated and contained violence. The jihadists' violence is enacted under the cover of the divinity, on whose behalf they deploy violence, aggregating the power of violence to the jihadist state or group. In this way, the aim of the jihadists is to establish a totalitarian state justified under the omnipotent power of the re-sacralized deity. Though such a system cannot last, it provides a potent answer to the dilemma of modernity, especially when justified with reference to the Abrahamic God and Islamic doctrine and practice. I have suggested that reference to God in jihadism is a projection of sacred violence that distorts and weaponizes the belief of the Abrahamic traditions in a God who stands with victims. Such a weaponized God is a potent, though ultimately ineffective, way of addressing the personal and collective identity issues manifest in jihadism. In this sense, jihadism is a totalitarianism "in service of nothingness," lacking positive value, and dependent on an idolatry of absolute rivalry and violence.[30]

While I have identified the anthropological dimensions of jihadist totalitarianism in this section, there are further metaphysical and theological dimensions that require exploration. In particular, the distinctive characteristic of jihadist totalitarianism—its reference to God—requires further examination. While I affirm Girard's account of the sacred to explain the reference to the divine or the supernatural in both archaic and modern forms of violence, I believe there is an underlying metaphysical and theological dimension to this attribution that is not fully identified in Girard's work or, more generally, in work on militant jihadism. This metaphysical dimension is present in the jihadists' reference to God in commissioning their violence. Girard hints at this dimension, but his work needs further development, in order to fully understand the nature of the modern reference to God in sacred violence. Thus, in the next section, I take up the task of analyzing the metaphysical and theological dimensions of sacred violence. Following Chapter 9, I then conclude this study with some reflections in Chapter 10 on how sacred violence can be countered within the Islamic tradition and the Abrahamic traditions more broadly by cultivating a way of life imbued with "the holy."

[illegible]

Part III

The Idolatry and Future of Militant Jihadism

9

Why is God Part of Human Violence?

The Idolatrous Nature of Militant Jihadism

In the previous section, I argued that there are two overlapping crises out of which militant jihadism emerges: the crisis of modernity, connected to the breakdown of sacred structures; and the crisis in the Muslim-majority world, connected to the colonial and postcolonial experience, the advent of the nation-state, and certain trends in Islamic thought. The answer to these crises provided by militant jihadists takes the form of an Islamic modernity structured around a totalitarian system. This jihadist totalitarianism is based on a modern form of sacred violence justified in reference to God, which directly challenges efforts to desacralize God in the Abrahamic traditions. As part of this sacred totalitarian violence, jihadists are willing to execute violence in ruthless and indiscriminate ways, supported by a conspiratorial and apocalyptic worldview.

A central claim of militant jihadists is that they are the only legitimate actors on behalf of God, which licenses apocalyptic and indiscriminate forms of violence. In this claim, a perennial question arises: Why does violence need to be justified with reference to God (or the divinity/the sacred/the supernatural)? As discussed, René Girard argues that collective human violence is invariably connected to some point of transcendent reference—what he calls "the sacred"—which is a projection and justification for scapegoating violence. While this account helps to explain the reference to God in jihadist violence, I argue that there is a further dimension that can shed light on the question of divinely commissioned violence. It is the neglected metaphysical dimension to Girard's work that presents an underlying or natural sense of the divine Other inherent in human consciousness, which coincides with forms of natural theology. I demonstrate this natural sense of the divine through an analysis of the nature of mimetic relations and sacred violence (with respect to the divinization of the victim), while also surveying approaches in the cognitive science and evolution of religion. I further argue that the effort at violent re-sacralization of God in jihadism is inconsistent with the Abrahamic traditions, which seek to reveal the innocence of the victim and promote a nonviolent, merciful God. In this way, jihadist groups can be shown to be idolatrous in both an anthropological sense and a theological sense, which is significant in that this undermines their own claims to speak and act for God.

"Why God?" Reflections on Cognitive Science and Evolutionary Studies

Though I have argued that militant jihadism is modern in its totalitarian structure and violence, the jihadist reference to God seems to be contrary to secular trends in modernity. Partly for this reason, jihadists enthusiastically embrace it as a form of resistance to modernity. Nevertheless, despite its mimetic and conflictual character, it is important to recognize that militant jihadists, on the whole, have a sincere belief in God. What kind of God they believe in has been heavily critiqued in this study, but they believe in some kind of monotheism nonetheless. This monotheistic belief, as I have argued previously, is heavily determined and colored by what Girard calls the violent sacred. Yet, this belief seems deeply held within the jihadist movement, and more broadly, within the Islamic world. Moreover, it provides the foundation for jihadist ideology and violence.

In this sense, there remains a question about why humans specifically resort to the category of the divinity (or the sacred) to justify and even motivate their own violence, beyond the mimetic dynamics of such an attribution. As Girard rightly points out, the category of the sacred (expressed in human cultures as gods, demons and, various spirits) provides a repository for violent transcendence against a victim. Yet, as Gil Bailie asks, why does "a suddenly hushed mob" mistake "its hapless victim for a god" and not some other type of being?[1] Why do humans not postulate an impersonal force or a really powerful human, animal, or spirit as the cause of their violence? Why is the category of divinity—as opposed to other types of agents—even part of the human worldview? For Girard, this also seems to be a question, because in one of his later works, he seems less definitive about the sacred as only being a projection. Girard states the sacred is "possibly tied" to the "emotional and cognitive event" of scapegoating.[2] Girard is not questioning that the violent sacred is a projection of human violence, but he may be suggesting that there is more underlying or informing it.

The question of the divine and supernatural world has increasingly occupied the attention of scholars in evolutionary studies, cognitive science, and psychology. Atran and Norenzayan note that belief in supernatural gods is universally present across known cultures, in what they call a "counterfactual and counterintuitive manner."[3] These beliefs involve costly public and material commitments and rituals, which seem to assuage existential anxieties.[4] In seeking to account for belief in the supernatural, they argue that religion is a "cultural by-product of the complex evolutionary landscape" that uses "ordinary cognitive processes" to display a commitment to the worlds governed by supernatural agents.[5] For example, the readiness of humans to perceive agency in diverse phenomena about which they experience uncertainty suggests to these authors an explanation for the universality of supernatural agents.[6]

The kind of evolutionary and cognitive explanation for the supernatural that scholars such as Atran and Norenzayan construct relies on the human capacity to discern intentionality and agency, and the propensity to ascribe both to nonrational or nonhuman agents. While Atran and Norenzayan discuss the emotional and existential dimensions of religion, their explanation for the prevalence of the supernatural essentially revolves around cognition and intentionality:

> In sum, supernatural agents are readily conjured up because natural selection has trip-wired cognitive schema for agency detection in the face of uncertainty. Uncertainty is omnipresent; so, too, is the hair-triggering of an agency-detection mechanism that readily promotes supernatural interpretation and is susceptible to various forms of cultural manipulation. Cultural manipulation of this modular mechanism and priming facilitate and direct the process. Because the phenomena created readily activate intuitively given modular processes, they are more likely to survive transmission from mind to mind under a wide range of different environments and learning conditions than entities and information that are harder to process. As a result, they are more likely to become enduring aspects of human cultures, such as belief in the supernatural.[7]

Atran and Norenzayan are leading figures in the field of psychology and evolution of religion, and they present compelling arguments for the "problem" of the prevalence of the supernatural across human cultures. They essentially argue that our cognitive abilities provide the grounds to discern intentionality and agency, which could then lead to formulations of supernatural agents to explain phenomena (as part of which cultures direct and manipulate this capacity). For example, the invisibility of the causality for the agency that humans identify with the supernatural (e.g., the stirring of wind[8]) may lend itself to postulating invisible entities.

Atran and Norenzayan present a kind of "god of the gaps" assumption that ascribes agency and causation to supernatural beings, in the absence of other evidence, or a scientific approach to explaining the world. This explanation for belief in the supernatural seems to make a large leap. It moves from humans who have naturally selected cognitive abilities with implicit agency detection, to humans who suddenly formulate a complex notion like a supernatural agent to satisfy this agency detection. How and why would humans do this? It is tempting to make this leap because humans stubbornly ascribe agency to a range of transcendent (nonphysical) supernatural entities (which in traditional forms can be resistant to natural causation). Nevertheless, these entities need not be gods, as is demonstrated by the range of nonhuman entities that humans ascribe agency to, including large animals, hybrid creatures, monsters, or impersonal forces such as karma. Moreover, not all supernatural entities are invisible. People or groups across time and cultures claim to have seen them or experienced them in some way. Humans also identify a range of physical actions with the gods or other supernatural entities that have clear physical causation (even actions that ostensibly originate from a human agent).

In a similar way, other arguments that seek to account for belief in God and religion in a determinative way contain problems. For example, those that posit content bias as the basis for religion, such as for reasons of memory, fitness or plausibility, still fail to adequately and fully address why gods and other supernatural entities are even thought of, compared to other possibilities.[9] In these kinds of arguments, there seems to be an automatic equation of belief in the supernatural with human cognitive capacities which leaves questions begging and intermediate steps unexamined.

While the above approach from Atran and Norenzayan (and others) could explain the preconditions for thought and belief about the supernatural, it is not a complete explanation for the particular historical manifestation of such thought and belief in all their variety and complexity. It may be true that humans are inclined toward meaning-making and are able to detect or discern agency, causation, and purpose. These capacities, moreover, may have given humans a means to understand the physical world and to discern a deeper structure, agency, and power to life than the physical world. Yet, a propensity for agency detection does not automatically equate with the production of the idea of God or the gods (in the sense of a transcendent, non-earthly entity/being), especially a God or gods with various characteristics such as being "all-powerful." One is not necessarily causative of the other, as Barrett stresses: a capacity does not give rise to its object.[10] To argue that a capacity does give rise to an object is already to assume that the object does not exist and to replace it with a deterministic solution.

Furthermore, a study of the history of religions presents one with a variety of supernatural beings with varying abilities and forms. It also presents a range of debates and different perspectives on how to exactly understand the divinity or supernatural world, especially because those in religious contexts have had particular rational, ritualistic, and evidential concerns or philosophical and theological pre-occupations. To ignore these is to reduce the nature and variety of human thought and belief to a series of cognitively determined steps.

Another problem that is not faced by Atran and Norenzayan is the nature of knowledge and interpretation. To posit that humans have capacities for discerning supernatural agents or realms requires defining what type of knowledge is involved and how humans came to such knowledge. Human intellectual capacity opens people to the possibility of knowledge about the world and the deeper structures of life, but it requires cultural formation and social symbolic systems to actualize. It also involves rational and meaningful deliberation.[11] To argue that humans think of the most powerful being possible to address their agency detection of strange events or forces still leaves the question of knowledge and interpretation begging: how and why did humans *think* of these beings (within the context of their symbol-making systems) rather than just automatically formulate them based on some kind of agency detection? Detection of objects and formulations of agency require some kind of interpretation, based on a symbolic system that is culturally formed.

Thus, there are still fundamental questions to answer about why humans refer to the divine or supernatural realm. At best, the mental capacities of humans only explain the likely preconditions for receptivity to certain ways of thinking about the supernatural. They do not fully account for the process within individuals and social contexts for the actualization of religious beliefs. It may be that, as Barrett argues, human minds have evolved in such a way that encouraged them or left them open to receive a notion of the gods and other supernatural agents, however, this does not determine its outcome or historicity.[12] This propensity may be because of common mental tools or structures (such as agency detection, meaning-making, and purpose discernment). The cognitive "tool-kit" of the human, Barrett suggests, indicates a natural disposition for contemplation of and belief in the supernatural (as well as other types of phenomena), which provides the basis for reflective thinking about God in human cultures.[13] While this toolbox theory is contested, Barrett largely avoids the deterministic mistake that would draw a direct line between a capacity and a particular object.[14]

Thus, an approach that focuses solely or primarily on the human mind does not adequately account for the historical manifestations of supernatural concepts and their attendant beliefs, as well as their variability and contestations. It fails to account for the complex rational discussions and traditions around the supernatural, as well as how the religious and cultural experiences of the supernatural (what might be called outside stimuli) influence the mind. Moreover, it does not explain the nature and passion of faith in God or gods.[15] To take the potentialities and conditions of the human mind as the sole reason for why the supernatural appears in human consciousness is to provide a reductionist answer to a complex issue. Ultimately, it simplifies and reduces the rich experiences and conceptualizations of the supernatural in a form of cognitive determinism.[16]

In this regard, special care and rigorous thinking are required to understand the nature of human knowledge and interpretation, especially with regard to God. Human knowledge is not merely generated automatically by cognitive capacities nor is such knowledge just concerned with abstract concepts. Human knowledge and understanding are embedded in meanings and values that operate at different levels: material, social, cultural, religious, and so on.[17] Knowledge of the supernatural is connected to the capacity that humans have for transcendent meaning and interpretation. In this sense, religious experience and knowledge are important to address in their specificity, especially as they attempt to address the experience and capacities of the whole human person (and his/her experience, interpretative capacity, and nature). This knowledge is broader than intellectual or cognitive capacities alone. Thus, to account for the supernatural requires more than an account of the mind; it requires an account of the full human person in their capacity for meaning, relationality, and transcendence.

Why Is God Involved in Human Violence?

To begin grappling with the human engagement with God and why God is used to support human violence, one must recognize the complexity and richness of human thought about the superntural. Even though supernatural entities in some forms are universally posited by human cultures, it seems strange to the scientific mind that these entities appear so consistently and in the forms that they do—in their diversity, and in comparison to the many other possibilities that they could have taken. Yet, a scientific approach (whether cognitive or biological) struggles to address this phenomenon. In order to ask why the supernatural is relevant to human lives and cultures, we must consider the following questions, at least as a starting point: Why have humans conceived of supernatural agents when they could have just explained reality by reference to powerful animals, creatures, or natural forces like the wind? Why is such powerful personal agency ascribed to supernatural agents (in specific places and times) and not ascribed in the same way to an unknown powerful human agent or to superhumans (e.g., superheroes or giants) or to an unknown species of physical beings (e.g., more powerful primates or aliens)? Why would humans use the supernatural or divine category at all, as opposed to other types of categories? Even in a "scientific age," there are a variety of nonhuman agents (e.g., nation-states, the market, spirits, deities, superheroes, angels) that so-called modern people refer to or believe in, in order to speculate about the nature of the universe or explain various phenomenon, systems, or events.[18]

There is a sense to these questions that there is a sheer strangeness and audacity to supernatural language and thought. This strangeness is particularly pronounced in a secular context where naturalism predominates, making supernatural terms and concepts "counterintuitive" and contradictory. The modern scientific age seems to challenge awareness of the supernatural, particularly by demanding empirical proofs. Moreover, it does not universally contain a cultural default belief in or intuition about the supernatural.[19] In this context, then, it is easy to produce simplistic explanations for complex phenomena such as religion and belief in the supernatural that seem strange, alien, and even irrational to a certain construction of the scientific worldview.

There is, however, a natural-ness to the consciousness of the supernatural for many of those who believe in and relate with God or gods. There is also a rationality to it for those who have reasoned about God's origins and existence, such as Thomas Aquinas. Moreover, traditions such as Christianity and Islam have considered the origins of the consciousness and desire for God (or the supernatural) in order to determine the basis for religious experience and knowledge about God. Like the cognitive science of religion, natural theology seeks to explain why people universally think about the supernatural, but it does so by taking the belief in God(s) seriously.[20]

As mentioned, the capacities and orientation of the human mind offer some insights into the preconditions for thought and belief about the supernatural. However, we need to broaden the inquiry into the question of God by reflecting more generally on the nature of human beings. Something of an answer to this dilemma is suggested in Girard's own account of human desire, violence, and religion. His mimetic understanding suggests a deeper level underlying the question of God and divinely sanctioned violence.

As discussed, the sacred provides order to human relations as a projection of scapegoating violence. It does so by (temporarily) answering the existential dilemma and yearning of humans for definitive mimetic transcendence and fulfillment in relationship with the other. The sacred is not merely a sociological device, but it concerns our very being in mimesis. Moreover, the ontological drive or need that underlies mimetic violence particularly manifests itself in the human subject's attempt to grasp at the other's object of desire. It is, fundamentally, an effort to gain the metaphysical or existential depth that the model seems to have in possessing a certain object. This ontological or metaphysical dimension of the subject–model relationship, which can manifest in positive (admiring) or negative (envious) forms, gives humans their distinctive capacity for self-determination and relationship with the other. This ontological dimension, which Girard calls "metaphysical desire," orients the subject to yearn for and seek perfect or self-sufficient being.[21] Each human being, in other words, seeks the fulfilment and perfection of their lives, and they historically actualize this search through their mimetic relations with others. Because the human subject does not possess this self-sufficiency, he/she seeks it in others—a process that is generally unsuccessful because of the imperfection of other human models. Nevertheless, the human subject remains in search of a perfect, self-sufficient model. Thus, humans are inherently and naturally orientated toward this search, that is, they feel its ontological urgency and need. In a sense, then, the following statement from Girard can be made more comprehensible: "Mimetic desire is also the desire for God."[22]

This general search for the perfect Other must be actualized in a symbolic system in which a historical agent is at the center. According to Girard, this agent is the divinized victim. This victim prompts an identification with the perfect Other as human groups encounter the victim's manifest power in the process of scapegoating. The victim is the transcendent referent, and so, fulfils the role of absolute Other gifted with supernatural powers. The victim, who is regarded as having reconciled a warring group following scapegoating, becomes, then, the center of a symbolic system in which he/she becomes the very definition of "in and out," "right and wrong," "good and evil." The supernaturalized victim contrasts to the human group which could not even reconcile itself:

> The victim is the focal point of the whole scapegoating event because these hominids are more or less "aware" that they have committed something "wrong," and are at the same time struck by the restored peace and the blissful bond they perceive as a result of the killing of the victim. This complex system of instinctual patterns and emotional effects produces a form of "short circuit" in their perception, which has to be elaborated on a higher level. First of all, even though the mechanism is totally endogenous, it is perceived as something *external*. ... Then, the focal point of the mechanism is, again, the victim—a natural source of this "something" that has to be treasured, becoming *sacred*.
>
> This "gift" of restored peace and the blissful bond also induced the primitive mind mimetically to *repeat* this event, perceived as the most effective way of acquiring peace and solidarity within the group in moments of crisis. In the "superstitious" repetition of the event, a form of "staging" in the shape of a killing of a surrogate victim had to be set in place. ... It is *the first symbolic sign* ever invented by these hominids. It is the first moment in which something *stands* for *something else*. It is the ur-symbol.[23]

The first victim is divinized, then, and made the absolute center of the human symbolic system. The human group sees itself as totally dependent on the victim-Other for life, stability, and prosperity—for everything that its members implicitly yearned for prior to the scapegoating. The divinization, in this sense, is undergirded by the group's discovery of mimetic unity and their drive for mimetic fulfilment.

Inherent in Girard's view of mimetic desire and the victim's divinization is *transcendence*. Humans are outwardly oriented and seek to move their material existence into a higher plane of mimetic and spiritual fulfillment in unity and reconciliation with the Other and so all others. This transcendence is culturally defined and culturally defining as it brings people together (or disunites them) in fundamental ways. Girard argues that cultures have been conventionally based around "deviated transcendency" that sacralizes powerful horizontal relations (scapegoating).[24] While this transcendence is deviated (as it is violent and persecutory), it is a form of transcendence that commonly recurs across human cultures, suggesting a common search for properly orientated vertical transcendency. Because humans struggle in this search, they revert to the only vertical relations they believe they've encountered, that of the encounter with the divinized victim. Yet, the use of "sacred violence," and the attempt to project cultural or religious structures as sacred, is contradictory and unsatisfying: it gains temporary mimetic fulfilment and unity through the expulsion of the other. The unsatisfying nature of this deviated transcendency is manifest in the temporary nature of the sacrificial resolution. Humans must resort to sacrificial violence again and again because they don't ultimately achieve long-lasting personal integration or cultural cohesion from it. By contrast, Girard associates "genuine religion" with the (divine) revelation of the innocent victim and what he calls "vertical transcendency," that is, properly orientated mimetic relationship with the divine model.[25]

Thus, the search for the perfect Other, which becomes part of the projection of the sacred onto the victim, is historically unfulfilled. Mob violence never delivers permanent mimetic transcendence and fulfilment. This unfulfilled yearning and search for the perfect Other can be regarded as the fundamental anthropological basis for religion and for the reference to divinity in human cultures. However, the way in which the sacred or the divinity is constructed historically in human cultures—through scapegoating violence—is a distortion or displacement of the sense of the perfect Other. This distorted conception arises as a result of violent mimetic relations and consciousness. In the sacred victim, humans believe they have found the perfect Other—the divinity as they conceive of it—in the powerful, though morally disconcerting, effects of scapegoating a victim. The victim is regarded as the ultimate self-sufficient being: the one who sits outside human insecurity and disorder to manipulate and resolve it. Thus, the victim is regarded as a god who has ultimate power and the fullness of being that we all seek (divinity). The divinized victim has the ultimate power over mimetic affairs as the self-sufficient one at the heart of the human symbolic system. Subsequent victimizations, following the failure of the temporary ritualistic system to imitate effectively the original "ur-event," produce more gods.[26]

The confusion of mimetic self-sufficiency (divinity) with human violence, then, leads to the construction of a divinity who is temporary and false but who has absolute power and violence ascribed to him/her. In this way, the transcendent yearning for being and communion, which manifests as a search for the perfect Other, is historically actualized as a projection onto another—a human victim—in what the Bible calls "idolatry." In other words, the truly transcendent Other—the one with authentic self-sufficient being, for which humans long—is replaced with lesser beings.

Thus, instead of the real "God," or religion per se, justifying violence, it is distorted desire, driven by the yearning for being, which justifies violence through the construction of a certain type of the divinity ("the sacred"). Violence fuels belief in this divinity through a deviated transcendence fundamentally motivated by a search for greater being and communion. This deviated transcendence is, moreover, justified by and attracted to a discourse that identifies and scapegoats enemies, as is evident in violent jihadism. Jihadists refer to God to justify its violence, then, by constructing a false notion of divine self-sufficiency to center its system of signification around absolute power and coercion. They do this in order to refuel the sacred violence that has lost its efficacy in modernity.[27]

The search for the Other (and being) is prior to human violence ontologically, though not necessarily historically.[28] The perfect Other is what humans are really searching for as a result of their unresolved and "ontologically needy" mimetic nature. The divinized victim is a historical instantiation of this perfect Other and catalyst for this search, but it is only a temporary and imperfect representation whose credibility is effective only as long as the scapegoating works to unite the members of the group. Once the effect of the scapegoating wears off, new scapegoats must be found to be make new gods (new centers of unity and signification), or new rituals of offering must be enacted to the gods. The search for God (and being) continues, but the particular instantiation changes. Thus, in this sense, the search for God is prior to the particular instances of scapegoating violence that result in divinized victims.

Thus, divinity need not just be a functional projection or creation of the human mind. The mimetic nature of humans and the scapegoating mechanism indicate that there is some deeper natural tendency in humans to search for divinity—for the ultimate and absolute being who can provide a true center to personal and collective identity. This divinity provides the group with meaningful and ultimate transcendence, which overcomes all mimetic problems and existential angst. In ascribing divinity to their victims, human groups inherently search for a Being that is greater than themselves, who knows and controls life in some fundamental way and who possesses perfect mimetic life. This search may be illusory, but I argue it is a natural and organic part of being human and mimetic—of the ontological necessity to seek answers to the chaotic dilemma of what it means to be human in mimetic relationship with others. This search for fulfilment and perfect being ("metaphysical desire") ultimately comes by way of communion with a Being who can provide definitive mimetic direction (*telos*), which is greater than the chaotic social life and unanimous violence human groups generally enact. In this way, a metaphysical or theological account of the natural desire for God is implicit within the psychological and anthropological account of desire and being that Girard provides.

God and Idolatry

The desire for God, then, seems to be implicit in mimetic transcendence and is even referred to by Girard as the desire for God.[29] Based on Girard's thought, what traditional Christian theology has termed the "desire for God" can be argued to be ultimately concerned with the orientation of human being in mimetic transcendence toward a properly constituted vertical relation (with the divine) in pacific mimesis.[30] However, this transcendent or religious orientation can be deviated toward powerful horizontal relations (e.g., mob violence) that seem to provide vertical orientation but which is only temporary and ultimately unfulfilling. In this sense, mimetic rivalry seeks to take divinity from the wrong place—from the victimized other—and scapegoating seeks to manufacture it through false or deviated transcendence. These relations are organized around a metaphysical yearning for divinity—for fullness of being and communion—and a developing insight that human life is mimetically dependent on the Other—on a prior Being who is the only one ultimately capable of answering the yearning and call of human desire.[31]

Religious and cultural forms involve an explicit or implicit acknowledgment of the divine priority (however construed) and are orientated toward it.[32] Idolatry is when the divine priority and transcendent orientation of human beings are replaced by the false or violent sacred, such as the divinized victim in archaic rituals, or sacred ideology, market or nation in modernity. I identify jihadism in the latter category as replacing the divinity with their violent and sacred construction. This conception deviates from the Islamic tradition in important ways and is fundamentally orientated by powerful horizontal relations: by the transcendent power of social violence.

The identification of the transcendent orientation of humans and its idolatrous offshoots is not at odds with social science or critiques of "religion." Rather, it allows for a necessary recognition of human nature as grounded in a transcendent orientation (toward the divine), which is enacted through social relationships. Without this recognition, anthropology and other social sciences are ultimately incomplete in their ability to understand human phenomena, especially violence. This recognition only involves an acknowledgment of a "religious" form to culture in the sense of a transcendent orientation that attempts to cope with the implications of mimetic desire, metaphysical yearning, and social relationships. Girard shows that human cultures have generally been formed based on "archaic" religious forms centered on the sacred. He also identifies those religious forms, such as the biblical/Abrahamic traditions, that have sought to resist and demythologize the violent sacred. These traditions seek to transcend sacred violence (though they struggle to do so) in order to provide a permanent means to satisfy the transcendent yearnings of the human.

Girard has charted the development of the nonviolent revelation of the victim within Judaism and Christianity, as it struggled to emerge alongside historical recourse to sacred violence (e.g., in "historical Christianity"). In this, Girard presents that these traditions have a hermeneutical center that is shifting away from sacred violence toward the innocence and forgiveness of the victim. Palaver sees this same shift in Islam. These traditions, however, grapple with the power and legacy of sacred violence and can be twisted by such violence at times when their members revert to it. In particular places and times, these traditions have been drawn back into providing transcendent justification for sacred violence to restore social order.

It is in this sense that jihadism uses Islam as a modern vehicle for the restoration of a virulent form of the violent sacred by reinterpreting God as perpetrating and commissioning violence. By claiming to defend victims, jihadists appropriate the moral and transcendent power of the Abrahamic traditions in an effort to reinstitute sacred horizontal relations. This is a totalitarian effort as re-sacralizing horizontal relations in modernity requires harnessing the unstable power of mimetic rivalry and internal mediation. This effort involves a total and (semi-) conscious "mobilization" of violence to resuscitate the violent sacred as the center of culture, order, and power. Jihadism, like other totalitarianisms such as fascist nationalisms, communism, or reactionary fundamentalisms, seeks to substitute idolatrous and extreme forms of violent horizontal relations for vertical transcendence. Rabbi Jonathan Sacks calls these totalitarianisms the "substitutes" for religion.[33]

God and Jihadist Violence

It is significant that there is an explicit transcendent focus on the divinity in traditions such as Judaism, Islam, and Christianity. Militant jihadists seek to subvert and manipulate this element. Girard's theory suggests that this divine element reorientates the Abrahamic traditions, and the cultures under their influence, toward sympathy for and solidarity with the victimized. The particular problem that the Abrahamic traditions face, though, is that this sympathy for the victim, and the God who is claimed to seek it, can be manipulated by those who wish to re-sacralize them and use their trans-cultural reach to violently radicalize people. The very injunction to transcend sacred violence makes such traditions vulnerable to such a struggle because of the personal, cultural, and transcendent uncertainty that can result from rejecting sacred violence. Ironically and tragically, the transcendent orientation to the divine that defines them becomes contested as a means to re-sacralize violence, especially as other modern alternatives have failed such as that of totalitarian nationalism (Nazism) and ideology (communism).

Jihadist groups, then, are the latest effort to re-sacralize violence, but this time it is through the direct assault on and distortion of the traditions that have undermined sacred violence. Jihadism is like communism or Nazism in that they are all based on false transcendence, but by contrast, jihadism directly grows out of and distorts an Abrahamic tradition (Islam). Rather than rejecting God or conventional religion (as previous totalitarianisms have done), jihadism represents a new totalitarian tactic: to use and transform belief in God and Islam to justify an ugly and virulent form of the violent sacred. For this reason, I have sought to take account of the jihadists' emphasis on God and their doctrinal beliefs and show how they are distorted by the jihadists' deep connections with violence. Violent jihadism, then, is a totalitarian religiopolitical ideology—it seeks to become the only worldwide state—that is centered on the false transcendent of sacred violence that distorts who God is and how to worship God.

The appropriation of God and Islamic tradition for the purposes of violence can be understood with greater clarity, then, if the context of sacred violence is appreciated. The breakdown of sacred violence set off by the Abrahamic traditions (and expanding beyond them into secular and non-Western contexts) has, in an unintended manner, led to an effort to reconstitute that sacred violence by distorting the central tenets of the Abrahamic traditions—the relationship with God and the awareness of the innocent victim. Militant jihadists make unabashed claims for their violence based on the appropriation of the divine mission—it is they who are doing the true work of God to defend the victimized through sacred violence and bring about a new order of divine justice based around a caliphate. This divine commissioning for jihadists is seen as justifying their sacred violence in defense of the righteous victims against the enemy apostates and infidels.

The attempts to re-sacralize human violence and culture by jihadists are directly aimed at countering the effects of desacralization. As discussed in Chapter 8, the transcendent effects of violence are ascribed to the monotheistic God (rather than to the victim), and by way of God, to the jihadist group and its "religious system." Because jihadists cannot divinize their victims, they attempt to re-sacralize the divinity by association with the transcendent effects of their own violence—exalted as righteous and God-like. For this reason, they are much more explicit about their violence than those in traditional cultures. In contrast to archaic cultures, violence is not unconsciously pharmaceutical for the jihadist but rather is (semi) consciously seen as necessary and righteous surgery. This is an important move as it seeks to re-sacralize the God of the Abrahamic traditions—who, according to Girard and Palaver, reveals the nature of human violence and fundamentally stands against it. The jihadist views his/her construction of God as possessing absolute power to restore proper order—an order structured by insiders (true Muslims) and outsiders (apostates) and fueled by transcendent violence. Yet, this God does not undertake direct violence himself but rather divinely commissions the jihadists to have power over and "legitimately" execute violence. The jihadist becomes the true image of the transcendent God, who now demands violence rather than stands against it. The jihadist absolutely controls who God is and what God wants and does in the world—which is the ultimate idolatry.

In this way, the jihadist uses the violently re-sacralized category of divinity to fill deep existential and social gaps in modernity. Yet, while the jihadist solution may work for a time, it will be ultimately ineffective because its underlying diagnosis is wrong. The jihadist believes that the divinity requires violent worship so to bring about a true social order, whereas the real problem lies with the modern inability to use violence unanimously—that is, to attract and coerce all people into violence so the victims can be sacralized. Thus, militant jihadism cannot replicate the gods of old; it can only offer more victims in a vain effort to re-sacralize the God of victims. However, if jihadists reflected on God's association with victims in the Islamic tradition, it would be possible to realize that the God of victims could not really want more victims—and certainly not part of a misguided effort at divine justice and totalitarian order. To claim so is contradictory and misunderstands the God of the Abrahamic traditions.

This misunderstanding is the heart of jihadism's failure. Their God is not convincing—at least not for most Muslims and non-Muslims. Thus, as they fail in their efforts at a global order under the spell of their sacred violence, jihadists demonstrate a violent and frenetic grasping for being and identity. This same grasping, according to Girard, is at the heart of all human violence and has been exposed and accelerated by the desacralization caused by the revelation of the innocent victim. Unfortunately, this frenzied grasping will only escalate, until militant jihadism has exhausted its violence in a total disintegration of its unity and worldview.

Conclusion

This chapter has outlined how mimetic transcendence, which is undergirded by a metaphysical desire for divinity, is the essential driver in human identity, relations, and violence. It has proposed that the use of the category of the divine in sacred violence is related to the way that it arises in human consciousness through the influence of mimesis and metaphysical desire. It arises because of the universal, mimetic search for being and the Other, which is historically manifested in the construction of the violent sacred based on the transcendent effects of mob violence. Yet, this construction is idolatrous. Moreover, because scapegoating has been exposed and weakened, attempts to revive it take more extreme forms. In this way, the sacred reemerges in a new guise, unprotected by its previous sacred covering, but reenergized by its perversion of that which revealed it. Militant jihadism is a prominent purveyor of this perversion, seeking to distort and obscure the legacy of the Abrahamic traditions, which reveals human violence through a God who is in solidarity with all victims.

10

The Sacred and the Holy

Alternatives to Escalating Violence

My analysis has indicated that there is a battle at the heart of "secular" modernity, particularly with those utilizing forms of sacred violence that seek a return (of a modern kind) to the archaic sacred. While they have gained territory and still are a threat in a number of places, militant jihadists have failed in the short term to bring about a global order under their violent deity. Even ISIS's supposed Caliphate has lost its territory in the Middle East. The dynamics of mimetic rivalry that are evident in militant jihadism, which seek to bring the concept of absolute war to reality, have been repressed by an alliance of nation-states led by the United States. The question is whether this repression will last and what needs to be understood and done in the meantime with regard to militant jihadists beyond defeat on the battlefield.

In contrast to the previous chapters which have been primarily diagnostic, this chapter is constructive in that it reflects on what is fundamentally at stake in the battle with militant jihadism and proposes pathways to address the implications of militant jihadism both within Islam and, more broadly, in modernity. In particular, I conclude this study by reflecting on alternatives to the violent sacred worshipped in jihadist totalitarianism and ways in which sacred violence can be transcended. In doing this, I reflect in a more theological and mimetic key on the particular way that jihadism engages in sacred violence—that is, by distorting the insight into the innocent victim for violent purposes, which is projected on to God and results in the rejection of the nonviolent ethos developed in the Abrahamic traditions. On this basis, I discuss what in the Abrahamic traditions could counter this distortion of God and victimhood. Following this, I identify specific issues in Islam that are exploited or provoked by militant jihadism which seem to have led to the mis-use of the Islamic tradition as a vehicle for a re-sacralized modernity. I, then, go onto outline alternatives to sacred violence which I argue need to be grounded in properly orientated transcendence. This transcendence involves cultivating what Girard, based on Emmanuel Lévinas, refers to as "the holy," as the pacific mimetic alternative to "the sacred."[1] It can involve a nonviolent "secular" ethos (in the sense of eschewing the violent sacred), which itself can be imbued with a nonviolent vertical transcendence orientated to God. On this point, I reflect on Girard's notion of "innermost mediation" as important for orientating pacific forms of mimesis, as well as ways "the holy" can be embedded in politics and social practices. In this way, this chapter acts as a summary of and conclusion to the study.

Countering the Distortion of the Abrahamic Revolution

I have argued that militant jihadists seek to resuscitate the violent sacred in an intentionally totalitarian form, in order to transcend the supposed "corruption" and disorder of modernity. Yet, they do so in a thoroughly mimetic way—through the dynamics of rivalry and the mechanism of scapegoating, which is no longer effective and can only exacerbate the violent sacred's decline. The idolatry of jihadism is revealed in this totalitarian effort: for the God who sides with victims, jihadists substitute a false or deviated transcendence that resuscitates the false sacred of archaic cultures in an extreme and intentional manner. Ironically and tragically, the adherents of false transcendence believe they are actually avoiding idolatry and doing the work of God by eliminating corrupt apostates who they accuse of causing suffering, injustice, and evil. This sacred "work" or duty is discharged by jihadists by imposing more violence and suffering (which they judge to be good and cleansing) on the "bad" persecutory violence of their enemies.

Simone Weil sums up the sense of the Abrahamic God that jihadists implicitly or explicitly reject: "The false God changes suffering into violence; the true God changes violence into suffering."[2] In other words, one of the essential insights of the Abrahamic traditions is that God does not react to violence with violence. Rather, they come to understand that God takes on violence, with or as the victim, and suffers it on behalf of others. Thus, the Abrahamic traditions inaugurate an alternative to violence, though they struggle to embody it consistently.

Moreover, because humans don't easily discover their victims, they require help to confront their victim-making violence. The availability of this help is the distinctive trait of the Abrahamic traditions. The insistence of these traditions on resisting idolatry is particularly associated with rejecting false notions of God bound up with violence. The movement away from idolatry and violence is slow, but within the scriptural traditions of the Abrahamic faiths, the further one goes along this path, the more they discover the nonviolent love and mercy of God.[3] This anti-idolatry is not just a philosophical insistence on the oneness of "God" but rather involves a personal and cultural discovery of the Other (in, e.g., "the lamb slain since the foundation of the world" [Rev. 13:8; cf. 1 Pet. 1:19-20]), who creates an alternative transcendence not dependent on violence.

Yet, because jihadists misunderstand the nature of the Abrahamic God, they construct a false and violent notion of God that they think will restore social order, justice, and peace through violence. Hence the adherents of militant jihadism and other similar religious or secular extremists have not learned the message of the Abrahamic faiths—that only God can bring about the kingdom of peace and justice and does so *alongside*, and even, *as* the victim. Human cooperation is necessary for this kingdom to come, but this cooperation involves resisting and transcending the violent dynamics of one's own distorted desire and sacrificial context. This kind of transcendence is to be found in solidarity with our victims, which involves the pursuit of justice and may even mean suffering. Such cooperation aligns with natural law (basic forms of goodness) and the call of conscience and is always held with a sense of humility and imperfection.

This kind of cooperation contrasts to the grasping and destructive form of "cooperation" with the divine undertaken by militants and extremists. It moves from cooperation to control, whereby jihadists place themselves in the position of God as God's agents who infallibly bring about God's rule and dictates. Such cooperation invariably involves inflicting violence and suffering in the name of God and those who are claimed to be victims (e.g., of Western, apostate, or sectarian oppression). By contrast, pacific transcendence and true cooperation with the divine involves recognizing one's own victims and complicity in distorted desire.

To resist, then, the different forms of violent sacralization that underlie all forms of idolatry—whether they be explicitly "religious" (in the modern sense) or "secular" in appearance—requires an awareness of one's involvement in unjust victimization. For Girard, the recognition of the innocence of the victim is the great breakthrough of human civilization, most particularly pioneered by the biblical/Abrahamic traditions. This breakthrough—most evident in the life, death, and resurrection of Jesus—leads to a gradual deconstruction of sacred violence and the false distinctions that it gives rise to: "the mob and the victim," "us and them," "self and other." Nevertheless, it is important to note that the Abrahamic traditions do not stand in violent opposition to archaic social systems but rather are part of them. It is from inside the system of the violent sacred that humans begin to discover their own idolatry in light of the revelation of the one God and gradually understand its implications. Thus, it is from inside these traditions that the slow and messy movement away from sacred violence occurs. This movement involves being undistorted and redirected away from a misguided search for unity and peace. It means confronting the victims of our own violence in mercy and forgiveness so that deviated transcendency can be transformed and the good within a culture and person can be liberated and properly cultivated.[4] Thus, for any society wishing to resist sacred violence, the resources of the Abrahamic traditions can be important, both in cultivating a deeper attentiveness to violence and victimization and in providing an alternative way of relating that is nonviolent.

One of the most important resources of the Abrahamic traditions is that, according to Girard, those who live within them can undergo repentance from their distorted desire and violence.[5] For example, in the encounter with the risen and forgiving victim, Jesus Christ, humans are given faith to believe in a nonviolent, loving God and so an ability to see themselves in a new way—that they are lovable and loving, and that this is enough to satisfy their mimetic existence. They discover a faith in the Other who loves them and wants to share life with them, even as their innocent victim. The chasm between creature and Creator is overcome: the Creator has become a creature—a brother—in order to overcome humanity's rejection of him in sacred violence and to share his life with them. One could expand Girard's claim to include Islam, at least in the sense that Islam also has a sense of the victim who God privileges. For example, Afsaruddin argues that scapegoating is not part of the Islamic tradition, especially because of its emphasis on and understanding of justice.[6] As mentioned, Palaver argues that the consciousness of the innocent victim is present in Islam, such as in the Qur'anic rendition of the Joseph story, which is combined with a forgiving ethos based on a merciful notion of God.[7] In this sense, the awareness of the victim can be associated with mercy, justice, and repentance in Islam.

This is not to claim that Christianity and Islam are identical, but that they have a broad similarity in the way they conceive of God in positive relation to the victim, who is shown to be innocent (in contrast to the violent sacred), and in their emphasis on justice, mercy, and repentance. Nevertheless, each tradition ultimately conceives of God's relationship with the victim and what this relationship produces in different ways. The relationship becomes one of complete identification in Christianity—with God as forgiving victim. While

God is on the side of the victim, God in Islam remains transcendent and absolute in his life and mercy, not reduced to human terms.

Nevertheless, Girard suggests that balancing the immanence and transcendence of God is crucial for resisting sacred violence. This balance avoids God becoming too remote from humans to make a difference to human lives, violence, or injustice, or too close to humans, in which God becomes identified in commissioning violence. In the right balance, God can be seen as providing a transcendent revelation to disrupt the unanimity of the scapegoat mechanism, while still relating with human beings to forgive and love them.[8] This radical immanence combined with an absolute transcendence—both infused with gratuitous love for the other—is the ultimate antidote to violence. Anything less—any tradition that cannot marry the absolute transcendence of divine love (untainted by human sin) with the immanent embodiment and practice of self-giving love—risks becoming distorted and twisted into sacred violence.

The Problems and Implications of Militant Jihadism

There are a number of specific challenges that the Islamic tradition faces in regard to jihadism, which I briefly address here.[9] Most important is the challenge of the violent sacralization of God, who leads to the commissioning of sacred violence. This association between God and sacred violence must be challenged and undermined. Cowdell identifies the problem in Islam being "a more amenable host nowadays than Christianity" to the violent sacred which Islam has not "offloaded" to the same degree as other Abrahamic traditions.[10] In this regard, Girard states that "parts of the Muslim world have retained pre-Muslim sacrifice" in the sense of the violent sacred, in contrast to Christianity.[11] Muslims have also been part of a period in history where colonial and postcolonial regimes were oppressive, leading to some Islamists using the Islamic tradition to justify sacred violence. Nevertheless, like the other Abrahamic traditions, there are resources in Islam that can counter these violent elements by emphasizing a conception of the merciful God that reveals and stands in nonviolent solidarity with the victim. These theological and social resources center on the mercy and benevolence of God who reveals our violence and encourages the spiritual jihad of "patient forbearance."[12]

The violent sacralization of God also connects to an overemphasis by jihadists or fundamentalists on the transcendence of God whose sacred "monarchial" rule results in a violent immanence. An overly transcendent God—who is totally removed from the "depraved" condition of human life so that there is little identification or sympathy with it—can give rise to an understanding of a remote, monarchial God who polices our every thought and action. This monarchial notion of God is, ironically, vulnerable to being distorted by false transcendence in which the will of God is interpreted violently—either against oneself or others (or both).[13] This vulnerability occurs because there is no connection between God and human nature—no analogy between the divine and human life in philosophical or theological terms—but only an emphasis on the "evil" that is the life of humanity—either identified in oneself or others. In this view, evil must be eradicated for divine rule to truly take effect. Almost any means are justified. These external impositions are consistent with the externalization of violence that characterizes the violent sacred who policies and commissions violence.

This sense of the transcendence of God and the depraved human condition is demonstrated in the following testimony of Armin Navabi about his childhood as a Muslim fundamentalist in Iran:

> I want to explain what that was like. You are always ashamed, from age four or five, of what you are thinking, you are always apologising. It is a kind of mental torture, I think, to push religion on to small children, who will believe everything you say.
>
> There are so many rules and you can't ever be good enough. You feel so disgusted with your thoughts every day. And you know the punishment. If you sin—and you are always sinning—even in your thought, you will burn forever. And how does it feel, to burn forever? I had to know, so I burned myself, held a fire to my arm, and I could hardly stand it, not for one second, so how will it feel forever?
>
> It scared me so much.[14]

For Navabi, the internalization of violence through external rules and laws led to his own failed effort at suicide. He attempted suicide because he believed he would reach heaven and avoid the age of responsibility for sin and of reason.[15] This kind of literalism, undergirded by the internalization and externalization of violence, is related to the problem of how God is conceived. The transcendence of God—who only provides an external solution to the human imperfection—is absolutely emphasized. In a strange way this transcendent God becomes immediate and immanent but as a kind of superego who polices and punishes. This kind of transcendence, then, leads to a violently orientated immanence. This could be avoided with a view of God that is both rational and relational, that is, with a God who relates with humans in a rational, nonviolent and merciful manner, and identifies with the human condition God created.

Furthermore, the self that Navabi relates in his testimony seems to be characterized by what Girard calls the romantic "lie of spontaneous desire"—that one's own desire is self-generated and not dependent on others (or even God).[16] This means that one neglects the social dimension of one's desire and instead takes absolute responsibility for it. One becomes an island to project evil onto the self, without any sense of one's goodness—which fundamentalists like Navabi risk—or, alternatively, project onto the other—as the jihadist does. In this view, external impositions save one from one's own "evil self," or alternatively, from the evil of the other.

This moralistic and fundamentalist fear of being contaminated by evil leads some Muslims to strictly place and police boundaries between themselves and the "un-righteous." It has, moreover, led jihadist groups to develop strict and exclusive doctrines, especially regarding non-Muslims and those Muslims not part of the jihadist group. Through the use of *takfir* and the development of the doctrine *al-wala' wa-l-bara'*, they have also undermined the claims of others to be Muslims if they do not follow the strict and idiosyncratic brand of Islam propagated by jihadist groups. These doctrines rely on a violent and exclusive interpretation of God, which believes that God wants any perceived opposition to Islam violently wiped out. Addressing these doctrinal areas, and the underlying violent exclusivism, with alternative notions of God and Islamic law (as being grounded in mercy and relationship, not on moral purity or exclusivism) is crucial for delegitimizing the strict attitude of righteousness and condemnation present in Islamist groups.

The strict transcendent view of God and Islamic law, moreover, leads to a form of a radical voluntarism in which the will of God is un-related to any rational criteria. Only what is said to be from God is important in taming the evil of the human species. This approach attempts to safeguard God and God's will as eternal and absolute, but it also means a radical discontinuity between God and God's creation. In this view, it is not necessary for God's will to be consistent with any rational criteria or definitions of good and evil. In one application of this view, reason can be seen as unimportant (at least regarding God's will) and only submission regarded as important. In another application, this kind of voluntarism gives license to arbitrarily construct, apply, and abrogate divinely commissioned rules to suit the purposes of a jihadist construction of God.[17]

The practice of abrogation is common in jihadist thought as a way to resolve contradictions or inconsistencies in the tradition, especially related to the Prophet Muhammad and the Qur'an. This principle suits the particular bias of the interpreter, especially the militant jihadist who wishes to support the sacralization of violence.[18] The principle of abrogation has traditionally meant in Islam that, for example, certain Qur'anic texts (or those from the Sunnah) can supersede others, resulting in such situations as God "licensing" a form of behavior for a time but then banning it (e.g., the drinking of alcohol).[19] Afsaruddin argues that the use of abrogation leads to selective readings that suits the bias of the interpreter and obscures the holistic meaning of the Qur'an:

> Ultimately, as far as their interpretive undertakings are concerned, one of the main differences between the modern thinkers and activists ... is their adherence or lack of adherence to the principle of naskh, usually translated as "abrogation," in relation to key Qur'anic verses. The irenic and peacemaking thrust of the Qur'an—as upheld by 'Aṭā' b. Abī Rabā ḥ in the first/seventh century extending to Muḥammad 'Abduh in the nineteenth century and Jamāl al-Banna in our own time—is primarily established by taking *all* its verses into consideration, especially in connection with the terms jihād and ṣabr and their derivatives. Read as an unabrogated whole, the Qur'anic text—simply and purely—advocates only limited, defensive fighting when peaceful overtures and stoic, non-violent resistance have failed and the adversary attacks first. The religious affiliation of the adversary in itself is irrelevant. To establish the opposite premise—that the Qur'ān actually advocates offensive attacks against non-Muslims qua non-Muslims regardless of whether they are peaceful or hostile—requires that a majority of verses that counsel peaceful, even amicable relations with non-belligerent non-Muslims be considered null and void. Ultimately, the yet unresolved dispute between militant and irenic factions today—as was also true in the past—hinges on their divergent attitudes towards the Qur'anic text and its interpretation. Should the Qur'an holistically engaged remain the final arbiter and source of Muslim ethical and legal deliberations or must its text be mediated—even truncated—by exegeses that defer to specific historical circumstances for the political and material gain of particular Muslims? The debate continues.[20]

While voluntarism on its own does not cause violence, forms of voluntarism and abrogation can be combined with a sense of indoctrinated submissiveness to provide the conditions for violence to occur. Submission to the one God can be a sublime act, but it can also be a remote one—where God is vastly transcendent and unknowable—which opens up possibilities for particular pathologies to develop. In this way, the utter transcendence of God can lead to a spiritual and existential submissiveness that can be exploited and manipulated. Through the instruction of a jihadist leader, submission to divine law may be construed to justify certain types of violence. In the jihadist vision, only submission to the divine will is absolute, intention to serve that will is paramount, and any means are legitimate.[21]

In addition to the above, interpretation of sacred texts and Islamic history contributes to sustaining or undermining a violent view. As Cook points out, Islamic peoples face a fundamental challenge to come to terms with the legacy of violence in their tradition, in order to address violent notions of the divinity and divinely commissioned violence. This problem is concentrated in two major areas of interpretation. First, it concerns the early history of conquest from the life of the Prophet into the early generation of Muslims (not only in the imperial ambitions of later Muslim states, which is often blamed for distorting Islam). Second, in the theological and legal literature around jihad as a violent, expansionary activity, not only an action that is defensive.[22]

These two areas of interpretation are connected to the way that mediation and imitation operate in Islamic contexts, which establish the parameters for Islamic traditions and authorities. As I have discussed, imitation is a powerful force in social and religious life and enables both cooperation and competition, cohesion and violence. To imitate requires interpreting the actions and intentionality of the model. In the case of the Islamic tradition, imitation particularly centers on the legacy of the Prophet Muhammad and the early generation of Muslims. The Prophet Muhammad is held up as the exemplar of the Muslim tradition, with Sunni groups regarding him as the Perfect Man[23] to imitate, and Shia groups regarding him (and others) in high devotional esteem. The Prophet Muhammad's life and the lives of the early generations of Muslims set important precedents, with militant jihadists placing almost sole focus on this period to the exclusion of some hadiths and later developments of the Islamic tradition. The character and model of the Prophet Muhammad needs to be carefully interpreted and evaluated in popular and academic discourse, with some scholars already arguing for a more realistic and less idealized treatment of the Prophet's actions.

In this regard, the Prophet Muhammad's actions regarding defensive and offensive conflict, alongside some texts of the Qur'an, provide material that is used to justify violent jihad. The actions of the Prophet Muhammad in his Median period (his raiding and defensive actions) and his takeover of Mecca are particularly referenced. How one interprets the Prophet Muhammad's persecution in this period, alongside the Prophet's teaching and armed actions, is crucial for how violence may or may not be justified in the Islamic tradition. Moreover, the early expansion and conquests of Islam can be interpreted to justify contemporary sacred violence. For example, the early "rightly guided" (*Rashidun*) Caliphs undertook raids (*ghazu*) and expansionary military activity that increased Arab-Muslim territory.[24] Umar ibn al-Khattab took the title as *amir al-muminin*—Commander of the Faithful—when he united the Arab tribes in raids and military expansion, which, as Armstrong argues, also ensured their fidelity and provided an outlet for internal divisions and tensions to be channeled.[25] Cook argues that this legacy of violence needs to be addressed by the mainstream Islamic tradition—and not just by Muslim scholars in the West—if violence in the name of Islam is going to be marginalized to an illegitimate fringe.[26]

In this sense, Islam has a distinct tradition and past which must be theologically and hermeneutically addressed. In this regard, the Islamic tradition has been heavily involved in the sociopolitical life of the societies in which it has been present, including with a founding figure who brought unexpected positive and peaceful change to his own society but engaged in violent and nonviolent means to do so.[27] The aim of the Prophet Muhammad was (and is) lofty in that he sought to cultivate "a society which puts into practice God's desires for the human race."[28] Yet, sociopolitical involvements bring the risk of becoming involved in the use of power and violence as well as the social machinations of rivalry and scapegoating. This issue, more broadly, relates to the relationship of the political and theological/religious, which is a challenging and contested area for Islam. In interpreting Islamic history, what is authentically Islamic, and what are the contingent dictates of social and political regimes, is a challenging hermeneutical dilemma—and perhaps impossible to fully differentiate.

Nevertheless, some reflection on this dilemma is required in order to know what Islam requires of particular persons and societies in different situations. For example, does Islam require a "total society" that commands all the loyalty of faithful Muslims, no matter how brutal and ahistorical? Many Muslims have objected to this total system and offered alternative versions of mosque–state relations. Moreover, there are alternative historical approaches. However, many Muslim-majority states still claim their legitimacy from Islam, perhaps in questionable ways. In this regard, Roy argues that Islam actually suffers from the domination of the political over the religious.[29] At the least, the further development of theo-political visions across the Muslim world that distance Islam from totalitarian positions is important, particularly ones that can champion justice in the name of victims in constructive and nonviolent ways.[30]

Furthermore, the nature of authority in Islam, especially regarding interpretation of Islamic law and texts, has shifted in modernity. Militant jihadists have been able to claim authoritative interpretations, though they often have no official leadership position. The increased literacy and education in modernity has given the abilities for jihadists to challenge, distort, or exploit mainstream scholarship.[31] Moreover, because of the dispersed nature of its authority structures, Islam may be susceptible to individual people or groups claiming to be true interpreters.[32] In this regard, Islam can be construed as involving a complete break from one's cultural context or past, which contributes to a puritanical reformist tendency that is typical of modernity.[33] This can result in sect-like tendencies that deny any positive elements within past or present cultural contexts.

Though militant jihadists have exploited dispersed structures in Islam, they have also found support for some of their theological or political positions within Islamic scholarship or from authorities in the Muslim-majority world. For example, Islamist and jihadist groups were politically useful at times for regimes in the Muslim-majority world, such as to counter radical left-wing groups in Egypt.[34] They were also useful for geopolitical purposes, such as for the United States, Pakistan, and Saudi Arabia in Afghanistan to repel the USSR.

Resisting Sacred Violence in Islam

While I have briefly reflected on areas in the Islamic tradition that militant jihadists have drawn on and exploited to justify their violence, it is important to emphasize that the phenomenon of sacred violence is larger than Islam and cuts across cultural and religious traditions. Protagonists of sacred violence use certain aspects of such traditions to legitimize their violence. For example, Girard discusses how "historical Christianity" has repeatedly engaged in sacred violence and distorted the revelation of the innocent victim with a "sacrificial" interpretation of the biblical texts.[35] Moreover, Girard's major theological contribution has been to argue that in focusing on the nonviolent God of the Cross and Resurrection, Christianity can authentically interpret its own tradition to avoid sacred violence. In a similar way, Islam has a tradition of recognizing the innocence of the victim and cultivating nonviolent forms, based around a transcendent God who is just and merciful. In this regard, legal, exegetical, theological, moral, ritual, and communal resources can contribute to authentically (re-)interpreting the tradition (in consistency with its past) and avoid violent interpretations. In terms of academic works, Asma Afsaruddin has provided an example of how to undertake the work of interpretation with regard to jihad. To engage in authentic Islamic practice, as Afsaruddin argues, jihad must revolve around justice, mercy, and patient forbearance.[36] These areas contribute to genuine jihad based on nonviolent and just ways of living.

Related to this, the interpretation of the Qur'an and other important texts as well as the Prophet's life, Islamic history, and the legal tradition, within a consistent theological hermeneutic, is crucial. This hermeneutic could be centered, at least in part, on the perfect mercy and justice of the one God—which humans don't control or manage, but to which they surrender in the hope of salvation from human imperfection, sin, and violence. The struggle with sacred violence within a tradition requires a central point of reference that expands over time to expose violence and evil. In the Christian tradition, this central point is Jesus' death and Resurrection, which has over time led to the exposure of sacred violence within this tradition. For Islam, the source of ultimate transcendence and life—Allah and his Prophet—provides this point of reference.

In this endeavor of interpretation, Qur'anic and legal scholars, theologians, and Muslim leaders have a particularly important role. As Cook suggests, hermeneutical and theological clarity around violence within Islamic scholarship and leadership is crucial.[37] Though scholars, clerics, and civil leaders are not the only authoritative interpreters of the Muslim tradition (as has been witnessed to great effect in the militant jihadist groups), they still have an influential role in modern Islamic societies in guiding popular interpretations and marginalizing or allowing for extremist interpretations. They—along with any Muslim or person of faith—can live, teach, and interpret in the way of God's mercy and love, in solidarity with the innocent victim, so to help humanity to resist sacred violence. It is to this universal task of resisting sacred violence that I now turn.

The Sacred and the Holy

In the remainder of this chapter, I reflect on ways in which contemporary traditions, particularly derived from Abrahamic roots, can transcend and transform their sacred violence. In particular, the Abrahamic traditions reflect ways of exposing false transcendence and engaging nonviolent forms of transcendence. For Girard, the revelation that emerges from the Judeo-Christian tradition transforms and subverts like a leavening agent: always undermining violence even as violence seeks to re-justify itself.[38] This leavening agent opens spaces free from sacred violence and enables people, communities, and traditions to transcend such violence. We can refer to these spaces and people as partaking of what Weil calls, and Girard emphasizes, as "the holy."[39]

The option for "the holy" provides a way to avoid escalating violence in the long-term by reorientating the victim consciousness away from violence toward forgiveness and nonviolence. The holy is based in pacific transcendence and involves a pattern of life modelled by figures such as Jesus (important to both Christianity and Islam) who have avoided sacred violence from the enlightened position of the Abrahamic faiths. This way of life is the alternative to apocalyptic violence, which Girard fears could be the more likely path for a species still enthralled with violence. This sense of the holy, grounded in an alternative form of mimetic transcendence to that of sacred violence, answers the human existential and social dilemma in a nonviolent, integrative manner. Though based in a difficult choice and involving demanding practices and habits, "the holy" provides the foundation for resisting resentful, escalating violence (that over-rides reason and distorts habit). It can also support a functioning cultural and political system that does not rely exclusively or primarily on violence. It does so by building a social system imbued with a sense of the victim through a non-resentful, forgiving ethos, open to the loving transcendent.

"The holy," then, is never divorced from its social context—it is both revelatory and incarnational as it enters into, disrupts, and transforms sacred violence from within the cultural structures of the sacred. Girard discusses this transformation with respect to the biblical texts and the way they look like myths. He shows how they typically share the same structure as myths but actually subvert mythical stories from the nonviolent perspective of the victim.[40] This transformative process is gradual and slow as humans discover the full implications of this perspective.

Thus, "the holy" is engaged in the slow opening and transforming of human identities and communities (and their stories and rituals) through the discovery of the implications of the nonviolent awareness of the victim.[41] In their struggle with sacred violence, communities and traditions carry the vestiges, biases, and wounds of sacred violence. They carry the risk of mimetic rivalry and sacred violence appropriating the awareness of the innocent victim for retributive violence, especially against perceived persecutors (as jihadists have done). In this appropriation, the awareness of the victim is combined with violent mimesis to bring about new forms of mob violence. The recognition of the mob's guilt, then, can only be a healthy one if a new type of mimetic solidarity and transcendence, grounded in loving sacrifice and forgiveness, accompanies it.

Undergirding this transformative process is an alternative form of transcendence that guides the awareness of the innocent victim toward pacific relations. The holy contrasts with the sacred precisely in the type of transcendence it engages, grounded in the forgiving spirit of the innocent victim. As I've discussed, the sacred relies on deviated transcendence derived from violent horizontal relations that externalize their violence in the form of a divinized victim. On the other hand, the holy partakes of pacific or loving transcendence—the shared mimesis of self-emptying and self-giving. This mimesis can be derived from and orientates people toward the eternal, self-offering divinity who reveals himself as the loving and merciful source and fullness of being itself.

Palaver argues that this distinction between the sacred and the holy corresponds to Weil's distinction between "gravity" as a type of religion determined by power and violence, and "grace" as "from a God who differs radically from such human projections of power":[42] "Grace refers back to the divine creator, whose renunciation and self-limitation created the world. Because God 'emptied a part of his being from himself,' he enabled his creation to fill the emptied space. In Christ, we discover this type of divinity exactly where he renounced it (Phil. 2:6-7)."[43] This divine renunciation and withdrawal—which Girard discusses in *Battling to the End*—is crucial both for creation and for its "redemption," that is, its saving from violence and destruction. Based on the German poet Holderlin's own withdrawal, Girard discusses the necessity of removing oneself from the patterns and influences of mimetic violence and rivalry. This withdrawal images Christ's own withdrawal from the world. Christ withdraws to resist rivalry and to enter more deeply into loving relationship with the Father. By doing this, Christ is, then, at the right distance to enter into relationship with humanity—removed from rivalrous relations and immersed into loving relations. In this, it is possible for humanity to imitate him as "brother" and perfect mediator rather than rivalrous sibling:

> The relationship [with the Father] sanctifies while reciprocity sacralizes by creating ties that are too strong. ... Christ is the only one who immediately places us at the right distance. He is simultaneously "near and difficult to grasp." His presence is not proximity. Christ teaches us to look at the other by identifying ourselves with Him, which prevents us from oscillating between too great proximity to and too great distance from the other whom we imitate. If we were to identify with the other, we would be imitating him in an intelligent manner. Imitating Christ thus means thwarting all rivalry, taking distance from the divine by giving it the Father's face: we are brothers "in" Christ. In this, Christ completed what the pagan gods had only sketched. As he sank into the withdrawal of his Father, Christ invited each of us to model our will on that of his Father. To listen to the Father's silence is to abandon oneself to his withdrawal, to conform to it. Becoming a "son of God" means imitating this withdrawal, experiencing it with Christ. God is thus not immediately accessible,

> but mediately: through his Son and the story of Salvation, which as we have seen takes on the paradoxical appearance of an escalation to extremes.[44]

Thus, through their mimetic fraternity with Christ, humans can enter right relationship with God and each other. A similar withdrawal is evident in Judaism and Islam, with God's being removed from human projection and idolatry. Withdrawing into relationship with God brings holiness that releases people from the intense reciprocity of rivalry. Instead, they are liberated into a relationship that is both "near and difficult to grasp" with the One who lives and models true *being*—the One who humans yearn for, but who they grasp at or try to control (which jihadists exemplify), rather than receive. Girard's reference to grasping in this passage denotes freedom from the oscillation between different proximities to the model—close or distant—which either keep rivalry at bay or intensify it. Withdrawal avoids these oscillations, though it does not mean abandonment or complete absence from mimetic relationships. In Christ, God is both immediately immanent but also transcendent, not within the grasp of rivalrous humans any more but always present in our deepest selves and in the other. Girard and Chantre call this "innermost mediation," which undermines internal mediation (that leads to rivalry) and turns it into the non-rivalrous relationship with and imitation of God (e.g., in Christ).[45]

In referring to "innermost mediation," Girard and Chantre are drawing on St. Augustine's understanding of God as being more present to the self than the subject is to his/her self. Here Girard moves to complete his spiritual approach to violence that began with his injunction to renounce violence in *Deceit, Desire and the Novel* (his first major work). In Girard's view, the subject is always disconnected from themselves by distorted mimesis. Grace that results in nonviolent forms of relationship and imitation integrates and gives back the self. It helps the self to discover its deepest meaning and fulfillment in loving mimesis, which is at the heart of creation and being. The divine Other, then, can be recognized as being present to the self in the most intimate relationality at the core of human being, freely exchanging love and opening up the self to holistic forms of relationship. This opening up of the self leads outward toward the human other (who Christians identify with Christ) to who one relates in the most intimate way through self-giving love.

The holy relies on a choice for a way of life that trusts the Other rather than being in rivalry with or sacred terror of the Other. This nonviolent faith is, then, able to be integrated with reasonable beliefs and virtuous action. By contrast, resentful mimetic violence overrides reason and distorts habit, thereby making politics impotent before the power of escalating violence, and transforming beliefs into mythic rationales for violence. In contrast, the revelation of the victim, combined with an ethic of transcendent love and forgiveness, liberates reason and belief from mythic delusion and frees politics from servitude to rivalry and war. Over time, the commitments of reason (expressed with and through deep convictions) and the efficacy of politics can be purified of violent misapprehensions and habits. However, this can only occur through the difficult journey of cultivating habits and relationships in nonviolent, gratuitous mimesis that resist and transform the habits of sacred violence. Each of the Abrahamic traditions provide well-developed ways and resources for this effort, centered on relationship with the divine who reveals the fullness of being in mercy and love. Christianity, for example, centers this task on the encounter with the forgiving God as crucified and risen victim. Islam focuses on the submission to the one, merciful God who entreats justice and humility, rather than tribal warfare and power.

In saying all this, Girard was rightly skeptical of humanity's capacity to want to break free from violence. He does not present a rosy picture of the holy as a simple solution to humanity's problems. However, Girard is both pessimistic and hopeful, that is, he trusts that nonviolent love will triumph, though only in the midst of the messy and potentially destructive struggle with violence. In this struggle, he discusses the possibility of a "positive undifferentiation"—the relations of self-giving love—that can effect positive social change. He is skeptical that politics on its own can prevent "negative undifferentiation" and mimetic violence, especially when human communities are engaged in escalating forms of rivalry that advance along the path of violent mimesis.[46] Nevertheless, Girard believes that resistance to rivalry is possible and that each human person can make a difference to forming a nonviolent alternative to mimetic contagion: "It is more than ever up to each one of us to hold back the worst; this is what being in an eschatological time means."[47]

In this struggle, Girard argues (along with Holderlin) for a "monotheism of reason and the heart" that brings together transcendence and intellect as an integrated whole.[48] In this way, desire becomes consistent with reason in the discernment of loving ways of being. Girard supported Pope Benedict XVI's Regensburg Address for highlighting the disconnect between reason and faith/religion in Westernized modernity, which effects militant jihadism.[49] Religion, as Benedict argued, should involve not violent compulsion, but rather should bring humanity into harmony with reason, and ultimately, with the *Logos*—the logic of creation—itself. This logic—that reveals the being and life humanity yearns for—is manifested in receiving and giving love, rather than grasping and taking in rivalry. In the biblical traditions, Girard identifies a clear expression of the pacific logic of creation—in revelation—in which the knowledge of the innocent victim is combined with a robust spiritual and communal ethic of forgiveness and love.

This unity of religion and reason, faith and virtue, has provided the transcendent motivation for Western and Islamic sociopolitical cohesion and development. Benedict provides a timely warning about the disintegration of the alliance of faith and reason in the West and in modernity more generally.[50] This warning seems to be ominously playing itself out with various forms of fissures in Western politics and in modernity more generally. Jihadism manifests these fissures in a stark way as it distorts the faith of the Islamic tradition and its awareness of the victim with a violent logic. It represents a fundamental mimetic crisis in which people grasp for identity by imbuing the belief in the one God with sacred violence. This projection involves identity markers (such as the willingness to commit certain acts of violence against infidels or follow certain laws) that create rival groups—even amongst the jihadists themselves—that vie for ideological purity and social and political power over one another. In the absence of a true transcendence, people manufacture false forms of transcendence based around idols that, because they are inherently defined over against others, lead to violence.

What Kind of Politics and Society without Sacred Violence?

If "the holy," grounded in pacific transcendence, is a real possibility in human life and can influence the structure of human relations, then it has implications for political and social practices. In *Battling to the End*, Girard is critical of the capacity of politics to resist the escalation of mimetic violence. As Girard warns, politics cannot "control the rise of negative undifferentiation," but it, along with civil society groups, can effect fundamental change and resistance to sacred violence before it escalates.[51] It is the particular task of politicians as well as civil society, and even more particularly churches and mosques, to model virtues and cultivate rituals and stories to encourage change. In this way they can build solidarity that is not dependent on sacred violence and that is in some way based on an ethic of sacrificial love.

In cultivating this ethic, Palaver argues that the positive/pacific and negative/violent forms of sacrifice should not be juxtaposed to each other in an absolute manner.[52] The Abrahamic traditions make the important discovery that the original form of desire and sacrifice is that of pacific self-giving—the kind that God enacts when God creates the universe and relates with it. The universe is enlivened by a loving gift that brings and maintains the universe in existence. Moreover, loving sacrifice is the fundamental mode of relationship, which satisfies the human's deepest yearnings for being and communion. The negative form of sacrifice—scapegoating that brings a false reconciliation—is a distortion of this positive form—just as the archaic religion of scapegoating was and is a distortion of the loving religion of communion. Loving sacrifice even confronts violence and suffering with a willingness to give oneself peacefully and with forgiveness: "Sometimes we have to undergo violence or suffering in order to avoid perpetrating violence against others. Whoever thinks they can avoid such dilemmas forever easily risks justifying the sacrifice of others in a disguised form."[53]

Militant jihadism is an exemplar of the avoidance of suffering in that it inflicts "just" punishment (suffering) on others—the so-called persecutors—to ensure the purity and well-being of the *ummah*, which has been historically victimized. This cult of the victim, as Palaver describes it, reengages with violent sacrifice in subtle ways—for example, by victimizing the perceived victimizer—because it lacks an accompanying ethic of forgiveness: "Escalation of conflicts in the realm of international politics ... can be overcome only by acts of forgiveness and the voluntary renunciation of claims and entitlements."[54] For example, Chris Fleming argues that Hiroshima became a sign of the consequences of total war, especially highlighting the civilian victims of modern violence, but also a sign of forgiveness and reconciliation following the war (e.g., Sadako Sasaki's paper cranes).[55] In this way, an awareness of the victims of violence could be combined with a reconciling ethic that contributed to Japan's moral, political, and economic reconstruction. Underlying this change was a conversion (in the Girardian sense) from defining one's self over against others to recognizing one's dependence on and violence toward the other. By contrast, jihadism appropriates the victim consciousness in a violent spirit under the power of a deviated transcendence rather than that of a true vertical transcendence. Lacking a nonviolent accompanying ethic, the revelation of the victim becomes a means for escalating violence.

Because of the way mimetic violence twists even the revelation of violence, Girard argues that politics is constantly playing catch up to violence and warfare and is usually eclipsed by them.[56] With the increasing breakdown of sacrificial violence in modernity, Girard argues that "only ethical relations could still found something."[57] Legal prohibitions are decreasingly effective in the face of mimetic violence, especially in escalating phases of violence and warfare. Security actions can prevent violence in the short-term, but only non-violent ethical relations can produce long-term positive results.

To concretize these ethical relations, political virtues and actions are required that freely express the positive forms of sacrifice that seek to de-escalate violence—to bring about what Girard calls "positive undifferentiation" of friendship, love and, solidarity.[58] In this regard, Palaver gives the example of Dag Hammarskjold who, following a proposal by Lester Pearson, helped to establish peacekeeping operations by the United Nations (UN). These operations had the aim to deescalate conflict and protect potential victims in a legal and proportionate manner (though imperfectly implemented at times). It has led to approximately three thousand people giving their lives in service of deescalation and peace.[59] Though guilty of major failures, UN peacekeeping operations, like the human rights discourse, represent an effort to avoid escalating violence by institutionalizing ways of positive, self-giving sacrifice.

Nevertheless, to resist sacred violence (in its many forms) requires a clear understanding of what violent actors like militant jihadists ultimately want to destroy: namely, the undermining of sacred violence and the slow and ambiguous emergence of a political order based on nonviolent solidarity with the innocent victim (rather than sacralization of the victim and violence). Resistance to groups like militant jihadists requires occasional and proportional defense with arms and peacekeeping operations. These efforts should be directed to protect the innocent and halt conflicts, in order to allow for space to cultivate social and political reconciliation. It should be understood that armies and security services are not enough to address the sacred violence of jihadists and the underlying cultural crisis motivating them. While military and police action can be effective in preventing terrorist attacks, they need to be combined with nonviolent community measures and forms of rehabilitation. Moreover, political, religious, and cultural efforts at inclusive governance and reconciliation—even if they don't include jihadists themselves, but do include those segments of society from which jihadists are drawn—are important for addressing the underlying conditions for jihadism.

In this sense, the international community needs to address the conditions that jihadists exploit to further their aims, namely, conflict in certain states and unjust political arrangements in these states. There also needs to be a careful reflection on the consequences of military or police actions by the West and other Middle Eastern nations and how defensive military action is going to be followed by concerted political efforts to ensure stability. The recent examples of Iraq and Afghanistan demonstrate that, while military action might bring initial victories, it must be followed by effective political action and reconciliation. When military intervention, good governance, and political reconciliation are effectively combined (such as following the 2007 Surge in Iraq), Kilcullen argues that it is possible to arrest the violent breakdown of a state or territory.[60] However, military action on its own may only lead to a stalemate or provoke civil conflict—as it did in Iraq following the 2003 invasion—of which jihadists can take advantage.

Furthermore, while defensive actions are necessary, it is important to avoid the way military and police actions can be construed as rivalrous and imbue the state with sacred power over against "evil" enemies or dissident groups. Justifications for state-based violence as "saving" the world from extremist "death cults" and "terrorists," who must be wiped out, are fraught with the kind of logic that William Cavanaugh has shown in *Myth of Religious Violence*: "good" state-based violence can restrain bad "religious" violence.[61] Kilcullen argues this has already occurred in Syria where President Assad intentionally labelled rebel groups as jihadist extremists and terrorists, which licensed his regime (and his international allies) to violently suppress any anti-government groups. Kilcullen states that this label was a lie at the beginning of the Syrian civil war to justify state-based violence. It became true because of the rise of jihadists in the Syrian conflict following the lack of an effective political solution.[62] Thus, individual states or groups of nation-states can easily fall into the trap of creating enemies and mirroring the terrorists to create order on their own terms and justify their power rather than taking the political opportunities and initiatives for reconciliation.

Sacralization, Secularization, and Sacrifice

Thus, it is the struggle to cultivate personal and collective identities around pacific and loving forms of mimesis, in solidarity with our victims, that is the challenge of our time. These identities, moreover, call for a proper secularization of the public domain that resists violent efforts at sacralization. In this regard, Girard's anthropology provides a helpful distinction between an unhealthy sacralization and a healthy secularization. A "secular" cultural space on a large scale is only possible as the violent sacred is subverted by solidarity with the innocent victim in an ethic of sacrificial love.[63] Both characteristics—the awareness of innocence and the inauguration of new mimetic spaces—are necessary otherwise the fruits of revelation itself become violent. The shocking aspect of militant jihadism is that it confronts us with the archaic roots of human culture and religion in sacred violence and seeks a kind of return to these roots.

While space does not permit a full analysis of secularity here, Scott Cowdell explores these issues in his book *René Girard and Secular Modernity*. He notes that modern secularity retains vestiges of the violent sacred: "Just as preserving the old sacred from anything profane had been necessary before the shift [to Christianity], the emerging modern world deemed a similar separation necessary so it could retain access to the archaic sacred."[64] Hence modern secularity became obsessed with keeping "religion" out of politics, which as Cavanaugh has extensively argued was an exclusionary move that blamed religion for modern violence and gave power to the state. As Cowdell explains, this move enabled a fundamental binary, based on an exclusion, that resuscitated the sacred: nothing "religious" (which is to blame for violence) could be allowed to infect the profane world of immanent flourishing, even as it became sacralized through its own violence. The rise of militant jihadism has seemed to support this view, as militants have violently objected to the immanent nature of Western secularism and put it under threat. This rivalry has produced a feedback system—as is typical of mimetic rivalry—in which Western and Muslim-majority states have sought to marginalize or oppress "religious" extremists, while these "religious" extremists object to such marginalization and the desacralization of their national and local spaces.[65]

While it is important to acknowledge that there are patterns of exclusion in the Westernized modernity, the causes of militant jihadism are more complex. While some in the Islamist movement have been persecuted, the core of the jihadist ideology is the objection to modern secularity in that it is not sacred or religious enough. In other words, modern secularism does not contain enough explicit sacred violence (or does not include jihadists in such violence) to satisfy jihadist terrorists and their disaffected allies. Thus, they seek to expel the "secular" in favor of the sacred, yet they mirror in reverse what they accuse their enemies of doing (namely, expelling the "religious"). The jihadists offer easy answers through a strict legalism and a social glue based on violent transcendence.

By contrast, a healthy secularism can be understood in terms of a desacralized space—a disenchanted world—that resists scapegoating violence. Yet, this desacralized space can never exclude the divine or supernatural—humans are too mimetic and transcendentally oriented to leave it as such. Jihadists have presented this transcendent and mimetic propensity in a stark form. However, a true vertical transcendence, like a true desacralized/secular space, does not involve sacred violence. This pacific vertical transcendence is exemplified in the nonviolent martyr, who provides a direct contrast to the jihadist martyr of sacred violence:

> The undermining of mythical beliefs begins with the acts of violence against those the Christians call *martyrs*. We see them as innocent people who are persecuted. This truth has been transmitted by history, and the perspective of the persecutors has not prevailed. … The innocence of the martyr is never in doubt. "They hated me [without a cause]." The Christian passion produces its first fruits. The spirit of vengeance leads vigorous rear-guard actions, but the martyrs nonetheless pray for their executioners: "Father, forgive them, they know not what they do."[66]

In contrast to the sacred violence perpetrated against "infidels" by suicide bombers or combatants named as so-called martyrs, the innocent death of the nonviolent martyr is closely linked to the martyr's self-giving, which is further accentuated by the martyr's forgiveness. The innocent death of the martyr highlights and is part of the self-giving act as the martyr stands in the place of the community in resistance to the unjust regime or social order, exposing its foundation in sacred violence. The remembering community comes to recognize this violent foundation in the innocence and self-giving of the martyr. Furthermore, the martyr witnesses to *a certain way of being* modelled in the Abrahamic faiths (particularly by figures such as Jesus), which extends the gift of self to both the remembering community and the mob that killed the martyr. In this way, the martyr enacts self-giving love which confronts a violent, destructive, and self-assertive way of being (in the form of the mob's violence) in that place where violence has reigned: namely, death.

Thus, the transcendent constriction of life and society by the violent sacred is resisted through the act and remembrance of the martyr. The martyr and remembering community resist sacred violence by together opening spaces that enact non-violent forms of solidarity, particularly through self-giving and forgiveness. This resistance can translate into general social forms in which self-sacrifice, forgiveness, and service are privileged as public virtues.

The important contrast, then, between the jihadist martyr and the nonviolent martyr is that in being innocently killed, the latter helps to reveal sacred violence through pacifically confronting persecution with sacrificial love that extends to all. The remembrance and reverence of the nonviolent martyr actually open up a space that desacralizes human culture and religion and thus provides for the *secular*. In other words, the secular is not in the first place created by a rational enlightenment or the separation of the church from the state. Rather it emerges from a transcendence (of the holy) that desacralizes human culture through putting into effect the desires, worldview, and practice of the forgiving victim. This transcendence opens up time and space beyond the confines of violence and enables a different kind of solidarity with the victimized in nonrivalrous and pacific forms of relationality. On this basis, the nonviolent martyr makes possible a nonviolent space, formed in the midst of violence, which can be participated in by a wide variety of people inspired by the example of the martyr.

The Future of Sacred Violence

While jihadism manifests a deep tension in modernity, there is a counterforce that can be a source for renewal: the recognition of one's own complicity in distorted desire and violence, accompanied by a commitment to self-sacrificial love, resulting in genuine and selfless actions for the common good. In this struggle, the Abrahamic faiths can be a positive force—if they are faithful to the central insights and practices of their traditions around solidarity, mercy, and love. Grounded in a common transcendence and forms of friendship, they can give rise to "positive undifferentiation"—to a recognition of our identity with each other in which all have inherent value in our common relationality. This relationality can allow for positive difference, uniqueness, and charity to flourish. This positive undifferentiation is reflected in the discourse of human rights at its best, in which dignity is recognized. Furthermore, it is reflected in the historic witness of the Abrahamic faiths to self-giving forms of charity (e.g., in hospitals, welfare networks, and schools for the poor) that gave a clear example of how to pursue the common good.[67]

In conclusion, the Islamic tradition and, more broadly, modernity is in the midst of a contestation regarding its theo-political vision and structure. Jihadists envisage a totalitarian political order, that absolutizes rivalry in sacred violence commissioned by God. Nevertheless, there are alternatives in the brave witnesses that confront violence and promote humble self-giving forms of mimetic identity.[68] These witnesses point to the capacity of "the holy" to peacefully resist and slowly transform the power of the sacred. This chapter has only begun to chart the potential of the Abrahamic traditions to bring forth the capacity of "the holy" in modernity. Ultimately, if the challenges of modernity are to be confronted, recognizing the importance of the victim and combining this awareness with forms of mimetic relationality will be crucial: it will either inspire nonviolent solidarity or sacred and apocalyptic violence.

Appendix: René Girard at a Glance

Scott Cowdell, Chris Fleming, and Joel Hodge

Note: *Terms in UPPERCASE are defined in the glossary.*

René Girard (1923–2015) was a French-American thinker and remains an *immortel* of *l'Académie française*. He honed a remarkable account of human culture and religion over fifty years of research across the humanities and social sciences. He began with modern realist fiction in the 1950s to uncover a novel account of human DESIRE as *mimetic* (see MIMETIC DESIRE). He went on to engage with foundational texts in anthropology, sociology, and ethnography in the 1960s, venturing a new approach to culture and religion that recalls the sociopsychological phenomenon of *l'esprit de corps*, in terms of an ersatz peace that SCAPEGOATING a victim introduces to human communities. He then set out an alternative account of religion, seen to emerge in the Judeo-Christian scriptures.

Human desire, for Girard, is desire "according to" the desire of another. Our desires, in other words, are borrowed from and stimulated by the desires of others. What Girard terms "mimetic desire" (or "triangular desire") means that the *subject* of desire imitates the desire of the *model* of their desire for an *object* of desire (see also MEDIATION). From Shakespeare and Cervantes to the great nineteenth-century novelists (Stendhal, Flaubert, Proust, Dostoevsky), a psychology is revealed in which the mimetic influence of others proves to be the true unconscious. Girard offers his own simplifying account of Freud's major conclusions to demonstrate the power of his approach, while, following Dostoevsky and Nietzsche, he explores various pathologies of the modern self.

These pathologies center on the distortion of desire into envy and rivalry, in which the subject seeks to acquire the object of desire from the model/rival. The subject risks being *scandalized* by the rival whenever his or her desire becomes a stumbling block to the fulfillment of the subject's desire (see DOUBLING). In such rivalry, the dependence of the subject/self on the other's desire is heightened yet repressed in increasingly unhealthy and obsessive ways, to the point that the object's value decreases as the subject advances in obsessive competition with the model/rival, resulting in the madness described by Dostoevsky and

Nietzsche. This pathological stage of MIMESIS is a manifestation of what Girard calls METAPHYSICAL DESIRE, in which the desire for being that underlies mimesis becomes clear. In this stage, the object eventually drops from view altogether and obsession with the model/rival becomes all-consuming. The subject in effect seeks the being of the model/rival. Explicating this state of thralldom allows Girard to theorize what he calls PSEUDO-MASOCHISM and PSEUDO-SADISM, along with self-destructive addictive behaviors, as mimetic phenomena.

Meanwhile, in the social context, the accumulation of mimetic rivalries risks wider mimetic contagion and disorder, threatening social breakdown. Girard argues that the mimetic escalation toward catastrophic violence in the protohuman group is contained by scapegoating, which founds and then maintains human culture. The contagion of mimetic violence comes to be focused on an individual or group arbitrarily chosen by the social whole, becoming a scapegoat upon which social chaos is focused and hence discharged. According to Girard, archaic cultures that manage by these means to survive their own violence show a common pattern in their myths, in which a violent crisis suddenly and miraculously gives way to peace and order. This change occurs as the hostile desires of "all against all" suddenly become the murderous desires of "all against one." Through this victimization, the community returns to peace and to differentiation around the slain victim. This victim is made SACRED and divinized by the mob, which transfers responsibility for the crisis and its resolution onto the victim—the two sides of the sacred (the destructive and the saving) that constitute Girard's original account of Rudolf Otto's *mysterium tremendum et fascinosum*. Religion is the part of culture that emerges from this single-victim mechanism to encode its beneficial effects in PROHIBITION, MYTH, and RITUAL.

Girard sees archaic religion emerging naturally in the evolutionary process as a necessary evil, containing rivalry's potentially catastrophic escalation by the memory of primal cathartic violence that scapegoating represents. Rooted in the management of our unfocused and unstable desiring, religion's targeted, culture-founding violence is both recapitulated and revivified through ritual (especially by sacrificial rituals), justified in myth, and safeguarded by prohibition and taboo—these latter elements regulate relationships and establish boundaries to avoid further mimetic rivalry and violence.

Yet, in the Judeo-Christian vision that comes to its climax in Jesus, Girard argues that religion overcomes its origins: the innocence of the victim is revealed, the scapegoat mechanism is exposed, and human desire is shown to be distorted and diverted from its true source in God the Father's gratuitous and self-giving love. Through analysis of many biblical texts, and especially the Gospels, Girard argues that the biblical revelation can be figured precisely thus: as a revelation from outside conventional human religion and culture that lifts the veil on human violence and distorted desire.

He does this through a distinctive hermeneutical approach that first identifies the common structural characteristics of mythical and biblical stories: (1) the presence of crisis, (2) the identification of a victim, (3) vulnerable characteristics associated with the victim (e.g., disfigurement or disability), (4) the climactic and unanimous violence of SURROGATE VICTIMAGE, and (5) the restoration of order and peace that follows this scapegoating violence. Then, on the basis of these structural commonalities, Girard identifies significant differences in the content and trajectory of mythical versus biblical accounts, showing that while archaic myths endorse the violent mob, the biblical narrative reveals and champions the victim's innocence.

In this way, according to Girard, the victim-making engine of all religions and cultures is sabotaged by the Bible, setting history on a secularizing path toward modernity. For Girard, this is Nietzsche's death of God properly understood: the collapse of religion's social function and the release of a dangerous instability evident in today's most pressing global challenges.

Glossary of Key Girardian Terms

Scott Cowdell, Chris Fleming, and Joel Hodge

Note: *Terms in UPPERCASE are defined within this glossary.*

Apocalypse/apocalyptic: Although present in his work on METAPHYSICAL DESIRE from the 1960s onward, the theme of "the apocalyptic" assumed increasing importance in Girard's oeuvre. Harking back to the etymology of the Greek term *apokalypsis*, apocalypse concerns the "disclosure" of something—a "revelation" or "unveiling." The term itself has biblical roots, and Girard's interest in it concerns the revelation of violence. Here Girard emphasizes violence as that which threatens human order and security because of its contagious nature, and he emphasizes the extent to which this revelation itself further undermines human order and security. That is, the biblical uncovering of human violence—the laying bare of SURROGATE VICTIMAGE—*itself* destabilizes culture and society. By desacralizing the principal mechanism by which humans have attained unanimity and social cohesion—SCAPEGOATING—human communities are thrown into chaos that, in the short and intermediate terms, can exacerbate rather than ameliorate violence. In this situation, Girard argues that the internal logic of mimetic violence plays itself out as the mimetic and contagious nature of violence generates an "escalation to extremes" that leads to destruction. Although Girard argues that his concept of apocalypse remains utterly faithful to the biblical tradition, it runs counter to a widespread understanding of apocalypse as divine violence against humanity.

Desire: Girard acknowledges that, while humans have evolved biological appetites that operate at the level of instinct, it is the further evolved capacity for MIMESIS that most fully accounts for the dynamics of human desiring, whether or not any particular desire builds on or directs a biological appetite.

Doubling: In Girard's schema, conflictual MIMESIS is characterized by "doubling." "Doubling" refers to the progressive and mutually reinforcing dedifferentiation of subjects that occurs by virtue of an intensification of mimesis. That is, mimesis encourages, through positive feedback, an increasing symmetry between antagonists, which emerges despite increasing attempts at differentiation; it tends toward the erasure of significant differences between individuals—those differences that mark their sociopsychological identity and position within a particular cultural order.

Mediation: For Girard, whose conception of DESIRE is not object-oriented, desire is always mediated via a third party (a model or mediator) through a process of MIMESIS. There are two primary ways in which such mediation occurs: externally and internally.

External mediation (*mediation externe*) occurs where the model or mediator is historically, socially, or ontologically distant from the subject such that conflict over the object of desire is precluded. Conversely, internal mediation (*mediation interne*) occurs where the desiring subject's object of desire and their model's object of desire overlap and thereby become a pretext for rivalry or "conflictual mimesis." In this instance there is a mutual convergence on a desired object and the model is designated a "model-rival" or "model-obstacle."

Metaphysical desire: Metaphysical desire (*le desir de metaphysique*) is an attraction to the very being of a mediator. In metaphysical desire, the object is merely a means by which the desiring subject can attain or absorb the mediator's (imagined) autonomy, uniqueness, or spontaneity. Metaphysical desire is particularly evident when the object of desire is honor or prestige directly and not just one of their concrete markers.

Mimesis/mimetic desire: The idea of "mimesis" is at the center of Girard's thinking. The etymology of the term can be traced to ancient Greece (μίμησις) (*mimesis*), from μιμεῖσθαι (*mīmeisthai*), "to imitate," and it has served a variety of purposes in theoretical discourse since at least Aristotle. In Girard's thought it refers to imitative desire (*le desire mimetique*). For Girard, desire is itself imitative: we desire what we desire because we imitate—consciously or not—the desires of others. Girard has called this a "mimesis of appropriation" (*une mimésis d'appropriation*). The other main area in which Girard sees mimesis operating is in SCAPEGOATING. Here, the form of imitation observed is that of members of a crowd or populace converging around a victim or group of victims. Girard has dubbed this a "mimesis of accusation" or a "mimesis of antagonism" (*une mimésis d'antagonisme*). Girard's conception of mimesis can be traced back to his very first work, *Deceit Desire, and the Novel,* where he posits a distinction between novelistic (*romanesque*) versus romantic (*romantique*) works; where the former reveal and demythologize the mimetic nature of social relations, the latter continue to propagate delusions about absolute human spontaneity and originality.

Myth: Myth is one of the three institutions of the SACRED—along with PROHIBITION and RITUAL. Myth is preeminently concerned with *narrating* the sacred. Myth is characterized by stories that possess a radically incomplete recollection of cultural degeneration and SURROGATE VICTIMAGE. Like rituals, myths represent stereotypically distorted accounts of both the cultural chaos associated with the sacrificial crisis and the cessation of this crisis through collective violence. Myths typically encode such mis-knowing (*méconnaissance*) by representing a primordial chaos—through, for example, "natural" and cultural calamities that signify the dissolution of difference, such as plagues or the appearance of warring twins or brothers (such as we see, for instance, in the mythical narrative of Romulus and Remus).

Prohibition: Prohibition is one of the three institutions of the SACRED—along with MYTH and RITUAL. For Girard, the main function of prohibition is to control mimetic contagion and thereby proscribe interpersonal conflict. Religious taboos/prohibitions commonly target mimetic behavior and the mythical transpositions of that behavior through representation. For instance, taboos are often focused on things such as behavioral mirroring, "imitative magic," representational art, and the problematic of "twins." By targeting these domains, prohibition is best seen as a sacred prophylactic that, although manifesting only dim self-awareness, is preoccupied with the forestalling of rivalry and the dissolution of differences that conflictual reciprocity engenders.

Pseudomasochism and **pseudosadism:** Pseudomasochism and pseudosadism represent two of the primary poles of psychopathology in Girard's understanding. The prefix "pseudo" in both cases indicates what deconstructionists would call terms "under erasure": terms that are considered necessary but problematic because of their traditional constructions. Here, Girard wants to distance himself from the Freudian conceptions under which the notions of masochism and sadism have been developed while wanting to retain something of their ambience or semantic field.

From one perspective, pseudomasochism can be seen as a kind of METAPHYSICAL DESIRE *in extremis*. In MIMETIC DESIRE, the prestige of the model is sometimes boosted by his or her seeming indifference toward others. The pseudomasochist concludes that their rejection by the mediator confirms the mediator's supremacy and the absolute desirability of what the mediator desires. The pseudomasochist looks for objects whose value is conferred and confirmed by the resistance encountered in attempts to attain them. Where a model serves initially as an obstacle to the consummation of a desire, the pseudomasochist eventually will seek the obstacle itself—the model is valued because of the obstruction that he or she can provide.

Pseudosadism involves what Girard calls a "dialectical reversal" of pseudomasochism: where the masochist will seek a mediator who will oppose him or her, the pseudosadist seeks masochists for the same end, of turning him or her into a demigod. The sadist seeks to be a mediator for imitators for whom he or she will provide violent opposition and, in so doing, hopes to turn this role of human divinity into a reality. For Freud such social pathologies are externalizations of internal disquiet; for Girard, these psychopathologies represent the internalization of external social dynamics.

Religion: See the SACRED.

Ritual: Ritual is one of the three institutions of the SACRED—along with PROHIBITION and MYTH. Ritual, along with prohibition, functions to control mimetic behavior. Both freeze into institutional form an imperfect comprehension of SURROGATE VICTIMAGE; they are distorted recollections of both the cultural chaos associated with a sacrificial crisis and its abatement through SCAPEGOATING. The primary form of ritual is sacrifice, which usually begins with carnivalesque features (masks, intoxication, the theatrical erasure or suspension of normal cultural codes, and so on) and concludes with the killing of an animal (or, in the past, a human or group of humans). Ritual is the institution of the sacred that is preeminently constituted by a performative restaging of a cultural crisis and its resolution through surrogate victimage, usually by means of a sacrifice.

(The) Sacred: Girard continually emphasizes the connections between religion, social structure, and culture, which he sees as holding firm in so-called primitive (or pre-state) cultures, in ancient cultures, and even in "modern" (so-called) secular cultures—although the way these features interconnect and function in each case is importantly different. There are two senses of the sacred (*le sacré*) in Girard's work. The first, evinced in early works such as *Violence and the Sacred*, is that the sacred is the anthropological correlate of the social; further, that violence lies at the basis of the sacred and that the institutions of the sacred—MYTH, RITUAL, and PROHIBITION—give institutional form and religious underwriting to the culture-forming power and ambit of human violence.

However, beginning with *Things Hidden since the Foundation of the World*, Girard develops a new conception of the sacred that doesn't so much overturn as supplement his earlier view. He develops this view by posing the question of how it is we came to know about the (violent) sacred and its effects. His answer is that this knowledge is the product of the radically desacralizing effect of the Judeo-Christian scriptures, beginning with the psalms, the Joseph story, Job, and the Servant Songs of Isaiah, and culminating in the Gospel narratives of Jesus' passion.

Girard posits a fundamental distinction between myth and biblical narrative; where the former narrates events structured by SURROGATE VICTIMAGE in a way that legitimizes violence, the latter takes the point of view of the victims of that violence—*thematizes* violence—in a way that undermines its legitimacy. In this sense at least, Girard acknowledges the breakthrough insight of nineteenth-century German philosopher, Friedrich Nietzsche (1844–1900), whose antithesis between "Dionysus" and "the Crucified" anticipates Girard's thesis in many respects—anthropologically, if not ethically, since Nietzsche repudiates Christian regard for victims in favor of Dionysian excess.

Scapegoating: Girard's use of the term "scapegoating" (scapegoat: *bouc émissaire*) is consistent in many ways with the commonsense uses of that term: the violent and arbitrary convergence around a victim or group of victims who are seen as uniquely responsible for a particular group's misfortunes. Although scapegoats need not be innocent in any strong sense of that word—that is, utterly blameless—they bear the blame for the social disorder surrounding them out of all proportion to their responsibility. In the *Scapegoat*, Girard argues that scapegoats are (mis)represented in remarkably similar ways—with what Girard calls "victimary signs"—and so we can see scapegoating in certain texts, even when authors do not see this themselves. Scapegoating is a central feature of SURROGATE VICTIMAGE.

Surrogate victimage: In Girard's thought, "surrogate victimage" (*mécanisme de la victim émissaire/le mécanisme victimaire*) names the principal mechanism by which cultures constitute themselves sacrificially. Where MIMETIC DESIRE denotes those dimensions of imitative behavior oriented by reference to acts of *appropriation*, surrogate victimage has its basis in an increasingly envious and rivalrous MIMESIS of *accusation*. Surrogate victimage is best encapsulated by reference to a hypothetical scenario where a contagion of rivalrous mimesis has swept through a protohuman milieu and leveled the identities of individuals, so that mutual suspicion and enmity become pandemic. In such a situation of pervasive DOUBLING, Girard proposes that what invariably occurs is that an individual or group will emerge that is seen to be different enough by the crowd to polarize it in an escalating mimesis of accusation. In other words, the SCAPEGOAT functions in a sociopsychological sense by reintroducing difference when all other differences or markers of identity are collapsing. The mob polarizes around the scapegoat, who is lynched or banished. (Of course, the persecuting community does not see their victim as a *scapegoat*. Rather they see *themselves* as scapegoats of those they are accusing.) The *esprit de corps* produced by the lynching or banishment then ends up justifying or legitimating the lynching to the mob, *post hoc*. This accounts for the origin of the SACRED, according to Girard, as the victim—formerly thought to be the malign source of violent contagion threatening the community—is experienced *post mortem* as the bringer of a seemingly miraculous order and stability by virtue of his or her murder, which spontaneously quenched the mob's mimetic violence.

Thus, religions begin with the deification of victims. Surrogate victimage is the mechanism that lies behind the primitive religiocultural nexus, giving rise to MYTH, RITUAL, and PROHIBITION—the three institutions of the sacred. Girard thus proposes that conflict rooted in rivalry better explains human violence and conflict than either "aggression" (the biological/zoological explanation) or "scarcity" (the economistic explanation).

Notes

Introduction

1 René Girard, *Battling to the End: Conversations with Benoît Chantre*, trans. Mary Baker (East Lansing: Michigan State University Press, 2010), 100. Modernity is used in a broad manner to denote the period since the rise of the nation-state (particularly following the peace of Westphalia), the Enlightenment, and industrialization, which has intensified in globalization. In a particular sense, modernity is marked by the desacralization of violence and the escalation of violence, which René Girard charts, and which I discuss in more detail in Chapters 1 and 2.

2 Though "Abrahamic traditions" is a contestable and general term, I use it in this study only in one particular sense: to denote the common insights into or revelation of violence against victims present in Judaism, Christianity, and Islam, which is associated with the monotheistic God. This revelation is based in some sense on the legacy of Abraham—present in these three traditions—which involves rejecting violent sacrifice in favor of fidelity to God. In this regard, see Wolfgang Palaver, "The Abrahamic Revolution," in *Mimetic Theory and World Religions*, ed. Wolfgang Palaver and Richard Schenk (East Lansing: Michigan State University Press, 2018), 259–78; Michael Kirwan and Ahmad Achtar, eds., *Mimetic Theory and Islam: The Wound Where Light Enters* (New York: Palgrave Macmillan, 2019).

3 Girard, *Battling to the End*, 72, 118, and 198.

4 René Girard, "Victims, Violence and Christianity," *The Month* 31, no. 4 (April 1998), 129.

5 Girard, "Victims, Violence and Christianity," 129.

6 René Girard was professor at Stanford University, chair in *L'Académie française* (The French Academy), and recipient of various awards, including the Modern Language Association's award for Lifetime Scholarly Achievement. His theory is one of the most important contributions to the understanding of violence, culture, religion, and the human person in the twentieth century, with Michel Serres naming Girard "the new Darwin of the human sciences." Michel Serres, "Receiving René Girard into the Académie Française," in *For René Girard: Essays in Friendship and in Truth*, ed. Sandor Goodhart, Jørgen Jørgensen, Tom Ryba, and James G. Williams. Studies in Violence, Mimesis and Culture (East Lansing: Michigan State University Press, 2009), 5.

7 Farhad Khosrokhavar, *Inside Jihadism: Understanding Jihadi Movements Worldwide* (Boulder, CO: Paradigm/Routledge, 2009), 251.

8 Gilles Kepel, *Jihad: The Trail of Political Islam*, trans. Anthony F. Roberts (London: I.B. Tauris, 2004), 5.

9 If "jihadist" is used on its own in the study, it denotes a militant jihadist. Using the term is not the normal practice in the study, but it is occasionally used as it can be cumbersome to repeat adjectives such as "militant" or "violent" next to the term, "jihadist," after having done so in the relevant section.

10 Asma Afsaruddin, *Striving in the Path of God: Jihad and Martyrdom in Islamic Thought* (New York: Oxford University Press, 2013), 1–34, 189–205, and 268–99; "Orientalists, Militants, and the Meanings of Jihad," *Renovatio: The Journal of Zaytuna College*, April 28, 2017, https://renovatio.zaytuna.edu/article/orientalists-militants-and-the-meanings-of-jihad.

11 Afsaruddin, "Orientalists, Militants, and the Meanings of Jihad."

12 Afsaruddin, *Striving in the Path of God*, 1–95; "Orientalists, Militants, and the Meanings of Jihad."

13 Samantha May, "Are We Really Seeing the Rise of a 'New Jihad'?," *The Conversation*, May 26, 2017, https://theconversation.com/are-we-really-seeing-the-rise-of-a-new-jihad-78422.

14 Federal Bureau of Investigation, *Terrorism 2002–2005*, U.S. Department of Justice, accessed March 11, 2019, https://www.fbi.gov/stats-services/publications/terrorism-2002–2005; Frederic Lemieux, "What Is Terrorism? What Do Terrorists Want?," *The Conversation*, June 2, 2017, https://theconversation.com/what-is-terrorism-what-do-terrorists-want-78228. The FBI's report *Terrorism 2002–2005* acknowledges there is no one definition of terrorism, however it is used for legal and policing purposes to distinguish certain types of activities:

There is no single, universally accepted, definition of terrorism. Terrorism is defined in the Code of Federal Regulations as "the unlawful use of force and violence against persons or property to intimidate or coerce a government, the civilian population, or any segment thereof, in furtherance of political or social objectives" (28 C.F.R. Section 0.85).

The FBI further describes terrorism as either domestic or international, depending on the origin, base, and objectives of the terrorist organization.

The lack of an agreed definition relates to the perspective one has on the political aims of the group labelled as terrorist. For this study, the designation "terrorist" or "terrorism" will be discussed in the context of irregular warfare in which non-state parties undertake violent activities that usually fail in some way to distinguish between civilian and combatant in pursuit of political and religious aims. Of course, nonreligious groups undertake terrorist acts, most infamously a range of fascist, far-right activists and groups.

15 See Richard Dawkins, *The God Delusion* (London: Bantam, 2006); Christopher Hitchens, *God Is Not Great: How Religion Poisons Everything* (New York: Twelve, 2007).
16 William Cavanaugh, *The Myth of Religious Violence: Secular Ideology and the Roots of Modern Conflict* (New York: Oxford University Press, 2009).
17 Scott Atran, "ISIS Is a Revolution," *Aeon*, December 15, 2015, https://aeon.co/essays/why-isis-has-the-potential-to-be-a-world-altering-revolution.
18 Olivier Roy, "Who Are the New Jihadis?," *The Guardian*, April 13, 2017, https://www.theguardian.com/news/2017/apr/13/who-are-the-new-jihadis.
19 Michael Cook, "The Appeal of Islamic Fundamentalism" (lecture), March 14, 2013, London, The British Academy, https://www.youtube.com/watch?v=X6dN6RC2J1Q.
20 Christopher Wray, "Current Threats to the Homeland: Statement before the Senate Homeland Security and Government Affairs Committee," September 27, 2017, Federal Bureau of Investigation, https://www.fbi.gov/news/testimony/current-threats-to-the-homeland.
21 Atran, "ISIS Is a Revolution."
22 Jonathan Cole, "The Jihadist Current and the West: Politics, Theology, and the Clash of Conceptuality," in *Does Religion Cause Violence? Multidisciplinary Perspectives on Violence and Religion in the Modern World*, ed. Scott Cowdell, Chris Fleming, Joel Hodge, and Carly Osborn (New York: Bloomsbury Academic, 2018), 207–28.
23 Cole, "The Jihadist Current and the West," 207.
24 Cole, "The Jihadist Current and the West," 216.
25 Cole, "The Jihadist Current and the West," 216.
26 Girard, *Battling to the End*, 214.
27 Girard, *Battling to the End*, 213.
28 Cole, "The Jihadist Current and the West," 216.
29 René Girard, Pierpaolo Antonello, and João Cezar de Castro Rocha, *Evolution and Conversion: Dialogues on the Origins of Culture* (London: Continuum, 2007), 113–24.
30 Girard, *Battling to the End*, 215.
31 "A Communiqué from Qa'idat Al-Jihad concerning the testaments of the heroes and the legality of the Washington and New York Operations," in David Cook, *Understanding Jihad* (Berkeley: University of California Press, 2005), 175–7.
32 Girard, *Battling to the End*, 15–17.
33 Cole, "The Jihadist Current and the West," 216.
34 See, e.g., Wolfgang Palaver and Richard Schenk, eds., *Mimetic Theory and World Religions* (East Lansing: Michigan State University Press, 2018).

35 Michael Kirwan, "René Girard and World Religions," in *Mimetic Theory and World Religions*, ed. Wolfgang Palaver and Richard Schenk (East Lansing: Michigan State University Press, 2018), 209.
36 Kirwan, "René Girard and World Religions," 210–11.
37 Cole, "The Jihadist Current and the West."
38 Mark Juergensmeyer, *Terror in the Mind of God: The Global Rise of Religious Violence* (Berkeley: University of California Press, 2000).
39 Cavanaugh, *Myth of Religious Violence*.

1 René Girard's Mimetic Theory

1 Girard's theory has been analyzed and critiqued at length. I have explored critiques elsewhere and refer the reader to the following: Joel Hodge, *Resisting Violence and Victimisation: Christian Faith and Solidarity in East Timor* (Farnham: Ashgate, 2012), 43–9. For a fuller introduction to Girard's mimetic theory (and criticisms), see René Girard, *I See Satan Fall Like Lightning*, trans. J. G. Williams (Maryknoll: Orbis Books, 2001); *The Girard Reader*, ed. James G. Williams (New York: Crossroad, 1996); Michael Kirwan, *Discovering Girard* (Cambridge, MA: Cowley, 2005); *Girard and Theology* (London: T&T Clark, 2009); Wolfgang Palaver, *René Girard's Mimetic Theory*, trans. Gabriel Borrud (East Lansing: Michigan State University Press, 2013).
2 René Girard, *Deceit, Desire, and the Novel: Self and Other in Literary Structure*, trans. Y. Freccero (Baltimore, MD: Johns Hopkins University Press, 1965), 4; René Girard, with Jean-Michel Oughourlian and Guy Lefort, *Things Hidden since the Foundation of the World*, trans. S. Bann and M. Metteer (Stanford, CA: Stanford University Press, 1987), 10.
3 Girard, *Deceit, Desire, and the Novel*, 4.
4 Jean-Michel Oughourlian, *The Puppet of Desire: The Psychology of Hysteria, Possession, and Hypnosis* (Stanford, CA: Stanford University Press, 1991), 1.
5 Aristotle, *Poetics*, trans. S. H. Butcher, http://classics.mit.edu/Aristotle/poetics.1.1.html, Part 4; *Aristotle's Poetics: Translated and with a Commentary by George Whalley*, ed. John Baxter and Patrick Atherton (Montreal: McGill-Queen's University Press, 1997), 57.
6 See, e.g., Scott R. Garrells, *Mimesis and Science: Empirical Research on Imitation and the Mimetic Theory of Culture and Religion* (East Lansing: Michigan State University Press, 2011).
7 Iain McGilchrist, *Master and His Emissary: The Divided Brain and the Making of the Western World* (New Haven, CT: Yale University Press, 2009), 247.
8 McGilchrist, *Master and His Emissary*, 249.
9 Oughourlian, *Puppet of Desire*, 10; James Alison, *The Joy of Being Wrong: Original Sin through Easter Eyes* (New York: Crossroad, 1998), 29.

10 Alison, *Joy of Being Wrong*, 29.
11 Ibid., 33.
12 Girard, *Deceit, Desire, and the Novel*, 83–112; *Things Hidden*, 295–8.
13 Alison, *Joy of Being Wrong*, 29.
14 By violence I am referring to a coercive act that physically, psychologically, spiritually, symbolically, or structurally results in injury, harm, or the clear diminishment of the actualization or flourishing of a person.
15 René Girard, *The One by Whom Scandal Comes*, trans. M. B. DeBevoise (East Lansing: Michigan State University Press, 2014), 4; *Battling to the End: Conversations with Benoît Chantre*, trans. Mary Baker (East Lansing, MI: Michigan State University Press, 2010), 31; "Violence, Victims and Christianity," *The D'Arcy Lecture*, University of Oxford, November 5, 1997, https://www.uibk.ac.at/theol/cover/girard/videos.html.
16 Girard, "Violence, Victims and Christianity."
17 Girard, *Deceit, Desire and the Novel*, 15–17.
18 Oughourlian, *The Puppet of Desire*, 20.
19 Ibid., 101–12; René Girard, *Violence and the Sacred*, trans. P. Gregory (Baltimore, MD: Johns Hopkins University Press, 1977), 159–60; Girard et al., *Things Hidden*, 12; Girard, *Battling to the End*, 31.
20 Girard, *I See Satan Fall*, 16.
21 Girard also discusses "appetites" (e.g., bodily needs) that operate alongside mimetic desire. Competition over resources to satisfy appetites is also a problem for human groups, though mimesis tends to even become part of these conflicts.
22 Girard, "Violence, Victims and Christianity."
23 Girard, *I See Satan Fall*, 9.
24 Girard, *Things Hidden*, 26.
25 Girard, *I See Satan Fall*, 16. For example, in 2011 the American Pastor, Terry Jones, burned a Qur'an that led to Afghani Muslims reacting with mob violence. In this rivalry, each became a scandal to the other. The object that each desired was the honor, protection, and supremacy of their tradition, and each believed that the other was an obstacle to achieving this desire. The Pastor's action can be understood in a context where he felt threatened religiously and culturally by the onset of Islamic claims to power and truth. As groups and traditions meet, they become aware of the relative nature of their truth claims and pretence at supremacy, which provokes the desire to achieve it as the other desires the same object.
26 Girard, *I See Satan Fall*, 119.
27 Girard, *Deceit, Desire, and the Novel*, 115.
28 Ibid., 107–25; René Girard, with Pierpaolo Antonello and João Cezar de Castro Rocha, *Evolution and Conversion: Dialogues on the Origins of Culture* (New York: Continuum, 2007), 240.

29 Girard, *I See Satan Fall*, 15–16.

30 Girard, *Violence and the Sacred*, 39–57.

31 Ibid., 68–88; René Girard, *The Scapegoat*, trans. Y. Freccero (Baltimore, MD: Johns Hopkins University Press, 1986), 17–38; *Things Hidden*, 130–4. I generally use "victim" and "scapegoat" interchangeably, following Girard's usage. Both terms have a technical meaning in Girard's thought: to denote a person (or people) who are unanimously blamed and expelled/killed to bring order to a group.

32 Some feminist scholars critique Girard's view of mimetic desire and violence as primarily or exclusively masculine. For example, it is claimed that the violence of the mob is primarily an action of males. Further, these scholars attempt to place the oppression of women as prior to the victimage cycle. See, e.g., a summary in Richard J. Golsan, *René Girard and Myth: An Introduction* (New York: Routledge, 2002), 113–16, and Palaver, *René Girard's Mimetic Theory*, 297–308. In response, Girard (in Golsan, *René Girard and Myth*, 141–6) argues that males and females share the same mimetic nature and engage in the same patterns of mimetic rivalry and scapegoating (whether within, across, or between gender groups). Girard also discusses the mimetic nature of sexual violence and is clear about the propensity for women to be targeted for victimization (*Violence and the Sacred*, 34–6, 118, 141, and 219–20). While men are responsible for a higher number of deaths in war and homicides, women are still participants in mimetic rivalry and violence, and engage in what is traditionally regarded as "male" forms of violence. For example, the number of women who are members of militant groups as willing supporters, combatants, and suicide bombers is significant. Risk assessment and home-grown terrorism expert, Jason Thomas, comments, "Women are no less capable of evil than men. One-third of Tamil Tiger suicide bombers during Sri Lanka's bloody civil war were women, including one pretending to be pregnant who was involved in an attack against Sri Lanka's military chief in 2006. Many women led the Islamic State enforcement brigades on the streets of Raqqa and some of the harshest enforcers were foreigners." (Jason Thomas, "Traitors Would Kill Us; It's in Their Nature," *The Australian*, March 28, 2019, https://www.theaustralian.com.au/commentary/traitors-would-kill-us-its-in-their-nature/news-story/91e76a9c521da7083cd99731c5e20ce3). It is argued that the historically oppressed position of women leads to certain pressures on them to participate in forms of mimetic violence dominated by men. The case of women who join jihadist groups, especially when they come from Western contexts, puts into question whether the cause is male oppression of women. For these women, there is a level of free choice, though an imperfect or limited one.

33 Girard, *Violence and the Sacred*, 257–64; *I See Satan Fall*, 71–2.

34 The terms "archaic" or "traditional" are not used in a chronological or pejorative sense but denote a premodern, traditional culture characterized by a singular

tradition of sacrificial rituals, myths, and prohibitions. Girard identifies these societies as based around the violent sacred and not affected by the revelation of the innocent scapegoat. Post-archaic or modern societies are affected by this revelation, such that violence can no longer be as effectively, unanimously, and unproblematically divinized and deployed. Furthermore, Girard does not seek to blame or scapegoat archaic cultures for victimage practices but rather identifies them as the means that humans used to convene and stabilize their cultural relations for a peaceful aim. Nevertheless, Girard does not condone the use of violence or scapegoating.

35 Girard, *Battling to the End*, 23.

36 Girard, *The Scapegoat*, 24.

37 Girard notes that not all cultures have been capable of maintaining the scapegoat mechanism and subsequently have not survived. See Girard, *Evolution and Conversion*, 67.

38 Girard, *Deceit, Desire, and the Novel*, 61. See also Girard, *I See Satan Fall*, 96–8, and *Deceit, Desire, and the Novel*, 53–82 and 153–9.

39 See Girard, *Things Hidden*, 141–280; *The Scapegoat*, 100–212; *I See Satan Fall*, 103–60.

40 Girard, *Things Hidden*, 144–9.

41 Ibid., 146–7.

42 Ibid., 144–9.

43 Ibid., 144–9; *I See Satan Fall*, 143–6; Gil Bailie, *Violence Unveiled: Humanity at the Crossroads* (New York: Crossroad, 1995), 138–40.

44 Girard, *Things Hidden*, 146.

45 Ibid., 149. While Cain is no longer worthy to remain in the Garden of Eden, it is important to note that God also protects Cain from retribution by placing a mark on him.

46 Girard, *Things Hidden*, 149.

47 Ibid., 155–6; *I See Satan Fall*, 28–30.

48 Girard, *Things Hidden*, 149–54.

49 Ibid., 180–280; *The Scapegoat*, 100–212; *I See Satan Fall*, 121–60; *Evolution and Conversion*, 196–213.

50 Girard, *Evolution and Conversion*, 218.

51 Girard, *The Scapegoat*, 109.

52 Girard, *Battling to the End*, 35; Scott Cowdell, Chris Fleming, Joel Hodge, and Mathias Moosbrugger, *René Girard and Raymund Schwager: Correspondence 1974–1991*, Violence, Desire, and the Sacred 4, trans. Sheelah Treflé Hidden and Chris Fleming (New York: Bloomsbury Academic, 2016).

53 Girard, *Evolution and Conversion*, 214–17.

54 Girard, *Things Hidden*, 233; *I See Satan Fall*, 130–1.

55 Girard, *Things Hidden*, 277.

56 Girard, *Battling to the End*, 214–16.

57 Ibid., 214.

58 Ibid., 215–16.

59 Ibid.

60 Ibid., 215.

61 Wolfgang Palaver, "The Abrahamic Revolution," in *Mimetic Theory and World Religions*, ed. Wolfgang Palaver and Richard Schenk (East Lansing: Michigan State University Press, 2018), 259. Palaver also points out that Girard's claim about Islam being a return to archaic religion requires clarification because Girard has also stated that there are no archaic religions remaining in the modern world (at least in societies that have undergone modernization).

62 Palaver, "The Abrahamic Revolution," 259–60.

63 Ibid., 260–67; Wolfgang Palaver, "Religious Extremism, Terrorism, and Islam: A Mimetic Perspective," in *Does Religion Cause Violence? Multidisciplinary Perspectives on Violence and Religion in the Modern World*, ed. Scott Cowdell, Chris Fleming, Joel Hodge, and Carly Osborn, Violence, Desire, and the Sacred 7 (New York: Bloomsbury Academic, 2018), 192.

64 Girard, *Things Hidden*, 224–62.

65 Girard, *I See Satan Fall*, 161–9; *Evolution and Conversion*, 258.

66 René Girard, *When These Things Begin: Conversations with Michel Treguer*, trans. Trevor Cribben Merrill (East Lansing: Michigan State University Press, 2014), 81.

67 Girard, *Battling to the End*, 198.

68 Ibid., 131.

69 Girard, *When These Things Begin*, 81; Paul Dumouchel, *The Barren Sacrifice: An Essay on Political Violence*, trans. Mary Baker (East Lansing: Michigan State University Press, 2015), 64 and 143–7.

70 Girard, *Evolution and Conversion*, 236.

71 Girard, *Battling to the End*, 1–25.

2 Violence in Modernity

1 In Chapter 1, I gave definitions for "archaic" and "modern" societies according to Girard's schema. In addition to being affected by desacralization, modernity serves as a chronological marker for a certain period in Western (and world) history (from approximately the fifteenth century onward) characterized by phenomena such as the rise of science and technology, industrialization, democratic revolutions, nation-states, and globalization. In philosophical terms, modernity is associated with certain philosophical tenets, such as an emphasis on rational truth. While modernity will be used in this study to denote a contemporary cultural condition

that results from these trends, I also note that what is referred to as "postmodernity" has resulted in distinctive philosophical and political emphases (on which there is an extensive literature), such as forms of relativism and pluralism. I will subsume all these trends under the term "modernity" for ease of reference.

2 René Girard, *Battling to the End: Conversations with Benoît Chantre*, trans. Mary Baker (East Lansing: Michigan State University Press, 2010), 9–10 and 35–42; Paul Dumouchel, *The Barren Sacrifice: An Essay on Political Violence*, trans. Mary Baker (East Lansing: Michigan State University Press, 2015), xxiii–xiv and 78–9.

3 Girard, *Battling to the End*, 6.

4 This is not to argue that there is moral equivalency between the parties of the world wars, especially of the Second World War. The Allies in the First World War and the Second World War, of course, stopped short of total destruction or domination of their enemies, but they still inflicted terrible forms of destruction in order to bring about surrender.

5 Girard, *Battling to the End*, 2.

6 Ibid., 2 and 22.

7 Ibid., 1–25.

8 Total warfare stands in contrast to formulations of just war, which represent the best of what Girard (*Battling to the End*, 2) calls "political rationality." Just war rationales ultimately seek to limit violence and injustice rather than exacerbate violence, though such rationales can be manipulated for political or ideological advantage.

9 Girard, *Battling to the End*, 154.

10 Ibid., 155.

11 Ibid.

12 Ibid., 157–93. In fact, Girard shows how French and German identities became dependent on their mutual antipathy and rivalry, into which the whole of Europe and the world were eventually drawn.

13 René Girard, *Deceit, Desire and the Novel: Self and Other in Literary Structure*, trans. Yvonne Freccero (Baltimore, MD: Johns Hopkins University Press, 1965), 121. The breakdown of aristocratic hierarchies is not lamented by Girard in a political or nostalgic sense but is analyzed for its cultural effects. Girard points to positive benefits in the movement for equality but also identifies its underside when equality breeds homogeneity that lacks "concrete difference or positive value" (Girard, *Deceit, Desire and the Novel*, 137).

14 Girard, *Deceit, Desire and the Novel*, 119.

15 Ibid., 119.

16 See Dumouchel, *Barren Sacrifice*, 96–110, for a discussion of how totalitarian regimes intensify and are exploited by internal rivalries.

17 Girard, *Deceit, Desire and the Novel*, 128. The French Revolution was similar to the Glorious Revolution in England in unleashing mimetic forces.

18 Girard, *Deceit, Desire and the Novel*, 137.
19 Ibid., 136–7.
20 Ibid.
21 Ibid., 92.
22 Ibid., 256–89.
23 Girard, *Battling to the End*, 65; Dumouchel, *Barren Sacrifice*, 79–81. See Carl Schmitt, *The Concept of the Political* (Chicago, IL: University of Chicago Press, 2007), 19–79.
24 Dumouchel, *Barren Sacrifice*, xviii–xiv.
25 Ibid., 78.
26 Girard, *Battling to the End*, 39.
27 Dumouchel, *Barren Sacrifice*, 80.
28 René Girard, *I See Satan Fall Like Lightning*, trans. James G. Williams (Maryknoll: Orbis Books, 2001), 158 and 180–1. The French Revolution developed its own religious rituals and doctrines based around the state, and later the Emperor, that evidences Girard's claim. These rituals started with scapegoating violence (executions and guillotining) in which the oppressed were celebrated and the oppressors denounced.
29 Wolfgang Palaver, "The Abrahamic Revolution," in *Mimetic Theory and World Religions*, ed. Wolfgang Palaver and Richard Schenk (East Lansing: Michigan State University Press, 2018), 267–9.
30 Dr. Abdul Aziz Rantisi, a founder of Hamas, in Mark Juergensmeyer, *Terror in the Mind of God* (Berkeley: University of California Press, 2000), 74.
31 Girard, *Battling to the End*, 1–2. Cf. Carl von Clausewitz, *Vom Kriege* (Bonn: Dummler, 1973), 8 and 199. See the translator's footnote on page 219 of *Battling to the End* (chapter 1, note 1) that draws a distinction between Girard's notion of "escalation to extremes" and Clausewitz's "trend" or "tendency to extremes."
32 René Girard, "'What Is Occurring Today Is Mimetic Rivalry on a Planetary Scale': René Girard on September 11" (with Henri Tincq). *Le Monde*, November 6, 2011. Translated by the Colloquium on Violence and Religion. Available at www.morphizm.com/politix/girard911.html.
33 Girard, *Battling to the End*, xvi.
34 Ibid., 198.
35 Ibid., 68. For a definition of terrorism, please see note 12 in the introduction.
36 Girard, *Battling to the End*, 215.
37 Girard, *Battling to the End*, 216. Technology can be understood here as an exemplar and carrier of Westernized modernity, which jihadists seek to master in destructive ways against the West.
38 Louise Richardson, *What Terrorists Want: Understanding the Enemy, Containing the Threat* (New York: Random House, 2006), 36.

39 Richardson, *What Terrorists Want*, 106.

40 Ibid., 36–7 and 106–7.

41 See Osama bin Laden, "Full Text: Bin Laden's 'Letter to America,'" *The Guardian*, November 24, 2002, https://www.theguardian.com/world/2002/nov/24/theobserver.

42 Girard, *Battling to the End*, 66; Carl Schmitt, *Theory of the Partisan* (New York: Telos Press, 2007), 4. It is argued that there are ancient precursors to modern terrorism, such as the Zealots, Assassins, and Thugi, who share similar destructive aims and methods to modern terrorists (Richardson, *What Terrorists Want*, 23–8). These groups share similarities with militant jihadists, but they also had strategic, operational, and religious limitations, especially in primarily targeting the "enemy occupier." For example, the Assassins share the ritualistic element of killing with jihadism, but the Assassins primarily killed "enemy" leaders or combatants. See Laurent Murawiec, *The Mind of Jihad* (New York: Cambridge University Press, 2008), 20–1.

43 Girard, *Battling to the End*, 66.

44 Ibid., 66. In ancient and medieval societies, warfare generally occurred between defined combatants. Killing civilians in combat was generally taboo. In ancient or traditional societies, there were rules around the treatment of civilians because of supernatural sanction and reciprocal ties (because of kinship ties, for example). Warfare was generally ritualized and often connected to sacrifice, e.g., prisoners of war were used for sacrificial purposes. Tribes or groups were generally connected by rules of reciprocity, which did not apply only if a group had little or no contact with another group. See Dumouchel, *Barren Sacrifice*, 51–9.

45 Girard, *Battling to the End*, 216.

46 Gilles Kepel, "The Origins and Development of the Jihadist Movement: From Anti-Communism to Terrorism," *Asian Affairs* 34:2 (2003): 91–108; *Jihad: The Trail of Political Islam*, trans. Anthony F. Roberts (London: I.B. Tauris, 2004), 5–20.

47 Hamish de Bretton-Gordon (a chemical weapons expert) in Joby Warrick, "Exclusive: Iraqi Scientist Says He Helped ISIS Make Chemical Weapons," *Washington Post*, January 21, 2019, https://www.washingtonpost.com/world/national-security/exclusive-iraqi-scientist-says-he-helped-isis-make-chemical-weapons/2019/01/21/617cb8f0-0d35-11e9-831f-3aa2c2be4cbd_story.html?noredirect=on&utm_term=.8465dd6fa0c6. See also Eric Schmitt, "ISIS Used Chemical Arms at Least 52 Times in Syria and Iraq, Report Says," *New York Times*, November 21, 2016, https://www.nytimes.com/2016/11/21/world/middleeast/isis-chemical-weapons-syria-iraq-mosul.html.

48 Gilles Kepel, *Beyond Terror and Martyrdom: The Future of the Middle East* (Cambridge, MA: Belknap Press of Harvard University Press, 2008), 114–20.

49 Girard, *Battling to the End*, 157–93.

50 Shiraz Maher, *Salafi-Jihadism: The History of an Idea* (London: Hurst, 2016).
51 Murawiec, *Mind of Jihad*, 18.
52 I explore these justifications in detail in Chapter 6.
53 Girard, *Battling to the End*, 117.
54 Ibid..
55 Girard, *Battling to the End*, 68–9.

3 The Islamic Modernity

1 Gilles Kepel, *The Revenge of God: The Resurgence of Islam, Christianity and Judaism in the Modern World* , trans. Alan Braley (Cambridge, UK: Polity, 1994), 24–5.
2 Gilles Kepel, *Jihad: The Trail of Political Islam*, trans. Anthony F. Roberts (London: I.B. Tauris, 2004), 66.
3 Jocelyne Cesari, *What Is Political Islam?* (Boulder, CO: Lynne Rienner, 2018), 2.
4 Cesari, *What Is Political Islam?*, 3.
5 Charles Tripp, "Islam and the Contingency of Politics," in *The Secular State and Islam in Europe*, ed. Kurt Almquist (Stockholm: Axel & Margaret Ax:son Johnson Foundation, 2007), 94–5.
6 Farhad Khosrokhavar, *Jihadist Ideology: The Anthropological Perspective* (Aarhus: Centre for Studies in Islamism and Radicalisation, Department of Political Science, Aarhus University, 2011), 165–9.
7 Ajami, Fouad. "The Way We Live Now: 10-07-01; Out of Egypt."*New York Times*. October 7, 2001.https://www.nytimes.com/2001/10/07/magazine/the-way-we-live-now-10-07-01-out-of-egypt.html.
8 Farhad Khosrokhavar, *Inside Jihadism: Understanding Jihadi Movements Worldwide* (Boulder, CO: Paradigm, 2009), 86.
9 Kepel, *Jihad*, 28. See also John L. Esposito, *The Islamic Threat: Myth or Reality?*, 3rd ed. (New York: Oxford University Press, 1999), 6–18.
10 Kepel, *Jihad*, 43–52 and 81–8.
11 Ibid., 52–60 and 168.
12 Ibid., 136–47.
13 Kepel, *Revenge of God*, 33–46.
14 Ibid., 35.
15 Kepel, *Jihad*, 81–2.
16 Kepel, *Revenge of God*, 24–5.
17 Ibid.
18 Kepel, *Jihad*, 46–7.
19 Ibid., 59–60.

20 Ibid., 52–7; Gilles Kepel, *The War for Muslim Minds: Islam and the West*, trans. Pascale Ghazaleh (Cambridge, MA: Belknap Press of Harvard University Press, 2004), 86.

21 Kepel, *Jihad*, 41.

22 Ibid., 52–60.

23 Khosrokhavar, *Jihadist Ideology*, 165.

24 Richard P. Mitchell, *The Society of the Muslim Brothers* (New York: Oxford University Press, 1969), 193–4; Laurent Murawiec, *The Mind of Jihad* (New York: Cambridge University Press, 2008), 33. This chapter refers to Egyptian examples throughout. The influence of the Muslim Brotherhood and Egyptian intellectuals such as Sayyid Qutb, as well as the long and significant history of Egyptian radicalism, has meant that the Egyptian Islamist movement has been internationally influential. The Egyptian example is studied by jihadist militants across the Muslim world and Egyptian militants have contributed substantially to international jihadist groups, such as al-Qaeda. Kepel, *Jihad*, 88.

25 Murawiec, *Mind of Jihad*, 33; Kepel, *Jihad*, 298.

26 Kepel, *Jihad*, 28.

27 Ibid., 33 and 52–60.

28 Ibid., 67.

29 Ibid., 67.

30 Ibid., 290–1.

31 Ibid., 290.

32 Ibid., 52–60, 110–3, 142 and 159.

33 Olivier Roy, "An Interview with Olivier Roy," *Colombia University Press*, accessed March 13, 2019, https://cup.columbia.edu/author-interviews/roy-globalized-islam.

34 Louise Richardson, *What Terrorists Want: Understanding the Enemy, Containing the Threat* (New York: Random House, 2006), 38–70.

35 Kepel, *Jihad*, 142–3.

36 Kepel, *Revenge of God*, 20.

37 Ibid., 33–5. The exact nature of this withdrawal and return has been interpreted differently by Islamist groups, with Qutb himself referring to an existential or spiritual withdrawal rather than a complete physical withdrawal from society.

38 Kepel, *Jihad*, 34–5.

39 Kepel, *Revenge of God*, 20.

40 Kepel, *Jihad*, 36–41.

41 Murawiec, *Mind of Jihad*, 34–7.

42 Kepel, *Revenge of God*, 34–6.

43 Kepel, *Jihad*, 24–32; David Cook, *Understanding Jihad* (Berkeley: University of California Press, 2005), 1–48 and 163–8; Asma Afsaruddin, *Striving in the Path of*

God: Jihad and Martyrdom in Islamic Thought* (New York: Oxford University Press, 2013). Cook argues that jihad has consistently had the sense of fighting or violence from the beginnings of Islam, while Afsaruddin argues that nonviolent, spiritual traditions have been present and are more prominent in a holistic reading of the Qur'an and related literature. This debate does not need to be resolved for or by this study, as it is enough to note that modern militant Islamists emphasize jihad as primarily or exclusively violent.

44 Fawaz A. Gerges, *The Far Enemy: Why Jihad Went Global*, 2nd ed. (New York: Cambridge University Press, 2009), 4–5. Gerges quotes from Sayyid Qutb, *Milestones* (Cedar Rapids, IA: Mother Mosque Foundation, n.d.), 17.

45 Cook, *Understanding Jihad*, 103.

46 Gilles Kepel, *The Roots of Radical Islam*, trans. Jon Rothschild (London: Saqi, 2005), 70–105.

47 Kepel, *Revenge of God*, 34–41.

48 Shiraz Maher, *Salafi-Jihadism: The History of an Idea* (London: Hurst, 2016), 42; John L. Esposito, *Unholy War: Terror in the Name of Islam* (Oxford: Oxford University Press, 2003), 64.

49 Qutb, *Milestones*, in Cook, *Understanding Jihad*, 105.

50 Cook, *Understanding Jihad*, 104.

51 Kepel, *Roots of Radical Islam*, 54–5.

52 Kepel, *Revenge of God*, 33.

53 Esposito, *Unholy War*, 61.

54 Kepel, *Jihad*, 154–6 and 170.

55 Ibid., 154.

56 Ibid., 153–8.

57 Kepel, *Revenge of God*, 22 and 25; Kepel, *Jihad*, 61–2.

58 Kepel, *Jihad*, 315.

59 Ibid., 315–16.

60 Esposito, *Unholy War*, 62.

61 With thanks to Professor Marcia Pally for discussions on this topic.

62 Scott Atran, "ISIS Is a Revolution," *Aeon*, December 15, 2015, https://aeon.co/essays/why-isis-has-the-potential-to-be-a-world-altering-revolution.

63 David Kilcullen, "Blood Year: Terror and the Islamic State," *Quarterly Essay* 58 (2015): 21–3, 72 and 78; "The Rise of ISIS and Its Threat: David Kilcullen in conversation with Robert Manne," La Trobe University Ideas and Society 2015, *The Monthly*, May 27, 2015, video, https://www.themonthly.com.au/video/2015/may/27/1432685877/rise-isis-and-its-threat-david-kilcullen-conversation-robert-manne.

64 David Kilcullen, *Blood Year: The Unravelling of Western Counterterrorism* (New York: Oxford University Press, 2016), 77.

65 Kilcullen, "Blood Year," 18–23 and 72; Zachary Laub and Jonathan Masters, "The Islamic State," *Council of Foreign Relations (CFR) Backgrounders*, May 18, 2015, http://www.cfr.org/iraq/islamic-state/p14811. ISIS also seems to have lower standards regarding their recruits and accept more of them than al-Qaeda.
66 Kilcullen, "Blood Year," 21–3.

4 The Militant Jihadist Response to Modernity

1 Wolfgang Palaver, "The Abrahamic Revolution," in *Mimetic Theory and World Religions*, ed. Wolfgang Palaver and Richard Schenk (East Lansing: Michigan State University Press, 2018), 267–73.
2 Farhad Khosrokhavar, *Jihadist Ideology: The Anthropological Perspective* (Aarhus: Centre for Studies in Islamism and Radicalisation, Department of Political Science, Aarhus University, 2011), 168.
3 Osama bin Laden, "Full Text: Bin Laden's 'Letter to America,'" *The Guardian*, November 24, 2002, https://www.theguardian.com/world/2002/nov/24/theobserver.
4 Shiraz Maher, "ICSR Insight – The Roots of Radicalisation? It's Identity, Stupid." International Centre for the Study of Radicalisation and Political Violence, King's College London, June 23, 2015, https://icsr.info/2015/06/23/roots-radicalisation-identity-stupid/.
5 Gilles Kepel, *The Roots of Radical Islam*, trans. Jon Rothschild (London: Saqi, 2005), 29.
6 Ibid., 26–32.
7 Ibid., 29.
8 Ibid., 30.
9 Gilles Kepel, *Jihad: The Trail of Political Islam*, trans. Anthony F. Roberts (London: I.B. Tauris, 2004), 254–6.
10 Samir al-Khalil (Kaneen Makiya), *Republic of Fear: The Inside Story of Saddam's Iraq* (New York: Pantheon Books, 1989), 52–3.
11 Kepel, *Jihad*, 87–8 and 91–8.
12 Ibid., 20–68. This repression began under the authoritarian despotism of Nassar's Arab nationalist regime, following the overthrow of the monarchy.
13 Farhad Khosrokhavar, *Inside Jihadism: Understanding Jihadi Movements Worldwide* (Boulder, CO: Paradigm, 2009), 248.
14 Ibid., 229.
15 Gilles Kepel, *The Revenge of God: The Resurgence of Islam, Christianity and Judaism in the Modern World*, trans. Alan Braley (Cambridge: Polity, 1994), 33–4.
16 Olivier Roy, *Globalized Islam: The Search for a New Ummah* (New York: Columbia University Press, 2004), 41; Khosrokhavar, *Inside Jihadism*, 59.

17 Sayyid Qutb, *Ma'alim fil tariq* (Signposts or The Signs of the Road), Minbar al Tawhid wal Jihad [website], in Khosrokhavar, *Inside Jihadism*, 23.

18 David Cook, *Understanding Jihad* (Berkeley: University of California Press, 2005), 93–100; Kepel, *Roots of Radical Islam*, 34–67 and 197–225.

19 Laurent Murawiec, *The Mind of Jihad* (New York: Cambridge University Press, 2008), 29–33 and 37.

20 Shiraz Maher, *Salafi-Jihadism: The History of an Idea* (London: Hurst, 2016), 181–3.

21 Ibid., 181–3.

22 Kepel, *Revenge of God*, 20–35.

23 Kepel, *Roots of Radical Islam*, 65.

24 Maher, *Salafi-Jihadism*, 181–3.

25 Kepel, *Revenge of God*, 31–2.

26 Maher, *Salafi-Jihadism*, 7 and 17; Kepel, *Roots of Radical Islam*, 34–67; Cook, *Understanding Jihad*, 93–110 and 163–6.

27 Maher, *Salafi-Jihadism*, 35–8.

28 Cook, *Understanding Jihad*, 164.

29 Maher, *Salafi-Jihadism*, 32.

30 On abrogation, see Asma Afsaruddin, *Striving in the Path of God: Jihad and Martyrdom in Islamic Thought* (New York: Oxford University Press, 2013), 296–7.

31 Khosrokhavar, *Inside Jihadism*, 76.

32 Afsaruddin, *Striving in the Path of God*, 268–99.

33 Kepel, *Roots of Radical Islam*, 25–6.

34 Ibid., 26.

35 Robert Manne, *The Mind of the Islamic State* (Carlton, AU: Redback Quarterly, 2016), 19; Kepel, *Roots of Radical Islam*, 25–6.

36 Maher, *Salafi-Jihadism*, 178–9; Kepel, *Revenge of God*, 20.

37 Maher, *Salafi-Jihadism*, 87–8; Khosrokhavar, *Inside Jihadism*, 94.

38 Maher, *Salafi-Jihadism*, 87–8; Kepel, *Roots of Radical Islam*, 63–7; Khosrokhavar, *Inside Jihadism*, 94.

39 Khosrokhavar, *Inside Jihadism*, 93–4.

40 Osama bin Laden, "Full Text: Bin Laden's 'Letter to America.'"

41 Kepel, *Jihad*, 86.

42 Murawiec, *Mind of Jihad*, 28.

43 Jonathan Sacks, *Not in God's Name: Confronting Religious Violence* (London: Hodder & Stoughton, 2015), 42.

44 Sacks, *Not in God's Name*, 42.

45 Ibid., 22.

46 Ibid., 22.

47 Chris Fleming, "The Apocalypse Will Not Be Televised," in *Mimesis, Movies, and Media*, ed. Scott Cowdell, Chris Fleming, and Joel Hodge (New York: Bloomsbury,

2015), 39. Fleming also argues that Hiroshima was another pivotal moment in a kind of end to modernity. It became a sign of the consequences of total war and the possibility of nuclear destruction and war. In this way, it became an inadvertent motivation for peace.

48 Eric Gans, "The Holocaust and the Victimary Revolution," in *Poetics of the Americas: Race, Founding, and Textuality*, ed. Bainard Cowan and Jefferson Humphries (Baton Rouge: Louisiana State University Press, 1997), 123–39.

49 Osama bin Laden, interview by John Miller, *Frontline*, May 1998, https://www.pbs.org/wgbh/pages/frontline/shows/binladen/who/interview.html.

50 Jean-Pierre Dupuy, "The Sacred Is Back—But as Simulacrum," in *Does Religion Cause Violence? Multidisciplinary Perspectives on Violence and Religion in the Modern World*, ed. Scott Cowdell, Chris Fleming, Joel Hodge, and Carly Osborn (New York: Bloomsbury Academic, 2018), 95–9.

51 Ibid., 99–100.

52 René Girard, *Battling to the End: Conversations with Benoît Chantre*, trans. Mary Baker (East Lansing: Michigan State University Press, 2010), 67.

53 Maher, *Salafi-Jihadism*, 64–5.

54 Scott Cowdell, *René Girard and Secular Modernity: Christ, Culture, and Crisis* (Notre Dame, IN: Notre Dame Press, 2013), 157.

55 Osama bin Laden, interview by John Miller.

56 Osama bin Laden, "Full Text: Bin Laden's 'Letter to America.'"

57 Khosrokhavar, *Jihadist Ideology*, 9.

58 Ibid., 9.

59 Ibid., 9–10.

60 Ibid., 10.

61 Murawiec, *Mind of Jihad*, 19–20.

62 Farhad Khosrokhavar, *Suicide Bombers: Allah's New Martyrs* (London: Pluto Press, 2005), 120.

63 Osama bin Laden, "Full Text: Bin Laden's 'Letter to America.'"

64 See, e.g., Peter R. Neumann, *Victims, Perpetrators, Assets: The Narratives of Islamic State Defectors* (London: International Centre for the Study of Radicalisation and Political Violence, King's College London, 2015).

65 Khosrokhavar, *Suicide Bombers*, 120.

66 Cf. Joel Hodge, *Resisting Violence and Victimisation* (Farnham: Ashgate, 2012), 112 and 114.

67 Algerian Salafist Group for Prayer and Combat (2005) in David Aaron, comp., *In Their Own Words: Voices of Jihad* (Santa Monica, CA: RAND, 2008), 86.

68 Palaver, "Abrahamic Revolution," 268–70. See also Elias Canetti, *Crowds and Power*, trans. C. Stewart (New York: Farrar, Straus and Giroux, 1984).

69 Palaver, "Abrahamic Revolution," 268 and 270; Murawiec, *Mind of Jihad*, 17.

70 Gilles Kepel, *Beyond Terror and Martyrdom: The Future of the Middle East* (Cambridge, MA: Belknap Press of Harvard University Press, 2008), 44.

71 Palaver, "Abrahamic Revolution," 271.

72 Ibid., 268–72. See also Charles Taylor, "Notes on the Sources of Violence: Perennial and Modern," in *Beyond Violence: Religious Sources for Social Transformation in Judaism, Christianity and Islam*, ed. J. L. Heft (Ashland, TN: Fordham University Press, 2004), 15–42.

5 The Globalization of Violent Jihad

1 Abu Musab al-Zarqawi in Shiraz Maher, *Salafi-Jihadism: The History of an Idea* (London: Hurst, 2016), 35.

2 Maher, *Salafi-Jihadism*, 34–5.

3 As discussed in Chapter 3, such a desire for a caliphate is a utopian ideal that seeks to address the political and cultural displacement of jihadists in modernity.

4 Maher, *Salafi-Jihadism*, 38.

5 Robert Manne, *The Mind of the Islamic State* (Carlton, AU: Redback Quarterly, 2016), 53–70.

6 Muhammad abd-al-Salam Faraj, *The Neglected Duty*, trans. Johannes J. G. Jansen (New York: Macmillan, 1986), 161, in John L. Esposito, *Unholy War: Terror in the Name of Islam* (Oxford: Oxford University Press, 2003), 63.

7 Gilles Kepel, *The Roots of Radical Islam*, trans. Jon Rothschild (London: Saqi, 2005), 201–6.

8 David Cook, *Understanding Jihad* (Berkeley: University of California Press, 2005), 108; Kepel, *Roots of Radical Islam*, 201.

9 Cook, *Understanding Jihad*, 108.

10 Kepel, *Roots of Radical Islam*, 204–11 and 235.

11 Cook, *Understanding Jihad*, 108.

12 Farhad Khosrokhavar, *Inside Jihadism: Understanding Jihadi Movements Worldwide* (Boulder, CO: Paradigm, 2009), 64.

13 Mustafa Köylü, *Islam and Its Quest for Peace: Jihad, Justice and Education* (Washington, DC: Council for Research in Values and Philosophy, 2003), 53; Marc Sageman, *Understanding Terror Networks* (Philadelphia: University of Pennsylvania Press, 2004), 17.

14 Kepel, *Roots of Radical Islam*, 206–8; Sageman, *Understanding Terror Networks*, 16.

15 Sageman, *Understanding Terror Networks*, 16.

16 Fawaz A. Gerges, *The Far Enemy: Why Jihad Went Global*, 2nd ed. (New York: Cambridge University Press, 2009), 10; Sageman, *Understanding Terror Networks*, 16–17.

17 Cook, *Understanding Jihad*, 94; Gilles Kepel, *Jihad: The Trail of Political Islam*, trans. Anthony F. Roberts (London: I.B. Tauris, 2004), 86.

18 Kepel, *Jihad*, 147.

19 Ibid., 318.

20 Ibid, 146–7.

21 Esposito, *Unholy War*, 64; Kepel, *Roots of Radical Islam*, 207–11; Maher, *Salafi-Jihadism*, 42.

22 Samantha May, "Are We Really Seeing the Rise of a 'New Jihad'?," *The Conversation*, May 27, 2017, https://theconversation.com/are-we-really-seeing-the-rise-of-a-new-jihad-78422.

23 Gilles Kepel, *The War for Muslim Minds: Islam and the West*, trans. Pascale Ghazaleh (Cambridge, MA: Belknap Press of Harvard University Press, 2004), 83.

24 Kepel, *Jihad*, 148–50 and 362.

25 Ibid., 219.

26 Maher, *Salafi-Jihadism*, 7.

27 Ibid., 11–12.

28 Ibid., 15–16.

29 Kepel, *Jihad*, 221.

30 Ibid., 299–301 and 317–18.

31 Maher, *Salafi-Jihadism*, 17–20.

32 Khosrokhavar, *Inside Jihadism*, 64–5; Laurent Murawiec, *The Mind of Jihad* (New York: Cambridge University Press, 2008), 5–58.

33 Olivier Roy, "Who Are the New Jihadis?," *The Guardian*, Apr 13, 2017, https://www.theguardian.com/news/2017/apr/13/who-are-the-new-jihadis.

34 Mohamed Merah in Roy, "Who Are the New Jihadis?"

35 Khosrokhavar, *Inside Jihadism*, 64–5.

36 Ibid., 65.

37 Maher, *Salafi-Jihadism*, 38; Sageman, *Understanding Terror Networks*, 17.

38 Khosrokhavar, *Inside Jihadism*, 75.

39 David Kilcullen, *Blood Year: The Unravelling of Western Counterterrorism* (New York: Oxford University Press, 2016), 61.

40 Kepel, *Jihad*, 276–98. Similar tactics of targeting foreigners and religious minorities (e.g., Jews) were undertaken in Algeria and Morocco (Kepel, *Jihad*, 307–8).

41 Kepel, *Jihad*, 295.

42 Ibid., 68 and 297.

43 Ibid., 363.

44 Ibid., 13 and 297. This focus on internationalizing the jihad may have led to a split between Azzam, who wanted to focus on the near enemy, and bin Laden and Zawahiri, who wished to focus on the far enemy. See Kepel, *Jihad*, 315–16 and 418, note 40.

45 Kepel, *Jihad*, 366.
46 Ibid., 254–75.
47 Kilcullen, *Blood Year*, 40–1; Joe Parkinson and Drew Hinshaw, "Islamic State, Seeking Next Chapter, Makes Inroads through West Africa," *Wall Street Journal*, February 3, 2019, https://www.wsj.com/articles/islamic-state-seeking-next-chapter-makes-inroads-through-west-africa-11549220824.
48 Kepel, *Jihad*, 272–5 and 297–8.
49 Gilles Kepel, *Beyond Terror and Martyrdom: The Future of the Middle East* (Cambridge, MA: Belknap Press of Harvard University Press, 2008), 118–19.
50 Kilcullen, *Blood Year*, 41–2.
51 Kepel, *Jihad*, 16.
52 For this reason, al-Qaeda has sought to be more strategic in its use of violence, in contrast to groups like ISIS, which have been more indiscriminate. However, the difference is not one of theology but primarily one of strategy.
53 Kepel, *Beyond Terror and Martyrdom*, 118–19. It is important to note that the GIA in Algeria tried at times (such as under Zitouni) to distance itself from the most extreme violent stances that some of its members had taken, such as the targeting of and retaliation against civilians. This effort was made as the GIA lost popular support and was criticized for going against the Islamic tradition. It failed in this reform effort as the dynamics of violence had already overridden their ethical and religious principles, resulting in continued extreme manifestations of violence (Kepel, *Jihad*, 269–75).
54 The Indonesian state and military attempted a similar effort in East Timor following the independence referendum in August 1999. The military and its allied militias massacred people, forcibly moved people to West Timor, and destroyed much of the country in order to punish the populace and to construct a situation of chaos. Because the Indonesian military claimed that the violence was being perpetrated by local Timorese factions, they argued that the Indonesian state was the only force capable of saving the Timorese from their own violence and restoring order. See Joel Hodge, *Resisting Violence and Victimisation* (Farnham: Ashgate, 2012), 96–7; Clinton Fernandes, *Reluctant Saviour: Australia, Indonesia and the Independence of East Timor* (Carlton North, AU: Scribe, 2004), 47–85.
55 Kepel, *Jihad*, 272–5.
56 Ibid., 272.
57 Ibid., 273; BBC News, "Antar Zouabri: A Violent Legacy," *BBC*, February 9, 2002, http://news.bbc.co.uk/2/hi/middle_east/1811194.stm.
58 Kepel, *Jihad*, 274–5.
59 Ibid., 362.
60 René Girard, *Deceit, Desire, and the Novel: Self and Other in Literary Structure*, trans. Yvonne Freccero (Baltimore, MD: Johns Hopkins University Press, 1965), 137–8.

61 Kepel, *Jihad*, 106–14, 175–6 and 361–76.
62 Ibid., 333.
63 Ibid., 263–7.
64 I explore the indiscriminate nature of jihadist violence in more detail in the next chapter.
65 Kepel, *Jihad*, 219–20.
66 Ibid., 18.
67 Ibid., 209–10.
68 Ibid., 316–7; Maher, *Salafi-Jihadism*, 43. For example, bin Laden had to flee from Saudi Arabia and Sudan because of international pressure. He eventually found safe haven in Afghanistan.
69 Kepel, *Jihad*, 208–19.
70 Maher, *Salafi-Jihadism*, 43. With the betrayal that was felt by jihadists following the end of the conflict in Afghanistan and the US "occupation" of Muslim lands in the Gulf War, the geographical and psychological distance between jihadists and Westerners was removed, and so, rivalry became more likely.
71 Kepel, *Jihad*, 205–17.
72 Ibid., 218–19.
73 Ibid., 207–8.
74 Maher, *Salafi-Jihadism*, 43.
75 Olivier Roy, *Globalized Islam* (New York: Colombia University Press, 2004), 1; *The Failure of Political Islam*, trans. Carol Volk (Cambridge, MA: Harvard University Press, 1994).
76 Kepel, *Jihad*, 320.
77 Ibid., 268.
78 Ibid.
79 Ibid., 231–2. Bin Laden and Zawahiri built an unusual alliance with the Taliban, a conservative Islamic movement derived from the Deobandi tradition in Pakistan and India. The Taliban was committed to jihad and sharia but was opposed to state-based forms of government. Kepel (*Jihad*, 223–36) argues that bin Laden had increasing influence over the Taliban up to 2001, influencing the Taliban's more extreme actions and positions.
80 The Taliban emerged from a different movement within Islam (Deobandi) in contrast to al-Qaeda and ISIS and also had a different political philosophy. However, their shared jihadist ideology led them to become allies (at least with AQ) and commit to similar violent activities, upon which they relied to maintain their political regimes. Cf. Kepel, *Jihad*, 231–2.
81 Osama bin Laden, "Full Text: Bin Laden's 'Letter to America,'" *The Guardian*, November 24, 2002, https://www.theguardian.com/world/2002/nov/24/theobserver.

82 Ibid.
83 Kepel, *Jihad*, 220–36.
84 Ibid., 137.
85 Osama bin Laden, "Full Text: Bin Laden's 'Letter to America.'"
86 Maher, *Salafi-Jihadism*, 180.
87 Ibid., 181.
88 Cook, *Understanding Jihad*, 25; Khosrokhavar, *Inside Jihadism*, 61–3. While Islamic scholars generally condemn compulsion, violence has been used by Islamic rulers and regimes to spread Islam and remove "obstacles" to the preaching of the faith.
89 Khosrokhavar, *Inside Jihadism*, 63. For example, see Associated Press, "They Asked Me to Convert to Islam, but I Told Them I Will Die a Christian," *New York Post*, December 23, 2016, https://nypost.com/2016/12/23/iraqs-christians-celebrate-christmas-amid-isis-hell/.
90 NBC News, "ISIS Tells Iraqi Christians to Convert or Die," *NBC*, September 14, 2014, https://www.nbcnews.com/watch/nightly-news/isis-tells-iraqi-christians-to-convert-or-die-329118275734.
91 Kepel, *Jihad*, 218–19.
92 Khosrokhavar, *Inside Jihadism*, 91–2.
93 Ibid., 92.
94 Ibid., 79–93.
95 Ibid., 82.
96 Ibid., 86–7.
97 Ibid., 87.
98 Maher, *Salafi-Jihadism*, 42–3.
99 Khosrokhavar, *Inside Jihadism*, 84 and 93.
100 Ibid., 92–3.
101 Kepel, *Jihad*, 14.
102 Ibid., 16–17.
103 Maher, *Salafi-Jihadism*, 45.
104 Girard, *Battling to the End*, 184.
105 Kepel, *Jihad*, 4–5, 272–5, 296–8, and 317.
106 Ibid., 320–1.
107 Kepel, *Beyond Terror and Martyrdom*, 114–19.
108 Kepel, *Jihad*, 201–8; Kepel, *Beyond Terror and Martyrdom*, 110–20. The weakness of the jihadist movement in a geopolitical sense does not fully explain the virulency of the movement, and its resentment of and rivalry with the West. I explore this question in more detail in Chapter 7, with reference to the jihadist obsession with violence and the underlying issues of mimetic identity.
109 Khosrokhavar, *Jihadist Ideology*, 237. In fact, there were meetings between Shia and Sunni radicals in the early stages of Islamism's development, including some

pioneered by Al-Banna and the Muslim Brotherhood. Murawiec (*Mind of Jihad*, 42) called this "an Islamic ecumenism based on radicalism."

110 Murawiec, *Mind of Jihad*, 42.

111 Kepel, *Jihad*, 110–13.

112 Ibid., 111.

113 Ibid., 112–13.

114 Ibid., 116; Khosrokhavar, *Inside Jihadism*, 66.

115 Kepel, *Jihad*, 109.

116 Ibid., 109.

117 Ibid., 116.

118 Ibid., 116–17.

119 Khomeini in Murawiec, *Mind of Jihad*, 43.

120 Khosrokhavar, *Inside Jihadism*, 66–7. Iraq's Baathist regime was ostensibly socialist in nature, and at that time, was supported by Western powers.

121 Khosrokhavar, *Inside Jihadism*, 70. This revolutionary theology and martyrdom mentality were taken to a particularly strange extreme during the Iran–Iraq war. Since the revolution had not spread beyond Iran, a group of devout young men from the Basiji organization felt their death could assuage their own guilt for their sins and for failing to bring about a world Islamic revolution. They felt that since service of Islam in life had not led to Islam's full flourishing, death and martyrdom could be the force for renewal by the pursuit of death (Khosrokhavar, *Inside Jihadism*, 66; Kepel, *Jihad*, 116–17). Instead of just making others the victims of Islamic expansion, these Iranians made themselves the victims, who were deserving of death, so that in their deaths they were in some way witnesses to the "true" Islamic way. Their embrace of death and victimization took Shia identity to an extreme—to an identification with a violent death that would be expiatory, purgative, destructive, and transformative all at once. Girard argues that one of the possibilities of mimetic rivalry and persecution is for the victim to participate in their own persecution and internalize the violence done to them, as the Basiji did.

122 Kepel, *Jihad*, 117; Khosrokhavar, *Inside Jihadism*, 66. According to Kepel, these human wave attacks were also an expedient way for Iran to defend itself and provide an outlet for the energy of the masses following the Iranian Revolution.

123 Kepel, *Jihad*, 117; Khosrokhavar, *Inside Jihadism*, 66. Interestingly, there are affinities and possibly even complementarity between Kepel and Olivier Roy on the point of a "death wish" (despite the public dispute between the two). Kepel regards this death wish in Islamic terms, while Roy regards such a death wish as a manifestation of the nihilistic attitude of Islamic extremists. Roy's diagnosis relies on the relatively recent and surface-level radicalization of many extremists from the West and East. It coincides with the victim-attitude of jihadists that leads them to undertake violently destructive jihad. However, Kepel's approach takes account of the theologically and politically constructive nature of jihadism. Such a

constructive vision of jihadism provides a justification for sacred violence, which distorts and manipulates the Abrahamic tradition ostensibly to construct a sacred order for apocalyptic purposes.

124 Khosrokhavar, *Inside Jihadism*, 66–70.

125 Kepel, *Jihad*, 117.

126 Ibid., 116–17 and 364.

127 Khosrokhavar, *Inside Jihadism*, 71.

128 Kepel, *Jihad*, 128.

129 Ibid., 128–30.

130 Farhad Khosrokhavar, *Suicide Bombers: Allah's New Martyrs* (London: Pluto Press, 2005), 236–7.

6 Jihadism and Violence

1 David Kilcullen, "Blood Year: Terror and the Islamic State," *The Quarterly Essay* 58 (2015): 55.

2 David Kilcullen, *Blood Year: The Unravelling of Western Counterterrorism* (Oxford: Oxford University Press, 2016), 29–35; "Blood Year," 20–1.

3 For example, an ISIS recruit, Omarjan Azari, who was convicted of plotting to kill civilians in Australia, was instructed by a senior ISIS recruiter, Mohammed Ali Baryalei, to kill Western tourists so to make "worldwide news." Elias Visontay, "Omarjan Azari yells Allahu Akbar, Refuses to Stand as He's Convicted on Terror Plot," *The Australian*, March 29, 2019, https://www.theaustralian.com.au/nation/omarjan-azari-yells-allahu-akbar-refuses-to-stand-as-hes-convicted-on-terror-plot/news-story/538cb3c4c1b7b996fc8eef24dac0e32b.

4 Laurent Murawiec, *The Mind of Jihad* (New York: Cambridge University Press, 2008), 9.

5 Shiraz Maher, *Salafi-Jihadism: The History of an Idea* (London: Hurst, 2016), 39.

6 Ibid., 32.

7 'Abdallah 'Azzam in Maher, *Salafi-Jihadism*, 34.

8 Maher, *Salafi-Jihadism*, 38; Marc Sageman, *Understanding Terror Networks* (Philadelphia: University of Pennsylvania Press, 2004), 17.

9 Murawiec, *Mind of Jihad*, 2.

10 Ibid., 5–8 and 10.

11 Ibid., 9–10 and 12.

12 Jean-Pierre Dupuy, "The Sacred is Back—But as Simulacrum," in *Does Religion Cause Violence? Multidisciplinary Perspectives on Violence and Religion in the Modern World*, ed. Scott Cowdell, Chris Fleming, Joel Hodge, and Carly Osborn (New York: Bloomsbury Academic, 2018), 99–100.

13 Itai Anghel, "No Free Steps to Heaven," *Four Corners*, Australian Broadcasting Corporation, April 27, 2015, http://www.abc.net.au/4corners/stories/2015/04/27/4222860.htm#transcript.

14 Peter R. Neumann, *Victims, Perpetrators, Assets: The Narratives of Islamic State Defectors* (London: International Centre for the Study of Radicalisation and Political Violence, King's College London, 2015), 1 and 10–11.

15 Murawiec, *Mind of Jihad*, 11.

16 For example, the Sunni and Shia engage in what Girard identifies as a rival twinning, i.e., they are closely related traditions that fight each other because they share similar beliefs and objects of desire.

17 René Girard, *Battling to the End: Conversations with Benoît Chantre*, trans. Mary Baker (East Lansing: Michigan State University Press, 2010), 15–19.

18 See Kilcullen, "The Blood Year," 50–1.

19 Neumann, *Victims, Perpetrators, Assets*, 1 and 10–11. Cf. John Simpson, "Isis Defectors Were Tired of Killing and Lack of Luxuries," *The Times*, September 22, 2015, http://www.thetimes.co.uk/tto/news/world/middleeast/article4563869.ece.

20 Patrick Cockburn, "Life under ISIS: Why I Deserted the 'Islamic State' Rather Than Take Part in Executions, Beheadings and Rape—The Story of a Former Jihadi," *The Independent*, March 16, 2015, http://www.independent.co.uk/news/world/middle-east/life-under-isis-why-i-deserted-the-islamic-state-rather-than-take-part-in-executions-beheadings-and-rape-the-story-of-a-former-jihadi-10111877.html.

21 Cockburn, "Life under ISIS."

22 James S. Morris and Tristan Dunning, "Islamic State Schooled Children as Soldiers—How Can Their 'Education' Be Undone?," *The Conversation*, 29 March 2018, http://theconversation.com/islamic-state-schooled-children-as-soldiers-how-can-their-education-be-undone-93266.

23 There is an essential feature in which jihadists do not mirror the Western-inspired state: that way in which the rights of victims are treated. While, the state's power is commonly used to cast social tensions onto certain categories of people, the state (especially in its legal system) is structured in a way that is aware of and seeks to guard against the power of mob violence. It even seeks to protect the rights of criminals and minorities against such violence.

24 Maher, *Salafi-Jihadism*, 67.

25 Ibid., 56–9.

26 Ibid., 49 and 59–61.

27 Ibid., 60–1.

28 Kilcullen, *Blood Year*, 29–36.

29 Maher, *Salafi-Jihadism*, 65 and 71. Abdul Wahhab is attributed with first re-introducing *takfir* as an active principle in Islamic life after centuries of restraint (Murawiec, *Mind of Jihad*, 37). Modern users of *takfir*, such as ISIS, reject a comparison that is often made to the Kharijites, who in the first century of Islam

used *takfir* in a freer manner than other groups. Jihadists reject this comparison because it is pejorative and puts into question the orthodoxy of a Muslim who uses *takfir*. Despite their rejection of this comparison, groups like ISIS seem to mirror the Kharijites in their liberal and hostile use of *takfir.*

30 Maher, *Salafi-Jihadism*, 71–3.

31 Ibid., 72.

32 Ibid., 65 and 72–3.

33 Farhad Khosrokhavar, *Inside Jihadism: Understanding Jihadi Movements Worldwide* (Boulder, CO: Paradigm, 2009), 61.

34 Maher, *Salafi-Jihadism*, 111–23. I thank Professor Daniel Madigan S.J. for pointing out the importance of this concept.

35 Maher, *Salafi-Jihadism*, 120–1. According to Maqdisi, the same lessons are present in the life of the Prophet Muhammad.

36 Maher, *Salafi-Jihadism*, 121.

37 Ibid., 138–40.

38 Ibid., 141.

39 Khosrokhavar, *Inside Jihadism*, 72.

40 Ibid., 73–4.

41 Kilcullen, *Blood Year*, 29–41; Maher, *Salafi-Jihadism*, 63. There were also numerous Sunni uprising against AQI which were brutally repressed.

42 Khosrokhavar, *Inside Jihadism*, 71–3.

43 Maher, *Salafi-Jihadism*, 59–67.

44 Ibid., 65.

45 Ibid., 51 and 61–7.

46 Ibid., 62–3.

47 Ibid., 64–5.

48 Ibid., 65.

49 Ibid., 59–67.

50 Ibid., 63.

51 Ibid., 65.

52 Ibid., 49.

53 Ibid., 50–1.

54 Osama bin Laden in David Aaron, comp., *In Their Own Words: Voices of Jihad* (Santa Monica, CA: RAND, 2008), 106.

55 Maher, *Salafi-Jihadism*, 49–52.

56 Osama bin Laden, "Full Text: Bin Laden's 'Letter to America,'" *The Guardian*, November 24, 2002, https://www.theguardian.com/world/2002/nov/24/theobserver.

57 Osama bin Laden, Interview by John Miller, *Frontline*, May 1998, https://www.pbs.org/wgbh/pages/frontline/shows/binladen/who/interview.html.

58 Kepel, *Jihad*, 333; Osama bin Laden, "Full Text: Bin Laden's 'Letter to America.'"
59 Maher, *Salafi-Jihadism*, 56–7.
60 Osama bin Laden, "Full Text: Bin Laden's 'Letter to America.'"
61 Maher, *Salafi-Jihadism*, 57.
62 Ibid., 57–8.
63 Ibid., 56.
64 Ibid., 54.
65 Osama bin Laden, "Full Text: Bin Laden's 'Letter to America.'"
66 Yusuf al-'Uyayri in Maher, *Salafi-Jihadism*, 51.
67 Maher, *Salafi-Jihadism*, 52–3.
68 Those who equate the logic of the West with jihadists do not properly account for the apocalyptic dimensions of jihadist thought. The West is not primarily apocalyptic in its logic but sacrificial: it uses violence to contain violent threats. It could be argued that the United States should be more responsible in its protection of civilians, but it does not seek apocalyptic victory or destruction. This point is clear in regard to WMDs (as Dupuy shows): the United States is primarily sacrificial in its logic regarding WMDs as a deterrent to violence and does not use WMDs indiscriminately, while, by contrast, jihadists profess an indiscriminate and apocalyptic logic regarding WMDs and are willing to use them as such.
69 David Cook, *Understanding Jihad* (Berkeley: University of California Press, 2005), 24.
70 Maher, *Salafi-Jihadism*, 63.
71 Farhad Khosrokhavar, *Jihadist Ideology: The Anthropological Perspective* (Aarhus: Centre for Studies in Islamism and Radicalisation, Department of Political Science, Aarhus University, 2011), 168.
72 Maher, *Salafi-Jihadism*, 54–6.
73 Ibid., 56.
74 Murawiec, *Mind of Jihad*, 17–18; Maher, *Salafi-Jihadism*, 31–68; Asma Afsaruddin, *Striving in the Path of God: Jihad and Martyrdom in Islamic Thought* (New York: Oxford University Press, 2013), 1–94 and 269–98.
75 Gilles Kepel, *Beyond Terror and Martyrdom: The Future of the Middle East* (Cambridge, MA: Belknap Press of Harvard University Press, 2008), 45. It is also worth noting that AQI also killed Sunnis, for strategic or repressive reasons. There were numerous Sunni tribal uprisings against AQI, which only succeeded when the American Surge occurred in 2006–7. See Kilcullen, *Blood Year*, 32–41.
76 For more about the way principle justifies rivalry and violence, see: René Girard, *Deceit, Desire, and the Novel: Self and Other in Literary Structure* (1961), trans. Yvonne Freccero (Baltimore, MD: Johns Hopkins University Press, 1965), 125–38; Joel Hodge, "Sacrifice in the Democratic Age: Rivalry and Crisis in Recent Australian Politics," in *Violence, Desire and the Sacred, Volume 2: René Girard and*

Sacrifice in Life, Love and Literature, ed. Scott Cowdell, Chris Fleming and Joel Hodge (New York: Bloomsbury Academic, 2014), 31–44.

77 Khosrokhavar, *Inside Jihadism*, 92–3.

78 Maher, *Salafi-Jihadism*, 55.

79 Ibid., 17.

80 Murawiec, *Mind of Islam*, 42; Maher, *Salafi-Jihadism*, 65; Farhad Khosrokhavar, *Suicide Bombers: Allah's New Martyrs* (London: Pluto Press, 2005), 49–50.

81 Khosrokhavar, *Jihadist Ideology*, 169–70.

82 Maher, *Salafi-Jihadism*, 42.

7 Violence and Identity

1 Scott Atran, "ISIS Is a Revolution," *Aeon*, December 15, 2015, https://aeon.co/essays/why-isis-has-the-potential-to-be-a-world-altering-revolution.

2 Scott Atran, "ISIS Is a Revolution"; *Talking to the Enemy: Violent Extremism, Sacred Values, and What It Means to Be Human* (London: Allen Lane, 2010).

3 Shiraz Maher, "ICSR Insight—The Roots of Radicalisation? It's Identity, Stupid," International Centre for the Study of Radicalisation and Political Violence, King's College London, June 23, 2015, https://icsr.info/2015/06/23/roots-radicalisation-identity-stupid/. See also Julian Droogan and Lise Waldek, "Religion, Radicalization, and Violent Extremism?," in *Does Religion Cause Violence? Multidisciplinary Perspectives on Violence and Religion in the Modern World*, ed. Scott Cowdell, Chris Fleming, Joel Hodge, and Carly Osborn (New York: Bloomsbury Academic, 2018), 173–90; Atran, *Talking to the Enemy*.

4 Pankaj Mishra, "Jordan Peterson & Fascist Mysticism," *New York Review of Books*, March 19, 2018, http://www.nybooks.com/daily/2018/03/19/jordan-peterson-and-fascist-mysticism/; Laurent Murawiec, *The Mind of Jihad* (New York: Cambridge University Press, 2008), 26.

5 Eva Nisa and Faried F. Saenong, "Female Suicide Bombers: How Terrorist Propaganda Radicalises Indonesian Women," *The Conversation*, June 25, 2018, http://theconversation.com/female-suicide-bombers-how-terrorist-propaganda-radicalises-indonesian-women-98143; V. G. Julie Rajan, *Women Suicide Bombers: Narratives of Violence* (Abingdon: Routledge, 2011).

6 Scott Cowdell, *René Girard and Secular Modernity: Christ, Culture, and Crisis* (Notre Dame, IN: Notre Dame Press, 2013), 158.

7 Maher, "ICSR Insight—The Roots of Radicalisation? It's Identity, Stupid."

8 Gilles Kepel, *Jihad: The Trail of Political Islam*, trans. Anthony F. Roberts (London: I.B. Tauris, 2004), 310.

9 Louise Richardson, *What Terrorists Want: Understanding the Enemy, Containing the Threat* (Random House: New York, 2006), 106–7.

10 Jonathan Sacks, *Not in God's Name: Confronting Religious Violence* (London: Hodder & Stoughton), 42. Cf. Atran, *Talking to the Enemy*.

11 Richardson, *What Terrorists Want*, 71–103.

12 Slavoj Žižek, "Slavoj Žižek on the Charlie Hebdo massacre: Are the Worst Really Full of Passionate Intensity?," *New Statesman*, January 10, 2015, http://www.newstatesman.com/world-affairs/2015/01/slavoj-i-ek-charlie-hebdo-massacre-are-worst-really-full-passionate-intensity. See also Slavoj Žižek, *Violence* (New York: Picador, 2008), 72–3.

13 René Girard, *Deceit, Desire, and the Novel: Self and Other in Literary Structure*, trans. Yvonne Freccero (Baltimore, MD: Johns Hopkins University Press, 1965), 73.

14 René Girard, *Battling to the End: Conversations with Benoît Chantre*, trans. Mary Baker (East Lansing: Michigan State University Press, 2010), 214.

15 Ibid., 115.

16 René Girard, *Violence and the Sacred*, trans. Patrick Gregory (Baltimore: Johns Hopkins University Press, 1977), 147–9.

17 Olivier Roy, "An Interview with Olivier Roy," *Colombia University Press*, accessed March 13, 2019, https://cup.columbia.edu/author-interviews/roy-globalized-islam.

18 René Girard, "Conflict," *Stanford Magazine* (Winter 1986), 60, in Cynthia Haven, *Evolution of Desire: A Life of René Girard* (East Lansing: Michigan State University Press, 2018), 91.

19 Kepel, *Jihad*, 316. Shiraz Maher, *Salafi-Jihadism: The History of an Idea* (London: Hurst, 2016), 43.

20 Kepel, *Jihad*, 317–18; Osama bin Laden, "Full Text: Bin Laden's 'Letter to America,' " *The Guardian*, November 24, 2002, https://www.theguardian.com/world/2002/nov/24/theobserver.

21 Kepel, *Jihad*, 317.

22 Ibid., 318.

23 "World Islamic Front Statement Urging Jihad against Jews and Crusaders," in Kepel, *Jihad*, 320.

24 Roy, "An Interview with Olivier Roy."

25 Olivier Roy, *Globalized Islam: The Search for a New Ummah* (New York: Columbia University Press, 2004), 8–9.

26 Ibid., 13–14.

27 Girard, *Deceit, Desire, and the Novel*, 185.

28 Ibid., 179–80.

29 Osama bin Laden, "Full Text: Bin Laden's 'Letter to America.' "

30 Ibid.

31 Sacks, *Not in God's Name*, 42.

32 Girard, *Deceit, Desire, and the Novel*, 255.

33 bin Laden, "Full Text: Bin Laden's 'Letter to America.'"

34 René Girard, with Pierpaolo Antonello and João Cezar de Castro Rocha, *Evolution and Conversion: Dialogues on the Origins of Culture* (New York: Continuum, 2007), 237–38.

35 René Girard, "'What Is Occurring Today Is Mimetic Rivalry on a Planetary Scale': René Girard on September 11," Interview by Henri Tincq, *Le Monde*, November 6, 2011, trans. the Colloquium on Violence and Religion, http://www.morphizm.com/politix/girard911.html.

36 Farhad Khosrokhavar, *Inside Jihadism: Understanding Jihadi Movements Worldwide* (Boulder, CO: Paradigm, 2009), 75.

37 Elisabetta Brighi, "Terrorism and Religion," in *The Palgrave Handbook of Mimetic Theory and Religion*, ed. James Alison and Wolfgang Palaver (New York: Palgrave Macmillan, 2017), 398–99.

38 Brighi, "Terrorism and Religion," 399.

39 Ibid.. Girard defines the "romantic self" as a delusion in which one believes one's desire is spontaneously produced by the self rather than dependent on others.

40 Brighi, "Terrorism and Religion," 399.

41 Peter Stork, *Human Rights in Crisis: A Cultural Critique* (Saarbrücken: VDM Verlag Dr. Mueller, 2007); Nathan Kensey, "Scapegoating the Guilty: Girard and International Criminal Law," in *Violence, Desire and the Sacred, Volume 2: René Girard and Sacrifice in Life, Love and Literature*, ed. Scott Cowdell, Chris Fleming, and Joel Hodge (New York: Bloomsbury Academic, 2014), 67–80.

42 Murawiec, *Mind of Jihad*, 3 and 150–68.

43 David Kilcullen, "Blood Year: Terror and the Islamic State," *The Quarterly Essay* 58 (2015): 19–20.

44 Girard, *Deceit, Desire, and the Novel*, 137–8.

45 Ibid., 138.

8 Sacred Jihadist Totalitarianism

1 Scott Atran, "ISIS Is a Revolution," *Aeon*, December 15, 2015, https://aeon.co/essays/why-isis-has-the-potential-to-be-a-world-altering-revolution.

2 David Kilcullen, "Blood Year: Terror and the Islamic State," *Quarterly Essay* 58 (2015): 61–2.

3 Ibid., 62.

4 Farhad Khosrokhavar, *Jihadist Ideology: The Anthropological Perspective* (Aarhus: Centre for Studies in Islamism and Radicalisation, Department of Political Science, Aarhus University, 2011), 237.

5 Ibid., 238–9.

6 Laurent Murawiec, *The Mind of Jihad* (New York: Cambridge University Press, 2008), 1 and 169–255.

7 Khosrokhavar, *Jihadist Ideology*, 239.

8 Ibid., 239.

9 Scott Cowdell, *René Girard and Secular Modernity: Christ, Culture, and Crisis* (Notre Dame, IN: Notre Dame Press, 2013), 154. In this sense, it represents one possible version of modernity, in contest with others (including alternative Islamic modernities) rather than a "clash of civilisations."

10 Scott Cowdell, *René Girard and Secular Modernity: Christ, Culture, and Crisis* (Notre Dame, IN: Notre Dame Press, 2013), 154–55. See also Charles Taylor, *A Secular Age* (Cambridge, MA: Belknap Press of Harvard University Press, 2007).

11 Cowdell, *René Girard and Secular Modernity*, 149–55 and 160; René Girard, "'What Is Occurring Today Is Mimetic Rivalry on a Planetary Scale': René Girard on September 11," interview by Henri Tincq, *Le Monde*, November 6, 2011, trans. the Colloquium on Violence and Religion, http://www.morphizm.com/politix/girard911.html.

12 Shiraz Maher, *Salafi-Jihadism: The History of an Idea* (London: Hurst & Company, 2016), 63.

13 Farhad Khosrokhavar, *Inside Jihadism: Understanding Jihadi Movements Worldwide* (Boulder, CO: Paradigm, 2009), 59.

14 Ibid., 60–1.

15 Murawiec, *Mind of Jihad*, 17.

16 Gilles Kepel, *Jihad: The Trail of Political Islam*, trans. Anthony F. Roberts (London, UK: I.B. Tauris, 2004), 229–31.

17 Ibid., 222–36 and 261.

18 Terror attacks have also been committed by violent fascists/white supremacists, such as in Norway and New Zealand, that purport to respond to jihadist attacks. They show similar traits to jihadism and other forms of totalitiarianism: an extreme and inflexible ideology that identifies enemies (e.g., invaders) and feeds off mimetic scandal and outrage, a glorification of violence to achieve a utopia, and the claim to do violence in the name of victims (e.g., of jihadism or immigration) to bring about a totalitarian vision. See, e.g., Rebecca Urban, "Fanatic Charted Growing Hate of 'Invaders' in Diary of Europe Trip," *The Australian*, March 16, 2019, https://www.theaustralian.com.au/news/nation/fanatic-charted-growing-hate-of-invaders-in-diary-of-europe-trip/news-story/ec53a72e730d037e396ec67320063bac. The background of fascist protagonists is similar to some jihadists, too: a rapid radicalization (usually men) following an ordinary and, at times, dissolute life.

19 Louise Richardson, *What Terrorists Want: Understanding the Enemy, Containing the Threat* (New York: Random House, 2006), 94–8.

20 René Girard, *Deceit, Desire, and the Novel: Self and Other in Literary Structure*, trans. Yvonne Freccero (Baltimore, MD: Johns Hopkins University Press, 1965), 138.
21 René Girard, *Battling to the End: Conversations with Benoît Chantre*, trans. Mary Baker (East Lansing: Michigan State University Press, 2010), 20.
22 Ibid., 20.
23 René Girard, "Apocalyptic Thinking after 9/11: An Interview with René Girard," interview by Robert Doran, *SubStance* 37, no. 1 (2007): 23.
24 Maher, *Salafi-Jihadism*, 169–206; Gilles Kepel, *Jihad: The Trail of Political Islam*, trans. Anthony F. Roberts (London: I.B. Tauris, 2004), 26; Khosrokhavar, *Inside Jihadism*, 65.
25 Joel Hodge, *Resisting Violence and Victimisation* (Farnham: Ashgate, 2012), 126.
26 See William T. Cavanaugh, *Torture and Eucharist: Theology, Politics, and the Body of Christ* (Oxford: Blackwell, 1998), 23–48; Hodge, *Resisting Violence and Victimisation*, 121–62.
27 Cf. Khosrokhavar, *Inside Jihadism*, 98, note 4.
28 Kilcullen, "Blood Year," 19–20.
29 Kepel, *Jihad*, 4.
30 Girard, *Deceit, Desire, and the Novel*, 137–8.

9 Why is God Part of Human Violence? The Idolatrous Nature of Militant Jihadism

1 Gil Bailie, "Raising the Ante: Recovering an Alpha and Omega Christology," *Communio: International Catholic Review* 35, no. 1 (Spring 2008): 98.
2 René Girard, with Pierpaolo Antonello and João Cezar de Castro Rocha, *Evolution and Conversion: Dialogues on the Origins of Culture* (New York: Continuum, 2007), 106.
3 Scott Atran and Ara Norenzayan, "Religion's Evolutionary Landscape: Counterintuition, Commitment, Compassion, Communion," *Behavioral and Brain Sciences* 27 (2004): 713. According to Justin Barrett, Atran and Norenzayan wrongly equate "counterintuitive" with a category mistake or contradiction and incorrectly place counterfactual alongside counterintuitive in regard to thought about the supernatural. In the field of cognitive psychology of religion, "counterintuitive" has taken on a technical meaning (derived from Boyer) in that some type of thought can go against common intuitive assumptions (e.g., scientific proofs can be counterintuitive as they often run counter to intuitions about how the world works). Atran and Norenzayan argue that the supernatural contradicts basic semantic meanings. Yet, as Barrett points

out, it is not clear that this is accurate. The example of God's omnipotence is used by Atran and Norenzayan ("Religion's Evolutionary Landscape," 720) to demonstrate counterintuitiveness: God as a nonmaterial being who is physically all-powerful is argued to be contradictory. Yet, monotheistic traditions such as Judaism, Christianity, and Islam understand God's omnipotence in much more sophisticated ways than merely physical power and account philosophically for God's omnipotence. Therefore, to demonstrate a factual contradiction would be to determine the truth of some area, whereas the category of "counterintuitive" is to only to be used to identify general assumptions or beliefs about reality (based on what seems natural) and those ideas or phenomena that run counter to those assumptions. Thus, to label belief in the supernatural as "counterintuitive" could imply that there is no evidence for the supernatural and that belief in it is not natural and rational. Yet, belief in the supernatural can only be counterintuitive in regard to a certain assumption or intuition. Atran and Norenzayan do not establish what this assumption of intuition is or could be, in regard to the supernatural. Justin L. Barrett, "Counterfactuality in Counterintuitive Religious Concepts," *Behavioral and Brain Sciences* 27 (2004): 731–2.

4 Atran and Norenzayan, "Religion's Evolutionary Landscape," 713.

5 Ibid.

6 Ibid., 720.

7 Ibid.

8 Ibid.

9 Cf. Will M. Gervais, Aiyana K. Willard, Ara Norenzayan, and Joseph Henrich, "The Cultural Transmission of Faith: Why Innate Intuitions Are Necessary, but Insufficient, to Explain Religious Belief," *Religion* 41, no. 3 (September 2011): 393–4.

10 Justin L. Barrett, "Why Would Anyone Believe in God?," YouTube Video, posted by "The Veritas Forum," February 26, 2012, https://www.youtube.com/watch?v=3I3GAaswAkc.

11 Furthermore, Barrett argues that if knowledge of the supernatural is determined by agency detection (in a strict naturalistic sense), it would be less likely that educated people in a scientific system (who are supposedly able to discern phenomena more accurately) would believe in the supernatural. However, this is not the case: religious belief is not predicted by education. Barrett, "Why Would Anyone Believe in God?"

12 Barrett, "Why Would Anyone Believe in God?"

13 Justin L. Barrett, *Why Would Anyone Believe in God?* (Walnut Creek, CA: AltaMira Press, 2004), ix and 139; Barrett, "Why Would Anyone Believe in God?"

14 Steven Engler, "Notes on Recent Publications: Why Would Anyone Believe in God?—Justin L. Barrett," *Religious Studies Review* 32, no. 2 (April 2006): 103–4. I would add that agency is also connected with causation in the human mind. In

other words, humans have the capacity to rationally discern causation alongside their capacity for agency-detection. Whatever led humans to become conscious of the supernatural is connected with the need to provide (reasonable or rational) causation for certain experiences and for the whole of life itself (because, e.g., humans are aware of their own contingency).

15 A similar problem occurs for Atran and Norenzayan (and others) when they argue that the propensity for humans to believe in minimal counterintuitive elements goes some way toward explaining the consistency of beliefs in the supernatural. Even those who put forward this argument, such as Gervais, Willard, Norenzayan, and Henrich, discuss its limitations for explaining the nature and fervor of faith. It also does not explain why the supernatural would be conceived of at all and how it can be classified as "minimally counterintuitive" compared to other possibilities. Atran and Norenzayan, "Religion's Evolutionary Landscape," 721–5; Gervais et al., "The Cultural Transmission of Faith," 389–95.

16 This kind of determinism reduces the problem of God/gods by arguing that the human mind evolved to be a (faulty) agency detector or overactive mind creating the feelings of transcendence and agency. This kind of argument is problematic because it reduces discussion of external phenomena to the mind or imagination. Effectively, it is an argument that either posits no reality outside the mind or implicitly rejects God or the supernatural as a possible externality to the mind without providing the necessary theological or philosophical arguments for such a stance. See Justin L. Barrett, *Cognitive Science, Religion and Theology: From Human Minds to Divine Minds* (West Conshohocken, PA: Templeton Press, 2011), 148–50.

17 Bernard Lonergan, *Method in Theology*, 2nd ed. (New York: Seabury Press, 1979).

18 In an interview with Time magazine, Bill Gates commented that modern people have the reductionist tendency to create heroes (and scapegoats) to explain reality, instead of understanding the complex systems that have actually contributed to improving the quality of life in modernity. This tendency has potential connections to the mythologizing propensity that Girard identifies in human cultures. Bill Gates, "Bill Gates Says This Book Is 'One of the Most Important' He's Ever Read," Interview by Sarah Begley, *Time*, April 3, 2018, https://time.com/5224618/bill-gates-hans-rosling-factfulness/.

19 Charles Taylor, *A Secular Age* (Cambridge, MA: Belknap Press of Harvard University Press, 2007).

20 For example, Thomas Aquinas's five ways suggest that questioning and understanding our physical reality can lead to the natural knowledge of God.

21 René Girard, with Jean-Michel Oughourlian and Guy Lefort, *Things Hidden since the Foundation of the World*, trans. S. Bann and M. Metteer (Stanford, CA: Stanford University Press, 1987), 296–7.

22 René Girard, "Violence, Difference, Sacrifice: A Conversation with René Girard," interview by Rebecca Adams, *Religion and Literature* 25, no. 2 (Summer 1993): 25.
23 Girard, *Evolution and Conversion*, 76–7.
24 René Girard, *Deceit, Desire, and the Novel: Self and Other in Literary Structure*, trans. Y. Freccero (Baltimore, MD: Johns Hopkins University Press, 1965), 61.
25 René Girard, *Battling to the End: Conversations with Benoît Chantre*, trans. Mary Baker (East Lansing: Michigan State University Press, 2010), 112; *Deceit, Desire, and the Novel*, 61.
26 Raymund Schwager, "Mimesis and Freedom," *Contagion* 21 (2014): 29–46.
27 The same phenomenon is present in totalitarian regimes. Violence is used to enforce and reinforce belief in the power of the "Absolute" (the state) through the transcendence of sacred state-sanctioned violence. See Joel Hodge, *Resisting Violence and Victimisation* (Farnham: Ashgate, 2012), 94–6.
28 James Alison, *The Joy of Being Wrong: Original Sin through Easter Eyes* (New York: Crossroad, 1998), 45–6; Gil Bailie, *God's Gamble: The Gravitational Power of Crucified Love* (Kettering, OH: Angelico, 2016), 40–50, 85–110.
29 Girard, "Violence, Difference, Sacrifice," 25.
30 Some may criticize this definition as being Western-centric. However, Eastern traditions such as Hinduism and Buddhism are also concerned with vertical orientation and the avoidance of unhealthy horizontal relations, though they may not be concerned with a deity (at least in some forms of Buddhism).
31 See Michael Casey, *Grace: On the Journey towards God* (Brewster, MA: Paraclete Press, 2018), 19 and 124.
32 Thus, while religion is a constructed category that has been used to marginalize, it is also possible to use the terminology of religion to identify a transcendent motivation to human relations—whether deviated toward the false sacred (because of murderous horizontal relations) or orientated toward the divine (understood as beyond time and space, and so, beyond our philosophical, scientific, and social categories).
33 Jonathan Sacks, *Not in God's Name: Confronting Religious Violence* (Hodder & Stoughton, 2015), 13–14.

10 The Sacred and the Holy: Alternatives to Escalating Violence

1 René Girard, with Pierpaolo Antonello and João Cezar de Castro Rocha, *Evolution and Conversion: Dialogues on the Origins of Culture* (New York: Continuum, 2007), 218; See also Emmanuel Lévinas, *Totality and Infinity: An Essay on Exteriority*, trans. Alphonso Lingis (Pittsburgh, PA: Duquesne University Press, 1969).
2 Simone Weil, *The Notebooks of Simone Weil: Volume Two*, trans. A. Wills, 2 vols. (London: Routledge & Kegan Paul, 1956), 507; See also Gil Bailie, "Raising the

Ante: Recovering an Alpha and Omega Christology," *Communio: International Catholic Review* 35: 1 (Spring 2008): 101.

3 I do not mean to claim that the Bible or the Qur'an are free from violence (including divine violence), but that the journey they chart is one of people encountering and discovering the nonviolent God in contrast to the violent sacred. For more on this point, see James Alison, *Jesus the Forgiving Victim: Listening for the Unheard Voice*, 4 vols. (Glenview: Doers, 2013); Gil Bailie, *Violence Unveiled: Humanity at the Crossroads* (New York: Crossroad, 1995); Raymund Schwager, *Must There Be Scapegoats? Violence and Redemption in the Bible*, trans. Maria L. Assad (San Francisco, CA: Harper and Row, 1987).

4 Wolfgang Palaver, "Abolition or Transformation? The Political Implications of René Girard's Theory of Sacrifice," in *René Girard and Sacrifice in Life, Love, and Literature*, ed. Scott Cowdell, Chris Fleming and Joel Hodge, Violence, Desire, and the Sacred 2 (New York: Bloomsbury, 2014), 17–30.

5 René Girard, "Are the Gospels Mythical?," *First Things: The Journal of Religion and Public Life* 62 (April 1996): 31.

6 Asma Afsaruddin, "Islam and Violence: Debunking the Myths," in *Does Religion Cause Violence? Multidisciplinary Perspectives on Violence and Religion in the Modern World*, ed. Scott Cowdell, Chris Fleming, Joel Hodge, and Carly Osborn, Violence, Desire, and the Sacred 7 (New York: Bloomsbury, 2018), 161–4.

7 Wolfgang Palaver, "The Abrahamic Revolution," in *Mimetic Theory and World Religions*, ed. Wolfgang Palaver and Richard Schenk (East Lansing: Michigan State University Press, 2018), 259–67. I do not wish to claim that the Abrahamic traditions are free of violence, but rather, that each grapples with violence and seeks to transcend scapegoating dynamics in their distinctive identification of the innocent victim.

8 René Girard, *The One by Whom Scandal Comes*, trans. M. B. DeBevoise, Studies in Violence, Mimesis, and Culture (East Lansing: Michigan State University Press, 2014), 59–60.

9 It is for Islamic scholars to comment and work in this area in more depth. I give a brief outline of theological and hermeneutical issues that could be addressed, which includes drawing on issues identified by existing literature on militant Islamism and jihadism.

10 Scott Cowdell, *René Girard and Secular Modernity: Christ, Culture, and Crisis* (Notre Dame, IN: Notre Dame Press, 2013), 154.

11 René Girard, "Apocalyptic Thinking after 9/11: An Interview with René Girard," interview by Robert Doran, *SubStance* 37:1 (2008): 31.

12 Asma Afsaruddin, *Striving in the Path of God: Jihad and Martyrdom in Islamic Thought* (New York: Oxford University Press, 2013), ch. 8.

13 This problem has also occurred in Christianity at different points when God's remoteness and transcendence were overemphasized. It remains a problem in forms of Christian fundamentalism and Pelagianism.
14 Caroline Overington, "Liberated by Lack of Faith," *The Australian*, January 23, 2019, https://www.theaustralian.com.au/news/inquirer/exmuslims-liberated-by-lack-of-faith/news-story/215aac5eaf78f46beef000c8c7e54245.
15 Overington, "Liberated by Lack of Faith."
16 René Girard, *Deceit, Desire, and the Novel: Self and Other in Literary Structure*, trans. Y. Freccero (Baltimore, MD: Johns Hopkins University Press, 1965), 16.
17 See Laurent Murawiec, *The Mind of Jihad* (New York: Cambridge University Press, 2008), 42.
18 Afsaruddin, *Striving in the Path of* God, 296–7; Shiraz Maher, *Salafi-Jihadism: The History of an Idea* (London: Hurst, 2016), 60–1.
19 Maher, *Salafi-Jihadism*, 60–1.
20 Afsaruddin, *Striving in the Path of God*, 296–7.
21 Murawiec, *Mind of Jihad*, 42.
22 See David Cook, *Understanding Jihad* (Berkeley: University of California Press, 2005), 163–8.
23 Karen Armstrong, *Islam: A Short History* (London: Weidenfeld & Nicolson, 2000), 21–6.
24 Armstrong, *Islam*, 23.
25 Armstrong, *Islam*, 23.
26 Cook, *Understanding Jihad*, 165–8.
27 Armstrong, *Islam*, 20. The Prophet Muhammad's conquest of Mecca contained a mixture of defensive and offensive actions (undertaken within the context of warring tribes), as well as nonviolent action (e.g., the march on Mecca which eschewed violence and relied on sheer numbers and the threat of force).
28 Armstrong, *Islam*, 20.
29 Olivier Roy, *Globalized Islam* (New York: Colombia University Press, 2004), 4.
30 The Western division of church and state has its own contested and idiosyncratic history, but it could be a reference point and dialogue partner. For example, some of the conflict in early modern Europe may contain similarities to the repressive actions of colonial regimes and Muslim-majority states after independence. Cavanaugh suggests that much of the conflict that occurred in early modern Europe (the so-called wars of religion) was centered on the emergence of the centralizing state (which related to, used, or marginalized churches depending on the context), rather than exclusively a fight over religious dogmas or practices. See William Cavanaugh, *The Myth of Religious Violence: Secular Ideology and the Roots of Modern Conflict* (New York: Oxford University Press, 2009), 123–80.

31 See Farhad Khosrokhavar, *Suicide Bombers: Allah's New Martyrs* (London: Pluto Press, 2005), 236.

32 Cook, *Understanding Jihad*, 163–5.

33 Palaver, "The Abrahamic Revolutions," 272.

34 Gilles Kepel, *Jihad: The Trail of Political Islam*, trans. Anthony F. Roberts (London: I.B. Tauris, 2004), 65–9; Khosrokhavar, *Suicide Bombers*, 236.

35 René Girard, with Jean-Michel Oughourlian and Guy Lefort, *Things Hidden since the Foundation of the World*, trans. S. Bann and M. Metteer (Stanford, CA: Stanford University Press, 1987), 224–62. Girard also discusses how under the influence of Christianity there is a gradual loosening of legal constraints and a decline in ritualized forms of scapegoating in cultures.

36 Afsaruddin, "Islam and Violence," 161–5; *Striving in the Path of God*, 179–204.

37 Cook, *Understanding Jihad*, 161–5.

38 René Girard, *When These Things Begin: Conversations with Michel Treguer*, trans. Trevor Cribben Merrill, Studies in Violence, Mimesis, and Culture (East Lansing: Michigan State University Press, 2014), 73.

39 Girard, *Evolution and Conversion*, 218. I am not specifically referring to religious conversion here but rather the opening up of spaces by all people of goodwill that resist and transform sacred violence through nonviolent/loving solidarity with the victim based on pacific forms of transcendence.

40 Girard, *Things Hidden*, 141–79.

41 James Alison refers to this process as that of a revealed discovery in what he calls an anthropology of wisdom, or conversion. James Alison, *The Joy of Being Wrong: Original Sin through Easter Eyes* (New York: Crossroad, 1998), 28–9.

42 Wolfgang Palaver, "Religious Extremism, Terrorism, and Islam: A Mimetic Perspective," in *Does Religion Cause Violence? Multidisciplinary Perspectives on Violence and Religion in the Modern World*, ed. Scott Cowdell, Chris Fleming, Joel Hodge, and Carly Osborn, Violence, Desire, and the Sacred 7 (New York: Bloomsbury, 2018), 200–1.

43 Palaver, "Religious Extremism, Terrorism, and Islam," 201.

44 Girard, *Battling to the End: Conversations with Benoît Chantre*, trans. Mary Baker (East Lansing: Michigan State University Press, 2010), 123.

45 Girard, *Battling to the End*, 133.

46 Girard, *Battling to the End*, 131. In the February 2019 conflict between Pakistan and India, Pakistan's prime minister, Imran Khan, made the following comment in a televised address to the Pakistan people that demonstrates Girard's point regarding politics as being impotent before escalating violence. Prime Minister Khan seems to use a euphemism—"miscalculations"—for the mistakes of a rivalrous mentality: "History tells us that in wars, there are miscalculations. … I have a question for the Indian government: The weapons that you and we

have, can we afford a miscalculation? Shouldn't we consider that if it escalates from here, where will it go? It won't be in my control or in Narendra Modi's [Indian Prime Minister] control." Prime Minister Khan also added, "At this time, better sense should prevail. We should solve our problems through dialogue." Thus, there was hope that dialogue—within the context of a global order of nation-states—could avoid conflict before it escalated to a point where reciprocity and victory become the ultimate logic. Saeed Shah and Rajesh Roy, "Pakistan, India Say They Have Shot Down Each Other's Fighter Jets," *Wall Street Journal*, accessed February 27, 2019, https://www.wsj.com/articles/pakistan-says-it-shot-down-two-indian-warplanes-11551251647.

47 Girard, *Battling to the End*, 131.

48 Ibid., 126.

49 Ibid., 206–10.

50 Benedict XVI, "Faith, Reason and the University: Memories and Reflections," (lecture, University of Regensburg, September 12, 2006), The Vatican, accessed September 16, 2019, http://w2.vatican.va/content/benedict-xvi/en/speeches/2006/september/documents/hf_ben-xvi_spe_20060912_university-regensburg.html.

51 Girard, *Battling to the End*, 131.

52 Palaver, "Abolition or Transformation?," 20–3.

53 Ibid., 25.

54 Ibid.

55 Chris Fleming, "The Apocalypse Will Not Be Televised," in *Mimesis, Movies, and Media*, ed. Scott Cowdell, Chris Fleming, and Joel Hodge (New York: Bloomsbury, 2015), 41.

56 Girard, *Battling to the End*, 142.

57 Ibid., 23.

58 Ibid., 131.

59 Palaver, "Abolition or Transformation?," 24–5.

60 David Kilcullen, *Blood Year: The Unravelling of Western Counterterrorism* (Oxford: Oxford University Press, 2016), 39–42.

61 Cavanaugh, *Myth of Religious Violence*, 181–230.

62 David Kilcullen, "Blood Year: Terror and the Islamic State," *Quarterly Essay* 58 (2015): 50–1.

63 Girard argues that individual breakthroughs from the sacred cult are possible (e.g., Socrates), however they do not result in widespread cultural change (and can remain locked in negative mimetic structures). In Greece, e.g., city-states remained wedded to the gods and a mythological worldview, despite the insights of philosophy.

64 Cowdell, *René Girard and Secular Modernity*, 110.

65 On the other side, however, there have been concerted efforts by political and community leaders and the media to separate radical Islam from mainstream Islam. This has been done to protect the Muslim population in the West from victimization and affirm its role in civil society.

66 René Girard, *The Scapegoat*, trans. Y. Freccero (Baltimore, MD: Johns Hopkins University Press, 1986), 198–9.

67 René Girard, *I See Satan Fall Like Lightning*, trans. James G. Williams (Maryknoll: Orbis Books, 2001), 169.

68 Here in particular I pay tribute to the bravery, humility, and faith of Muslims who have been persecuted unjustly and non-violently resist violence, especially friends and colleagues.

Bibliography

Aaron, David, comp. *In Their Own Words: Voices of Jihad*. Santa Monica, CA: RAND, 2008.

Abbey, Ruth. *Charles Taylor*. Teddington: Acumen, 2000.

Afsaruddin, Asma. "Orientalists, Militants, and the Meanings of Jihad." *Renovatio: The Journal of Zaytuna College*. April 28, 2017. https://renovatio.zaytuna.edu/article/orientalists-militants-and-the-meanings-of-jihad.

Afsaruddin, Asma. *Striving in the Path of God: Jihad and Martyrdom in Islamic Thought*. New York: Oxford University Press, 2013.

Ajami, Fouad. "The Way We Live Now: 10-07-01; Out of Egypt." *New York Times*. October 7, 2001. Accessed February 20, 2019. https://www.nytimes.com/2001/10/07/magazine/the-way-we-live-now-10-07-01-out-of-egypt.html.

Alison, James. *Jesus the Forgiving Victim: Listening for the Unheard Voice*. 4 vols. Glenview, IL: Doers, 2013.

Alison, James. *The Joy of Being Wrong: Original Sin through Easter Eyes*. New York: Crossroad, 1998.

al-Khalil, Samir (Kaneen Makiya). *Republic of Fear: The Inside Story of Saddam's Iraq*. New York: Pantheon Books, 1989.

Anghel, Itai. "No Free Steps to Heaven." *Four Corners*. Australian Broadcasting Corporation. April 27, 2015. http://www.abc.net.au/4corners/stories/2015/04/27/4222860.htm#transcript.

Antonello, Pierpaolo, and Paul Gifford, ed. *Can We Survive Our Origins? Readings in René Girard's Theory of Violence and the Sacred*. East Lansing: Michigan State University Press, 2015.

Antonello, Pierpaolo, and Paul Gifford. *How We Became Human: Mimetic Theory and the Science of Evolutionary Origins*. East Lansing: Michigan State University Press, 2015.

Aristotle. *Aristotle's Poetics: Translated and with a Commentary by George Whalley*. Edited by John Baxter and Patrick Atherton. Montreal: McGill-Queen's University Press, 1997.

Aristotle. *Poetics*. Translated by S. H. Butcher. 1994–2000. Accessed July 23, 2019. http://classics.mit.edu/Aristotle/poetics.1.1.html.

Armstrong, Karen. *Islam: A Short History*. London: Weidenfeld & Nicolson, 2000.

Associated Press. "They Asked Me to Convert to Islam, but I Told Them I Will Die a Christian." *New York Post*. December 23, 2016. Accessed February 1, 2019. https://nypost.com/2016/12/23/iraqs-christians-celebrate-christmas-amid-isis-hell/.

Atran, Scott. "ISIS Is a Revolution." *Aeon*. December 15, 2015. Accessed March 1, 2018. https://aeon.co/essays/why-isis-has-the-potential-to-be-a-world-altering-revolution.

Atran, Scott. *Talking to the Enemy: Violent Extremism, Sacred Values, and What It Means to Be Human*. London: Allen Lane, 2010.

Atran, Scott, and Ara Norenzayan. "Religion's Evolutionary Landscape: Counterintuition, Commitment, Compassion, Communion." *Behavioral and Brain Sciences* 27 (2004): 713–70.

Bailie, Gil. *God's Gamble: The Gravitational Power of Crucified Love*. Kettering, OH: Angelico, 2016.

Bailie, Gil. "Raising the Ante: Recovering an Alpha and Omega Christology." *Communio: International Catholic Review* 35, no. 1 (Spring 2008): 83–106.

Bailie, Gil. *Violence Unveiled: Humanity at the Crossroads*. New York: Crossroad, 1995.

Barrett, Justin L. *Cognitive Science, Religion and Theology: From Human Minds to Divine Minds*. West Conshohocken, PA: Templeton Press, 2011.

Barrett, Justin L. "Counterfactuality in Counterintuitive Religious Concepts." *Behavioral and Brain Sciences* 27 (2004): 731–2.

Barrett, Justin L. *Why Would Anyone Believe in God?* Walnut Creek, CA: AltaMira Press, 2004.

Barrett, Justin L. "Why Would Anyone Believe in God?" YouTube video. Posted by "The Veritas Forum," February 26, 2012. Accessed April 1, 2018. https://www.youtube.com/watch?v=3I3GAaswAkc.

BBC News. "Antar Zouabri: A Violent Legacy." *BBC*. February 9, 2002. http://news.bbc.co.uk/2/hi/middle_east/1811194.stm.

Benedict XVI, "Faith, Reason and the University: Memories and Reflections." Lecture, University of Regensburg, September 12, 2006. The Vatican, http://w2.vatican.va/content/benedict-xvi/en/speeches/2006/september/documents/hf_ben-xvi_spe_20060912_university-regensburg.html.

bin Laden, Osama. "Full Text: Bin Laden's 'Letter to America.'" *The Guardian*. November 24, 2002. Accessed February 15, 2018. https://www.theguardian.com/world/2002/nov/24/theobserver.

bin Laden, Osama. Interview by John Miller. *Frontline*. May 1998. Accessed February 15, 2018. https://www.pbs.org/wgbh/pages/frontline/shows/binladen/who/interview.html.

Brighi, Elisabetta. "Terrorism and Religion." In *The Palgrave Handbook of Mimetic Theory and Religion*, edited by James Alison and Wolfgang Palaver, 395–402. New York: Palgrave Macmillan, 2017.

Canetti, Elias. *Crowds and Power*. Translated by C. Stewart. New York: Farrar, Straus and Giroux, 1984.

Casey, Michael. *Grace: On the Journey towards God*. Brewster, MA: Paraclete Press, 2018.

Cavanaugh, William T. *Field Hospital: The Church's Engagement with a Wounded World*. Grand Rapids, MI: William B. Eerdmans, 2016.

Cavanaugh, William T. *Migrations of the Holy: God, State, and the Political Meaning of the Church*. Grand Rapids, MI: William B. Eerdmans, 2011.

Cavanaugh, William T. *The Myth of Religious Violence: Secular Ideology and the Roots of Modern Conflict*. New York: Oxford University Press, 2009.

Cavanaugh, William T. *Theopolitical Imagination: Discovering the Liturgy as a Political Act in an Age of Global Consumerism*. London: T&T Clark, 2002.

Cavanaugh, William T. *Torture and Eucharist: Theology, Politics, and the Body of Christ*. Oxford: Blackwell, 1998.

Cesari, Jocelyne. *What Is Political Islam?* Boulder, CO: Lynne Rienner, 2018.

Cockburn, Patrick. "Life under ISIS: Why I Deserted the 'Islamic State' Rather Than Take Part in Executions, Beheadings and Rape—The Story of a Former Jihadi." *The Independent*. March 16, 2015. Accessed May 1, 2015. http://www.independent.co.uk/news/world/middle-east/life-under-isis-why-i-deserted-the-islamic-state-rather-than-take-part-in-executions-beheadings-and-rape-the-story-of-a-former-jihadi-10111877.html.

Cook, David. *Understanding Jihad*. Berkeley: University of California Press, 2005.

Cook, Michael. "The Appeal of Islamic Fundamentalism." Lecture, March 14, 2013, London: The British Academy. https://www.youtube.com/watch?v=X6dN6RC2J1Q.

Cowdell, Scott. *René Girard and Secular Modernity: Christ, Culture, and Crisis*. Notre Dame, IN: Notre Dame Press, 2013.

Cowdell, Scott, Chris Fleming, and Joel Hodge. *Mimesis, Movies, and Media*. Violence, Desire, and the Sacred 3. New York: Bloomsbury, 2015.

Cowdell, Scott, Chris Fleming, and Joel Hodge, eds. *Violence, Desire and the Sacred: René Girard and Sacrifice in Life, Love and Literature*. Violence, Desire, and the Sacred 2. New York: Bloomsbury, 2014.

Cowdell, Scott, Chris Fleming, Joel Hodge, and Mathias Moosbrugger, eds. *René Girard and Raymund Schwager: Correspondence 1974–1991*. Violence, Desire, and the Sacred 4. Translated by Sheelah Treflé Hidden and Chris Fleming. New York: Bloomsbury, 2016.

Cowdell, Scott, Chris Fleming, Joel Hodge, and Carly Osborn, eds. *Does Religion Cause Violence? Multidisciplinary Perspectives on Violence and Religion in the Modern World*. Violence, Desire, and the Sacred 7. New York: Bloomsbury, 2018.

Dawkins, Richard. *The God Delusion*. London: Bantam, 2006.

Dumouchel, Paul. *The Barren Sacrifice: An Essay on Political Violence*. Translated by Mary Baker. East Lansing: Michigan State University Press, 2015.

Engler, Steven. "Notes on Recent Publications: Why Would Anyone Believe in God?—Justin L. Barrett." *Religious Studies Review* 32, no. 2 (April 2006): 103–4.

Esposito, John L. *The Islamic Threat: Myth or Reality?* 3rd ed. New York: Oxford University Press, 1999.

Esposito, John L. *Unholy War: Terror in the Name of Islam*. Oxford: Oxford University Press, 2003.

Federal Bureau of Investigation. *Terrorism 2002–2005*. U.S. Department of Justice. Accessed March 11, 2019. https://www.fbi.gov/stats-services/publications/terrorism-2002–2005.

Fernandes, Clinton. *Reluctant Saviour: Australia, Indonesia and the Independence of East Timor*. Carlton North, AU: Scribe, 2004.

Gans, Eric. "The Holocaust and the Victimary Revolution." In *Poetics of the Americas: Race, Founding, and Textuality*, edited by Bainard Cowan and Jefferson Humphries, 123–39. Baton Rouge: Louisiana State University Press, 1997.

Garrels, Scott R. ed. *Mimesis and Science: Empirical Research on Imitation and the Mimetic Theory of Culture and Religion*. Studies in Violence, Mimesis, and Culture. East Lansing: Michigan State University Press, 2011.

Gates, Bill. "Bill Gates Says This Book Is 'One of the Most Important' He's Ever Read." Interview by Sarah Begley. *Time*. April 3, 2018. https://time.com/5224618/bill-gates-hans-rosling-factfulness/.

Gerges, Fawaz A. *The Far Enemy: Why Jihad Went Global*, 2nd ed. New York: Cambridge University Press, 2009.

Gervais, Will M., Aiyana K. Willard, Ara Norenzayan, and Joseph Henrich. "The Cultural Transmission of Faith: Why Innate Intuitions Are Necessary, but Insufficient, to Explain Religious Belief." *Religion* 41, no. 3 (September 2011): 389–410.

Girard, René. "Apocalyptic Thinking after 9/11: An Interview with René Girard." By Robert Doran. *SubStance* 37, no. 1 (2008): 20–32.

Girard, René. "Are the Gospels Mythical?" *First Things: The Journal of Religion and Public Life* 62 (April 1996): 27–31.

Girard, René. *Battling to the End: Conversations with Benoît Chantre*. Translated by Mary Baker. Studies in Violence, Mimesis, and Culture. East Lansing: Michigan State University Press, 2010.

Girard, René. *Deceit, Desire, and the Novel: Self and Other in Literary Structure*. Translated by Yvonne Freccero. Baltimore, MD: Johns Hopkins University Press, 1965.

Girard, René. *Evolution and Conversion: Dialogues on the Origins of Culture* (with Pierpaolo Antonello and João Cezar de Castro Rocha). London: Continuum, 2007.

Girard, René. *The Girard Reader*. Edited by James G. Williams. New York: Crossroad, 1996.

Girard, René. *I See Satan Fall Like Lightning*. Translated by James G. Williams. Maryknoll: Orbis Books, 2001.

Girard, René. *The One by Whom Scandal Comes*. Translated by M. B. DeBevoise. Studies in Violence, Mimesis, and Culture. East Lansing: Michigan State University Press, 2014.

Girard, René. *The Scapegoat*. Translated by Yvonne Freccero. Baltimore, MD: Johns Hopkins University Press, 1986.

Girard, René. *Things Hidden Since the Foundation of the World* (with Jean-Michel Oughourlian and Guy Lefort). Translated by Stephen Bann and Michael Metteer. Stanford, CA: Stanford University Press, 1987.

Girard, René. "Victims, Violence and Christianity," *The Month* 31, no. 4 (April 1998), 129–35.

Girard, René. *Violence and the Sacred*. Translated by Patrick Gregory. Baltimore, MD: Johns Hopkins University Press, 1977.

Girard, René. "Violence, Difference, Sacrifice: A Conversation with René Girard." By Rebecca Adams. *Religion and Literature* 25, no. 2 (Summer 1993): 9–33.

Girard, René. "Violence, Victims and Christianity." The D'Arcy Lecture, University of Oxford, November 5, 1997. https://www.uibk.ac.at/theol/cover/girard/videos.html.

Girard, René. "'What Is Occurring Today Is Mimetic Rivalry on a Planetary Scale': René Girard on September 11." By Henri Tincq. *Le Monde*. November 6, 2011. Translated by the Colloquium on Violence and Religion. Accessed July 23, 2019. http://www.morphizm.com/politix/girard911.html.

Girard, René. *When These Things Begin: Conversations with Michel Treguer*. Translated by Trevor Cribben Merrill. Studies in Violence, Mimesis, and Culture. East Lansing: Michigan State University Press, 2014.

Golsan, Richard J. *René Girard and Myth: An Introduction*. Theorists of Myth. London: Routledge, 2002.

Goodhart, Sandor, Jørgen Jørgensen, Tom Ryba, and James G. Williams, eds. *For René Girard: Essays in Friendship and in Truth*. Studies in Violence, Mimesis and Culture. East Lansing: Michigan State University Press, 2009.

Haven, Cynthia. *Evolution of Desire: A Life of René Girard*. East Lansing: Michigan State University Press, 2018.

Hitchens, Christopher. *God Is Not Great: How Religion Poisons Everything*. New York: Twelve, 2007.

Hodge, Joel. *Resisting Violence and Victimisation*. Farnham: Ashgate, 2012.

Hodge, Joel. "Terrorism's Answer to Modernity's Cultural Crisis: Re-sacralising Violence in the Name of Jihadist Totalitarianism." *Modern Theology* 32, no. 2 (April 2016): 231–58.

Hodge, Joel. "Why Is God Part of Human Violence? The Idolatrous Nature of Modern Religious Extremism." In *Does Religion Cause Violence? Multidisciplinary Perspectives on Violence and Religion in the Modern World*. Violence, Desire, and the Sacred 7, edited by Scott Cowdell, Chris Fleming, Joel Hodge, and Carly Osborn, 39–55. New York: Bloomsbury, 2018.

Juergensmeyer, Mark. *Terror in the Mind of God: The Global Rise of Religious Violence*. Berkeley: University of California Press, 2000.

Kepel, Gilles, *Beyond Terror and Martyrdom: The Future of the Middle East*. Cambridge, MA: Belknap Press of Harvard University Press, 2008.

Kepel, Gilles. *Jihad: The Trail of Political Islam*. Translated by Anthony F. Roberts. London: I.B. Tauris, 2004.

Kepel, Gilles. "The Origins and Development of the Jihadist Movement: From Anti-communism to Terrorism." *Asian Affairs* 34, no. 2 (2003): 91–108.

Kepel, Gilles. "Political Islam: A Conversation with Gilles Kepel." By Michael Cromartie. *Books & Culture* 9, no. 3 (May–June 2003): 7.

Kepel, Gilles. *The Revenge of God: The Resurgence of Islam, Christianity and Judaism in the Modern World*. Translated by Alan Braley. Cambridge: Polity, 1994.

Kepel, Gilles. *The Roots of Radical Islam*. Translated by Jon Rothschild. London: Saqi, 2005.

Kepel, Gilles. *The War for Muslim Minds: Islam and the West*. Translated by Pascale Ghazaleh. Cambridge, MA: Belknap Press of Harvard University Press, 2004.

Khosrokhavar, Farhad. *Inside Jihadism: Understanding Jihadi Movements Worldwide*. Boulder, CO: Paradigm/Routledge, 2009.

Khosrokhavar, Farhad. *Jihadist Ideology: The Anthropological Perspective*. Aarhus: Centre for Studies in Islamism and Radicalisation, Department of Political Science, Aarhus University, 2011.

Khosrokhavar, Farhad. *Suicide Bombers: Allah's New Martyrs*. London: Pluto Press, 2005.

Kilcullen, David."Blood Year: Terror and the Islamic State." *Quarterly Essay* 58 (2015): 1–98.

Kilcullen, David. *Blood Year: The Unravelling of Western Counterterrorism*. New York: Oxford University Press, 2016.

Kilcullen, David. "The Rise of ISIS and Its Threat: David Kilcullen in conversation with Robert Manne," La Trobe University Ideas and Society 2015. *The Monthly*. May 27, 2015. Accessed July 1, 2015. Video. https://www.themonthly.com.au/video/2015/may/27/1432685877/rise-isis-and-its-threat-david-kilcullen-conversation-robert-manne.

Kirwan, Michael. *Discovering Girard*. Cambridge, MA: Cowley, 2005.

Kirwan, Michael. *Girard and Theology*. London: T&T Clark, 2009.

Kirwan, Michael, and Ahmad Achtar, eds. *Mimetic Theory and Islam: The Wound Where Light Enters*. New York: Palgrave Macmillan, 2019.

Köylü, Mustafa. *Islam and Its Quest for Peace: Jihad, Justice and Education*. Washington, DC: Council for Research in Values and Philosophy, 2003.

Laub, Zachary, and Jonathan Masters. "The Islamic State." *Council of Foreign Relations (CFR) Backgrounders*. May 18, 2015. Accessed February 1, 2019. http://www.cfr.org/iraq/islamic-state/p14811.

Lemieux, Frederic. "What Is Terrorism? What Do Terrorists Want?" *The Conversation*, June 2, 2017. https://theconversation.com/what-is-terrorism-what-do-terrorists-want-78228.

Lévinas, Emmanuel. *Totality and Infinity: An Essay on Exteriority*. Translated by Alphonso Lingis. Pittsburgh, PA: Duquesne University Press, 1969.

Lonergan, Bernard. *Method in Theology*. 2nd ed. New York: Seabury Press, 1979.

Maher, Shiraz. "ICSR Insight—The Roots of Radicalisation? It's Identity, Stupid." International Centre for the Study of Radicalisation and Political Violence, King's College London. June 23, 2015. Accessed August 13, 2019. https://icsr.info/2015/06/23/roots-radicalisation-identity-stupid/ .

Maher, Shiraz. *Salafi-Jihadism: The History of an Idea*. London: Hurst, 2016.

Manne, Robert. *The Mind of the Islamic State*. Carlton, AU: Redback Quarterly, 2016.

May, Samantha. "Are We Really Seeing the Rise of a 'New Jihad'?" *The Conversation*. May 26, 2017. Accessed May 26, 2017. https://theconversation.com/are-we-really-seeing-the-rise-of-a-new-jihad-78422.

McGilchrist, Iain. *Master and His Emissary: The Divided Brain and the Making of the Western World*. New Haven, CT: Yale University Press, 2009.

Mitchell, Richard P. *The Society of the Muslim Brothers*. New York: Oxford University Press, 1969.

Morris James S., and Tristan Dunning. "Islamic State Schooled Children as Soldiers—How Can Their 'Education' Be Undone?" *The Conversation*. March 29, 2018. Accessed March 29, 2018. http://theconversation.com/islamic-state-schooled-children-as-soldiers-how-can-their-education-be-undone-93266.

Murawiec, Laurent. *The Mind of Jihad*. New York: Cambridge University Press, 2008.

NBC News. "ISIS Tells Iraqi Christians to Convert or Die," *NBC*. September 14, 2014. Accessed March 1, 2019. https://www.nbcnews.com/watch/nightly-news/isis-tells-iraqi-christians-to-convert-or-die-329118275734.

Nelson, Craig, Habib Khan Totakhil, and Ehsanullah Amiri. "Nine Journalists among Dozens Killed by Kabul Bombs." *Wall Street Journal*. Accessed April 30, 2018. https://www.wsj.com/articles/deadly-blasts-hit-kabul-1525065495.

Neumann, Peter R. *Victims, Perpetrators, Assets: The Narratives of Islamic State Defectors*. London: International Centre for the Study of Radicalisation and Political Violence, King's College London, 2015.

Nisa Eva, and Faried F. Saenong. "Female Suicide Bombers: How Terrorist Propaganda Radicalises Indonesian Women." *The Conversation*. Accessed June 25, 2018. http://theconversation.com/female-suicide-bombers-how-terrorist-propaganda-radicalises-indonesian-women-98143.

Oughourlian, Jean-Michel. *The Puppet of Desire: The Psychology of Hysteria, Possession, and Hypnosis*. Translated by Eugene Webb. Stanford, CA: Stanford University Press, 1991.

Overington, Caroline. "Liberated by Lack of Faith." *The Australian*. Accessed January 23, 2019. https://www.theaustralian.com.au/news/inquirer/exmuslims-liberated-by-lack-of-faith/news-story/215aac5eaf78f46beef000c8c7e54245.

Palaver, Wolfgang. *René Girard's Mimetic Theory*. Translated by Gabriel Borrud. Studies in Violence, Mimesis, and Culture. East Lansing: Michigan State University Press, 2013.

Palaver, Wolfgang, and Richard Schenk, eds. *Mimetic Theory and World Religions*. Studies in Violence, Mimesis, and Culture. East Lansing: Michigan State University Press, 2018.

Parkinson, Joe, and Drew Hinshaw. "Islamic State, Seeking Next Chapter, Makes Inroads through West Africa." *Wall Street Journal*. Accessed February 3, 2019. https://www.wsj.com/articles/islamic-state-seeking-next-chapter-makes-inroads-through-west-africa-11549220824.

Qutb, Sayyid. *Milestones*. Cedar Rapids, IA: Mother Mosque Foundation, n.d.

Rajan, V. G. Julie. *Women Suicide Bombers: Narratives of Violence*. Abingdon: Routledge, 2011.

Richardson, Louise. *What Terrorists Want: Understanding the Enemy, Containing the Threat*. Random House: New York, 2006.

Roy, Olivier. *The Failure of Political Islam*. Translated by Carol Volk. Cambridge, MA: Harvard University Press, 1994.

Roy, Olivier. *Globalized Islam: The Search for a New Ummah*. New York: Columbia University Press, 2004.

Roy, Olivier. "An Interview with Olivier Roy." *Colombia University Press*. Accessed March 13, 2019. https://cup.columbia.edu/author-interviews/roy-globalized-islam.

Roy, Olivier. "Who Are the New Jihadis?" *The Guardian*. April 13, 2017. Accessed February 1, 2019. https://www.theguardian.com/news/2017/apr/13/who-are-the-new-jihadis.

Sacks, Jonathan. *Not in God's Name: Confronting Religious Violence*. London: Hodder & Stoughton, 2015.

Sageman, Marc. *Understanding Terror Networks*. Philadelphia: University of Pennsylvania Press, 2004.

Schmitt, Carl. *The Concept of the Political*. Chicago, IL: University of Chicago Press, 2007.

Schmitt, Carl. *Theory of the Partisan*. New York: Telos Press, 2007.

Schmitt, Eric. "ISIS Used Chemical Arms at Least 52 Times in Syria and Iraq, Report Says." *New York Times*. November 21, 2016. Accessed April 1, 2018. https://www.nytimes.com/2016/11/21/world/middleeast/isis-chemical-weapons-syria-iraq-mosul.html.

Schwager, Raymund. "Mimesis and Freedom." *Contagion* 21 (2014): 29–46.

Schwager, Raymund. *Must There Be Scapegoats? Violence and Redemption in the Bible*. Translated by Maria L. Assad. San Francisco, CA: Harper & Row, 1987.

Serres, Michel. "Receiving René Girard into the Académie Française." In *For René Girard: Essays in Friendship and in Truth*, edited by Sandor Goodhart, Jørgen Jørgensen, Tom Ryba, and James G. Williams, 1–18. Studies in Violence, Mimesis and Culture. East Lansing: Michigan State University Press, 2009.

Shah, Saeed, and Rajesh Roy, "Pakistan, India Say They Have Shot Down Each Other's Fighter Jets." *Wall Street Journal*. Accessed February 27, 2019. https://www.wsj.com/articles/pakistan-says-it-shot-down-two-indian-warplanes-11551251647.

Simpson, John. "ISIS Defectors Were Tired of Killing and Lack of Luxuries." *The Times*. September 22, 2015. Accessed October 1, 2015. http://www.thetimes.co.uk/tto/news/world/middleeast/article4563869.ece.

Spoerl, Joseph. "Jihad and Just War." *The Levantine Review* 2, no. 2 (Winter 2013): 159–87.

Spoerl, Joseph. "Muhammad and the Jews according to Ibn Ishaq." *The Levantine Review* 2, no. 1 (Spring 2013): 84–103.

Stork, Peter. *Human Rights in Crisis: A Cultural Critique*. Saarbrücken: VDM Verlag Dr. Mueller, 2007.

Taylor, Charles. "Notes on the Sources of Violence: Perennial and Modern." In *Beyond Violence: Religious Sources for Social Transformation in Judaism, Christianity and Islam*, edited by J. L. Heft, 15–42. Ashland: Fordham University Press, 2004.

Taylor, Charles. *A Secular Age*. Cambridge, MA: Belknap Press of Harvard University Press, 2007.

Tripp, Charles. "Islam and the Contingency of Politics." In *The Secular State and Islam in Europe*, edited by Kurt Almquist, 81–96. Stockholm: Axel & Margaret Ax:son Johnson Foundation, 2007.

Urban, Rebecca. "Fanatic Charted Growing Hate of 'Invaders' in Diary of Europe Trip." *The Australian*. Accessed March 16, 2019. https://www.theaustralian.com.au/news/nation/fanatic-charted-growing-hate-of-invaders-in-diary-of-europe-trip/news-story/ec53a72e730d037e396ec67320063bac.

Visontay, Elias. "Omarjan Azari Yells Allahu Akbar, Refuses to Stand as He's Convicted on Terror Plot." *The Australian*. March 29, 2019. https://www.theaustralian.com.au/nation/omarjan-azari-yells-allahu-akbar-refuses-to-stand-as-hes-convicted-on-terror-plot/news-story/538cb3c4c1b7b996fc8eef24dac0e32b.

Warrick, Joby. "Exclusive: Iraqi Scientist Says He Helped ISIS Make Chemical Weapons." *Washington Post*. January 21, 2019. https://www.washingtonpost.com/world/national-security/exclusive-iraqi-scientist-says-he-helped-isis-make-chemical-weapons/2019/01/21/617cb8f0-0d35-11e9-831f-3aa2c2be4cbd_story.html?noredirect=on&utm_term=.8465dd6fa0c6.

Weil, Simone. *The Notebooks of Simone Weil: Volume Two*. Translated by Arthur Wills. 2 vols. London: Routledge & Kegan Paul, 1956.

Wray, Christopher. "Current Threats to the Homeland: Statement before the Senate Homeland Security and Government Affairs Committee." September 27, 2017. Federal Bureau of Investigation. https://www.fbi.gov/news/testimony/current-threats-to-the-homeland.

Žižek, Slavoj. "Slavoj Žižek on the Charlie Hebdo Massacre: Are the Worst Really Full of Passionate Intensity?" *New Statesman*, January 10, 2015. http://www.newstatesman.com/world-affairs/2015/01/slavoj-i-ek-charlie-hebdo-massacre-are-worst-really-full-passionate-intensity.

Žižek, Slavoj. *Violence*. New York: Picador, 2008.

Index